ONE YEAR TO AN

ORGANIZED WORK LIFE

From Your Desk to Your Deadlines, the Week-by-Week Guide to Eliminating Office Stress for Good

REGINA LEEDS

MJF BOOKS
NEW YORK

Published by MJF Books
Fine Communications
322 Eighth Avenue
New York, NY 10001

One Year to an Organized Work Life
LC Control Number: 2014938448
ISBN 978-1-60671-267-2

Design by Jane Raese

This edition is published by MJF Books in arrangement with Da Capo Press, a member of the Perseus Books Group.

Printed in the United States of America.

MJF Books and the MJF colophon are trademarks of Fine Creative Media, Inc.

QF   10 9 8 7 6 5 4 3 2 1

This book is dedicated to all the kind men who
have graced my life, starting with my father, Nat.
Special thanks, however, must be extended to
Arno Frankel, Ariel Joseph Towne, and Joseph Walsh.
Their love and support contributed greatly
to the process of writing this book.
I am forever in their debt.

CONTENTS

A journey of a thousand miles
must begin with a single step.

—LAO-TZU

Introduction

I'm late, I'm late. For a very important date!

—ALICE IN WONDERLAND

AND THUS WHITE RABBIT PERFECTLY described the plight of the modern worker. Do you feel like him at times: always running here and there, never at ease, stomach in knots, frequently late? "You're going to be late for your own funeral!" Ever had a coworker, family member, or friend toss that one at you?

"But someday," you think, "this will be different. I'll be on time for appointments and with reports. I'll get enough sleep and eat three squares a day. Everyone will be so impressed with my efficiency—my sparkling office and clear desk. Why? Because I'm going to get organized!" Yes, you are. Today, in fact. Now begins the year-long adventure to change your work experience for the better. But my goal for you is deeper. I want to see you uncover and embrace your true passion in life. Joseph Campbell said it best: "Follow your bliss and don't be afraid, and doors will open where you didn't know they were going to be."

I see you working in a peaceful, well-organized space that serves you rather than ensnares you. I envision your files, projects, and all communications being the best quality they can be. I imagine you having a happier home life as your work days begin and end. After all, home and work are flip sides of the same coin: your life experience.

Am I living in Wonderland? Absolutely not! I know that life will throw you some curveballs. Some days you will inevitably get behind because of a tight deadline or a flu you can't shake. Positive things may also throw you off your game, from planning a wedding to the birth of a child. But just as you look around and think, 'My office looks just like it did before I got organized!" you will have a moment of clarity. Under all that chaos is a *system* waiting for you to restore order.

Still not convinced that I know you and your situation? Let's see if I can guess some of the issues you're facing:

You come to work with good intentions. Sometimes you even have the rudiments of a plan for your day in place. And then the phone rings, a colleague stops by, or you read your e-mail, voice mail, or snail mail. Suddenly you find yourself pulled in a hundred directions. At day's end your to-do list is a wish list.

You never have enough time to complete projects. Deadlines come upon you like rogue waves. You're forever wondering how your colleagues (seemingly!) stay on top of their workload while you're paddling to keep up.

The piles of papers on your desk hold valuable treasures. At least that's what you assume. One day you plan to do the equivalent of an archeological dig and get everything into folders. Until then you make duplicate and triplicate copies or printouts of everything in the futile hope that there is strength in numbers.

You go to social functions but your real date is your BlackBerry. You're known as an inseparable pair.

Your children complain that they never see you. Even when you are physically present, your mind takes you a million miles away, worrying about this assignment or that meeting. You know you're providing for their future but feel like you spend too much time at the office.

How did I do? If you identified with one or two of the preceding, you have the right book in your hands. Right about now, you may be feeling a bit guilty or inadequate. That's the knee-jerk response when the topic of organization—or lack thereof—comes up. Let's make a deal, shall we? Guilt and shame and any other negative emotion have no place in the world of Zen

organizing, the system of organizing I have developed over the past twenty years. Getting organized is a skill, not a talent we're born with. End of story. In my eyes you are a hero because you are doing the work to effect positive change in your life and career.

DEFINING ZEN ORGANIZING

Having grown up with an extremely organized mom, I had never seen piles of newspapers and magazines, closets teeming with clothes, or a pantry in disarray until I started working with clients. My mother didn't invent the slogan, "There's a place for everything and everything should be in its place," but she said it daily like a sacred mantra. She lived it and she made me live it. My mom trained me to be an organizer, but we didn't know that at the time.

From the first day I started working as a professional organizer, I noticed something that happened with clients. After every project was completed, obviously the home or office *looked* different, but there was something more. I finally noticed that the area *felt* different. I often wondered how I would describe this to people.

There are words for energy such as *chi,* but none were in common use in 1988. I feared no one would understand what I was talking about. One day a friend turned to me and said casually, "Oh you mean, it's Zen-like?" The lights went on and I screamed, "Yes! That's *exactly* what it's like." That day *Zen organizing* was born and I have been the *Zen organizer* ever since.

The average Westerner associates the word *Zen* with peace and calm. You don't have to become a Zen meditation practitioner to embrace this approach. You needn't be a yogi and twist your body into impressive positions. You don't have to live and work in a minimalist setting. The only requirement is your willingness to change.

If you don't like what you see around you now in your work space, don't fret. You created it, and you can therefore change it. Your physical environment is a manifestation of your inner world of thoughts and feelings. This year you will examine that world so that will you not only work in an organized environment but also experience less stress, greater ease, and, dare I say it, have more fun at your job!

Perhaps the simplest description of Zen organizing is this: It is a way to empower yourself to create the life you were born to live.

PARTS OF THE SAME WHOLE

It is written in Zen that "the way a man does one thing is the way he does everything." If you're struggling to be more productive at work, take a minute to look at your life as a whole.

It's frustrating when your heart and your drive tell you to work to the best of your ability but you fall short because you are constantly overwhelmed. Can you find the papers you need? Does your office look like a bomb just went off? Do you consistently miss deadlines? Do you set an agenda for the day that gets lost in a sea of e-mails or voice mails that steal your focus? We will examine how to handle all these common office issues, but first I'd like you to consider the problem from a holistic perspective.

I'm going to bet that your home looks a lot like your office. If stacks of papers decorate your desk and line the floor of your office, it's a good chance that clothes get draped over the chair in your bedroom, the bed never gets made, and you have no idea what's in your pantry.

If you have trouble completing assignments at the office, I expect that many tasks in your life could be in suspended animation. For example, do you open your dresser drawers and leave them ajar? Are the cabinet doors in the kitchen left open after you retrieve something?

Organizing goes deeper than how we place items in the environment. The minute I walk into an office, I know a great deal about the person. When I see papers and books occupying every square inch of the space, for example, I'm sure this client finds it hard to think clearly. It's as if all that stuff is making a loud racket. As we go through stacks of paper scattered around the desk, I find papers that could actually serve them languishing in piles. I wonder if the person has issues about success or failure. He or she certainly isn't set up to win in this environment. I presume too that the person needs to acquire the skill of being able to make decisions on the spot.

If I see coffee cups that need to be rinsed, food containers that should be tossed, or items that should have been returned long ago sitting in a corner, I know this person needs to understand the importance of completion. This disarray will be part of every facet of his or her life. Can you relate? Here are some other areas to consider.

Is your car a disaster? If your home and your office are a mess, your car may be a little scary as well. If you use your car in your business, is the trunk a treasure trove of old papers, forms, client folders, and maps? Do you avoid opening the glove compartment because an avalanche of stuff came pouring out the last time?

And let's not forget ye olde briefcase. Can you easily find what you need? Do you have six-month-old energy bars in secret compartments? Are papers from closed accounts still taking up space? Does your briefcase (or laptop bag, or handbag) weigh a ton because you never clean it out? No matter what mode of transportation you use to get to work, a briefcase that feels like you're transporting a rock quarry is going to slow you down.

Be honest with yourself. Remember, we're on a diagnostic quest, not playing the blame game. Getting organized is at its heart nothing more than a skill. You learn it the same way you acquire any skill, from dancing to swimming to playing the piano. A teacher breaks the skill down into a series of lessons. Your mastery grows over time commensurate with your willingness to learn and practice what you have been taught. When we care about ourselves, we care about the environment we set up for work and home. You care, because you're reading this book.

THE ONE-YEAR PLAN

You didn't get into this predicament overnight, so we're going to take the luxury of one year to effect lasting change. This plan is not the equivalent of a crash diet. It's a new way of living, experiencing, and contributing to life, especially that part called work. Real change is in the incremental steps we take forward. I tell my clients that even if time or money isn't an issue, it's still best to move slowly, systematically, and respectfully through any environment to effect change. Make that *permanent* change. I don't want you to tidy up your office and be back at square one in two weeks. I want you to replace your broken system with one that will not only support you but grow with you. And with your increased productivity, your growth will be off the charts!

You can benefit from reading *One Year to an Organized Work Life* no matter what your job. We'll be focused on the job that pays a salary, but the tools you acquire and the skills you learn can just as easily be applied to your volunteer positions and your home projects. Have you ever tackled a remodel? You are the one paying the money, but you had better be organized to reduce issues that may arise. If you are a parent, you can teach these principles to your children. Today it's a homework assignment; tomorrow it's a report for work.

Teaching children how to organize their world is the ultimate gift that keeps on giving. Organizing your work life will reap benefits you can't now imagine.

Although everyone can profit from this book, my heart goes out to the working moms among us. It is nothing short of a Herculean effort to maintain a home, advance in a career, and raise children. It is my sincere hope that this book can help moms everywhere experience less stress, find more time, and enjoy life more.

SECRETS OF A ZEN ORGANIZED WORK LIFE

It doesn't require more energy to get organized. In fact, chaos is a demanding taskmaster and time waster. Getting organized requires a *redirection* of energy away from one type of experience to another.

So the question arises: Why do we get caught up in chaos when we know better? The simple answer is: We're human! Aside from the obvious issues, life in the twenty-first century is unique in several ways. Here are a few to consider:

- We are bombarded by more methods of instant communication than ever before.
- To gain a competitive edge, companies of all sizes decide to place more work on fewer shoulders.
- With the advent of outsourcing, we are afraid to speak up when we feel overworked because any job feels better than no job.

We're only victims if we consciously refuse to acquire the tools to cope. Years ago, I heard something in a lecture that I never forgot: "There are no victims, only volunteers." When things happen that threaten to take you down the chaos road, stop yourself and redirect your energy. Volunteer to be successful. Choose to accomplish things with ease. Save your energy for what is truly important.

The path to getting organized and productive can be creative; you can have as much fun as you are willing to allow yourself. The following areas lay a solid foundation to ensure your success. Let's consider each in turn and then you can decide which you'd like to utilize. I hope, of course, you'll try them all.

Diet
Exercise
Meditation
A work life notebook
A dream board
Technology
Time-management skills
Good habits
Systems and routines
Rewards

Diet

How I wish I could have seen your face when you read the word *diet*. Here's the bottom line: We are what we eat. Food affects our ability to think clearly; it gives us the energy to stay alert throughout the day. So put away the candy bar and grab a piece of fruit. Reach for a bottle of water instead of that soda or your umpteenth cup of coffee. Add a tablespoon of cottage cheese to your breakfast toast or scramble some eggs to go with your morning coffee. Over time, small changes toward a healthier diet will make a difference in your energy level and improve your focus. The "Resources" section lists some great books to help you get started.

Exercise

Our bodies were not designed to sit for hours in front of a computer. If you are sedentary, a simple twenty-minute walk each day will change your life. Twenty minutes is the time it takes the average person to walk a mile. If you can't take twenty, begin with five minutes. Later you can build on that.

Ten or fifteen minutes of simple yoga postures will also revive you. You don't have to contort your body into positions only Gumby could master. Yoga has some simple, easy postures that can be of great benefit. Again, I have some direction for you in the "Resources" section. Of course the exercise you choose doesn't have to be walking or yoga. Find the type of exercise you enjoy so that sticking to your new regime will be easier.

Meditation

If you had a negative reaction to the word *meditation,* I understand. In the West we tend to think of meditation as something strange, exotic, and perhaps cultist. Let's see if I can't give you a fresh perspective on the practice itself, as well as some of its benefits. Meditation is a form of prayer. It's a key ingredient in Eastern philoso-

phies; the process by which we quiet our minds to connect with the Divine. However, you needn't use it to advance your spiritual life. You can gain enormous health benefits with as little as five minutes a day. Stressed at work? Close your office door and your eyes to restore calm to your body. Don't have a private office? Take an extra bathroom break. What happens in the stall stays in the stall.

Some of the major benefits of meditation that make it a worthwhile practice to incorporate into your life include the following:

- Reduces stress by releasing muscle tension. Often people with chronic headaches, including migraines, experience relief.
- Slows your heart rate while increasing oxygen consumption.
- Boosts your immune system. Research indicates that meditation increases the activity of "natural-killer cells," which kill bacteria and cancer cells.
- Sharpens your ability to focus.

When I suggest meditation to my clients and students, I hear two universal objections: "I tried but I kept falling asleep!" and "I can't meditate because my mind is too active." Allow me to assure you that everyone falls asleep in the beginning! It's part of the natural learning curve and comes to an end with practice, patience, and persistence. As for having an active mind, all I can say is: Who doesn't? Yogis have an expression to describe this state. It's called Monkey Mind. Your untrained mind is like a wild monkey in the forest swinging from branch to branch and tree to tree. It's far more powerful to have a mind you can harness at will.

You may also be wondering how you find a legitimate meditation instructor. I suggest that you research the location of a TM (transcendental meditation) institute near you. I have included the Web site address for the worldwide organization in the "Resources" section. This is a worldwide organization founded by the Maharishi Mahesh Yogi, who is famous for teaching the Beatles how to meditate in the sixties. If you can't find one of their teaching centers near you, you can get started with online classes. The "Resources" section also includes a few other organizations whose reputation I trust.

Work Life Notebook

In my previous book, *One Year to an Organized Life*, I confessed that I was once an arrogant reader of self-help books. You wouldn't catch me taking the time to write the answers to questions in a journal. After all, I knew exactly what I would say. Next! And then I had the good fortune to read John Bradshaw's wonderful book *The Homecoming*. For some reason, I decided that this one time I would make the exception and write my responses. What a surprise! The information that came pouring out of me was not at all what I expected. The act of surrendering my thoughts to pen and paper unleashed deeper feelings—thoughts I didn't realize I had.

It was so powerful that I immediately incorporated this technique into all my classes. So writing in a notebook plays a key role in getting organized this year, as you'll see in the first week of each month in the program. Feel stuck in the rut of "same old, same old" where your work is concerned? We're going to seek out the cause that set those reactions in motion. In this way, something far more powerful can be put in its place.

Dream Board

The dream board is another project that at first may seem worthless or to have little to do with organizing, but it can be revealing. Creating what I call a dream board allows you to see your goals before they come into physical reality. It's simple, creative, inexpensive, and powerful. How many things can you describe with those adjectives?

Here's what you do: purchase some posterboard and a glue stick at your local office supply store. Now sit down and go through a stack of magazines to find images that correspond to the life you want to create, your dream job, or the office space you desire. When you're finished, keep the board in a prominent place (it doesn't have to be at the office). You will be reminded and inspired on a regular basis about the direction you want to take. Don't be surprised if the images you are drawn to in the magazines surprise you. When you invite your inner thoughts and longings to rise to the surface, you will discover more of who you really are and what you'd like to manifest in your life. Embrace the surprises!

Now to the more familiar organizing and productivity tools.

Technology

In an effort to get organized, we often purchase gadgets and gizmos that we don't need but, due to advertising, feel we can't live without. In most chapters, we'll consider some items that might be of assistance to you—or are they time-suckers in disguise? Don't forget to consult your IT person (or someone like the Geek Squad at Best Buy) to see what he or she recommends. Technology changes so rapidly that by the time this book is published, new items will be available. The key question is: Do I *really* need this item? I was beside myself with joy the day I purchased a scanner. They were fairly new and the price was right. Guess what? I don't scan enough to have made that purchase worthwhile. I learned the "don't buy it unless you need it" lesson the hard way.

Time-Management Skills

Time is a precious commodity like food or money. When it's gone, it cannot be reclaimed. Why fritter your life away or, worse, give it to anyone who demands a piece? This year, learning time-management skills will play a huge role in your growing ability to create the work life you truly want, rather than enduring the one that seems to be happening to you.

Good Habits

For many years now I have seen the power of simple habits transform a client's relationship with his environment. Psychologists say it takes twenty-one *consecutive* days of repeating an *action* before it becomes a habit. The key ingredients are *consecutive* and *action*. If you miss a day, you need to start the count over. And the new habit needs to be an action, not an activity.

What's the difference? If I decide to straighten up my office each evening before I leave for the day, I am engaged in an activity. However, it has multiple *actions* that might include any or all of the following: place reference books on their designated shelves; return files to the file cabinet; wash my coffee cup in the office kitchen; empty the trash; water my plants; and perhaps send a few end-of-the-day report e-mails to colleagues. Often an activity is composed of a series of good habits strung together. Other words for a positive activity like this are routine, system, or even ritual. These routines are the heart of maintenance.

Another positive, repeatable activity in the office setting that has a positive effect is to *immediately* put away your personal property when you enter your work area. If your coat gets tossed across a chair, your lunch is forgotten on a bookcase shelf, or your boots are in a heap in the middle of the floor, you have just set the tone for the day: Anything goes! Instead, set the stage for success from the second you walk into your space. Respect your environment.

Systems and Routines

One of the most common questions I am asked when I teach goes something like this: "Regina, I get organized all the time.

And then two weeks later, it looks as though I haven't done a thing! Why should I bother?" I tell my students that they have not become organized; they have tidied up. To be organized means you have a system in place to keep your desk chaos-free. Another way of describing a system is to call it a routine. I would be willing to bet you have lots of routines in your life that bring you pleasure, such as getting ready to go out to a nice restaurant. What are some of the positive routines you follow now? We're going to insert a few that will keep your work life on track.

Rewards

It wouldn't be fair to ask you to do some hard work and not plan a reward at the end. We need something to look forward to when the going gets tough! I don't mean a trip to Tahiti after you master time management. I'm thinking about injecting a little joy into your life on a *consistent* basis.

Sometimes the simplest things bring us the most pleasure. For example, I have always loved animals. I know a horse who is a retired Olympic champion—as I write these words he's twenty-six, which for a horse is positively ancient. One of my favorite rewards is to drive out to see him. I turn him loose in the corral and sit down on the riding block and watch him. We're two old friends hanging out together. What simple, sweet experiences bring you joy? Can you turn them into rewards for a job well done?

THE YEAR UNFOLDS

If you are a person who wants to be fulfilled in life and not just show up at work for a paycheck; if you are overwhelmed by the way your work space currently looks; if you wish you knew how to handle the daily volume of communications that inundate you; and if more than anything else you long for a balanced life, you have found the right book.

Reading it is a step in the right direction. But you will need to make a commitment to change and take action to be successful. Nothing of value comes without a price. You'll have to inconvenience yourself sometimes and expend a considerable amount of elbow grease. In return, you will reap rewards beyond your wildest dreams. I've been organizing clients for over twenty years and have seen firsthand how these techniques work.

This next year you're going to improve the quality of your work life. You will save time, money, and that most precious commodity, energy. Whether it's physical, mental, emotional, or spiritual, energy is the sum and substance of who we are. What would happen if you were more productive? How would you spend the extra hours in your day? Where would the money you save go in your budget? What might you accomplish if you reduced your stress level? And why do you think this chaos was created in the first place? Grab your courage, your resolve, and yes, your notebook. We are about to find out.

1. JANUARY

Start Fresh

Let yourself be drawn
By the stronger pull
Of what you really love.
—RUMI

IF YOU FOLLOW THIS BOOK CHRONO-logically, you will be starting at the most propitious time of year to effect change. In December, most of us are exhausted from the extra demands the holidays have placed on us. As the month comes to an end, we're able to recharge our batteries. Now with the start of a New Year, vacation is over and it's back to work—but the energy and desire for change and growth fills the air.

Past experience, however, has probably taught you that emotion is only part of the equation. For example, I might be over the moon about the *idea* of losing weight. However, my excitement will get me started but only take me so far. How do we lose weight? We eat less and move more. To effect change, we need to know the bottom line. When it comes to your work experience, what's the bottom line for you?

- I'm going to leave for work earlier so I arrive on time this year.
- I want my undergraduate degree or master's degree or certification so I can make more money.
- My spouse/kids feel neglected. "All you do is work!" they say. There must be a more balanced way to live.
- This is the year I finally take control or get a raise or spend less time at the office.

If any of these sound familiar, take heart, because these laments all represent achievable goals. We're going to work systematically this year because many people get so overwhelmed at the very thought of making change that they stop all forward motion. The safety of "The devil you know is better than the devil you don't know" takes hold. You know what I say to that? Let's eliminate the "work devil" altogether!

At the end of this year, you will have streamlined your life and your physical space and moved closer to your career goals. Now, please don't attempt to achieve every work-related goal you've ever had! You want to build on your success over time. Likewise, the assignments and routines in this book build each week on a particular theme. And the themes themselves build over the course of the months. Let's consider January:

- The first week of this New Year, you'll take an inventory of your current situation. What exactly do you not like or want to change about your job? Complaints drain us. Specifics empower us.
- The next week, you'll figure out where you want to be in your work life and craft a plan to make it a reality. This gives you direction.
- You can't implement any plan without knowing how to schedule the steps that will take you out of the realm of wishes and dreams. To this end, we look at calendars in the third week.
- Finally, we close the month with the first routine: streamlining the morning experience so you go from rushed to rested.

Once you have a plan, you need to have an environment that supports your efforts. We'll spend February and March restructuring your physical work space as well as creating the perfect file system. The first quarter of the year is all about tools for change.

Looking ahead with fear only wastes energy. Remember that same physical and emotional energy could be harnessed to help you work on your assignments. I invite you to leave worrying behind like an old shoe that doesn't fit anymore and experience forward motion.

Change comes about when we successfully marry intention and action. I love change . . . provided I am the architect of the change that's occurring! When life throws a curve ball, change isn't quite so easy. But the great thing about the tools presented in this book is that once you use them for the changes you seek to make, they can serve you when life is turned upside down. This is the skill I most want you to master.

This month you'll start creating new, positive habits that you can also string together to form a system or routine. Our first habit, in week four, will be to create a morning ritual. After all, how you start the day often sets an indelible tone for the rest of the day. Start out stressed and in a rush, and often that's how work is too. I want to be sure that the aspects of life within your power to control are set up to support rather than sabotage you.

Each month, I will present two Zen organizing habits that I think are worth cultivating and that take only a few minutes. One habit relates to your work environment, but the other relates to your home and daily life. Because these areas work in concert—success in one feeds the other—you'll want to effect change in both. If the habit of the month is something you have long made a part of your routine, move on to the next. The key to new habit creation is twofold: You want to choose an *action* and you need to repeat it for twenty-one *consecutive* days (even weekends) so that it becomes second nature. But I'm not trying to clutter your life with more activities! It's also important to remember that developing these habits will, in the long run, make your workweek much easier.

WORK HABIT OF THE MONTH: LEAVE YOUR DESK

The work habit of the month is easy! Just take one break to move your body for five consecutive minutes every day. Walk around the block. Take the stairs. Close your door and do a few simple yoga postures while no one is looking. The break doesn't have to be fancy.

How does this qualify as a work habit? An exercise break recharges your "body battery." It helps you think more clearly. This simple five-minute break will make you more productive at work whether you are the cashier at a supermarket or the CEO of a large corporation. You are free to do more than five minutes if you have the time and the inclination. However, I'd rather see you build slowly than burn out, so if exercise is new to you, temper your enthusiasm and build on your success over time. Over the weekend, take a break from all the work you assigned yourself on the home front.

HOME HABIT OF THE MONTH: MAKE YOUR BED

Each day begins and ends not at the office, but in your bedroom. January's habit, therefore, is to make your bed every day. An unmade bed signals that there is no end to your day; you are dragging the activities, emotions, and energy of one day into the next without ever giving yourself the experience of a fresh start. When you make your bed, you will feel energized every time you walk into your bedroom.

You don't have to strip your bed and make military corners. Just use a top sheet and a comforter—it takes about a minute to pull them into place and fluff your pillows. (By the way, don't have too many pillows on the bed. They may unconsciously be your excuse not to bother making it.)

WEEK ONE

Chart the Course

This week, you can

- Give your career more conscious direction
- Introduce positive habits into your daily life

Time required: Thirty minutes

I HAVE A FRIEND WHO IS A PILOT FOR a major airline. Fred flies the same routes most of the time, but this doesn't mean that he gets into the cockpit without going over a flight plan, the controls, a check of the weather, and more. Can you imagine hearing the following announcement: "Ladies and gentlemen, welcome aboard. We'll be leaving LAX shortly en route for New York City. I fly to the Big Apple all the time but I like to see where the wind might take us. And I haven't done it in a week, but hey, I've got a great memory, so no worries. If we get off course, I'll probably be flying low enough so you can catch the sights while I scramble to get back to our route. Fasten your seatbelt because it's going to be an unconventional ride!" I think there would be a stampede for the exit.

You're probably thinking that's a silly idea. No reputable airline would allow an unprepared pilot to cowboy his way across country. Well, guess what? If you've been showing up for work each day without a routine—and then scrambling to get things under control—you're just like that crazy pilot. And you have less chance of achieving your longer-term career goals because, unlike our pilot, you don't have computers automatically adjusting your flight plan when you get off course. In the weeks ahead, we're going to be sure you know where you're headed . . . and why!

THE POWER OF INTENTION

Have you ever noticed that you walk in the direction you are facing? You also steer your car in the direction of your gaze. In the same way, you give your life direction with the thoughts you think. You can set your intention to succeed or to fail; the choice is always yours.

Sometimes feeling crazed in the workplace can stem from a sense of loss due to the "road not taken." Yes, chaos can be due to a lack of organizing skills, but it's also often a symptom of a lack of inner peace. We'll tackle both of these throughout the course of this year. "As within so without," said the ancient yogis. They weren't specifically referring to your physical environment, but their advice can be applied to our modern situation. Open yourself to finding ways to incorporate your original desires into your current reality.

Turning your life in a new direction is like docking one of those huge ocean liners. It takes time and effort. In your life, your thoughts are like those small but powerful tugboats that get the job done.

THE "YOU" INVENTORY

This first week, begin the basic outline of a plan that this year will bring you back to what you love. As the months go by, you can add elements and feel progress in your journey to bring order to your work life. Where will you start? In your mind. In life, what we give our attention to is what comes to fruition.

The tool you'll need this week is a notebook. It doesn't matter whether it's a school notebook you took from your kid's supplies or a leather-bound diary. For years I was in love with lined, yellow legal pads but these days my thoughts flow more quickly and effortlessly using a computer. The key ingredient to making the notebook a useful tool in your success arsenal is your willingness to commit to writing down your responses to the questions I provide.

Give yourself five minutes of uninterrupted time to respond to each of the following questions. I like to do this kind of work in a local coffee shop because being away from my home and work environment frees me. Perhaps it will do the same for you.

I'm giving you a short amount of time because I don't want you to think too deeply about your responses. Whatever flows first will be closest to the truth. If you are new to this type of exercise, you may be in for a surprise. What you write may be very different from what you think when you first read the question. Give it a try. Don't forget you can time yourself using your cell phone's alarm.

Where Am I Now?

Where are you in terms of your life? Where are you in your career path? Are you on target for the plan you made? (We all have one, especially when we are young). Or have you lost your way? Life has a way of imposing unexpected demands on you. Have you been able to weather the storms and stay on track, or are you surprised to find yourself in your current job or career? Please be as specific as you can.

How Did I Get Here?

Trace the literal circumstances that brought you to this point in time. Did a family illness derail you? Or are you following the fast track? There is no right or wrong answer. We just want to see the mechanics of the process in black and white. You may be surprised by what you discover.

Are you feeling stuck? Not sure what you should write? Here are some prompts to head you in the right direction. See if any of the following describe your current work situation:

- I got a job right out of college and never left. It's not what I wanted to do but the pay is adequate and I need the benefits.
- I was out of the work force raising a family and I'm lucky to have this job. At my age and with my responsibilities, I can't be picky.
- I love the work I do. It's the people I work with who wear me out.
- We're short staffed. If there were more people to pick up the slack, I'd say I had the perfect job.
- My job is okay. I work with nice people, the pay is good, and the benefits are great. But I hate the commute. I spend so much time on the road that I miss quality time with my family.
- I believed that having my own business was the ticket to freedom. Now I am overwhelmed with business, fam-ily, and social demands. In fact, my business demands are so overwhelming and all-encompassing that I no longer spend quality time with my family and my friends are up in arms over my prolonged absence.

Did you recognize yourself in any of these? Do you relate to more than one scenario? Take advantage of your five minutes and jot down your feelings about your current situation. If none of these capture the issue you have with your work life, take a minute to describe it in a few sentences.

We want to understand the macro experience rather than the micro one. If you fell into your job by chance, for example, massive positive changes in your day-to-day work life may not heal the hole in your soul. The idea is to be fulfilled. (And if you are one of the lucky few who are engaged in a profession you love and work for the company of your dreams, you can pat yourself on the back and be grateful!)

What Do I Love?

This is one of the most important questions in this book. Very often we are passionate as young people and then we are told that our passions are meaningless. Life, "they" assure us, is about a paycheck. Take a minute to write down and reconnect with your passions. It may be time to welcome them back into your life.

In college, I was a theater major with a minor in romance languages. My parents were deeply concerned. Exactly what job, they wondered, was I preparing myself for? When I was about to graduate, I registered with the job referral service at school to make my parents happy.

The college service sent me to interview for a job with the FBI. Not only was it a government position, I would be working directly with incoming visitors to the United States at JFK Airport. My parents saw this as a great way to make use of my romance language minor. For several days FBI agents canvassed our Brooklyn neighborhood, interviewing neighbors about me. I went to the office at the airport and was fingerprinted. My parents were beside themselves with joy when I was offered the job. A funereal pall settled over our home the day I turned it down.

Somehow at the tender age of twenty-one I had the courage to listen to the still, small voice within telling me that this profession was not for me. No matter how rocky the future might be, I had to believe in myself and try my luck in show business. I never did achieve great success, but I was a working actress for many years and I loved what I did. What comforts me is that I can look back and know the outcome of that challenge. It would have been terrible to end my days wondering what might have been.

Have you followed your dreams in life? Is your job a fulfilling one? It doesn't have to be a grandiose position for you to give a "yes" response—do you take pride in what you do, and at the end of the work day, do you feel tremendous satisfaction?

If you are in a profession or job that is far from your original goal for your life, can you make a switch? At the very least can you find a way to incorporate elements of that dream into your life now?

As a young girl in China, Dr. Linda Zhang loved to dance. At sixteen she told her parents that she wanted to be a professional dancer. Their reaction mirrored that of my parents: Get a real idea. Instead of becoming a dancer, she became an acupuncturist and a doctor of Oriental medicine, with a large and successful practice. Linda's passion for dance is fulfilled these days in the myriad number of dance classes she takes each week. Instead of a profession, it's how she stays in shape.

I know a man who always wanted to be an actor, but he took the more traditional road in life and had a successful career in corporate America. He's retired now and guess what? He spends his days participating in local community theatre.

Take five minutes and make a list of your passions—or even just one or two things that have always captured your imagination. Then list two or three *creative* ways you can incorporate your passions into your life today.

As this week draws to a close, take a look at what you have accomplished. If you are the least bit unhappy at work, you now have a much better understanding of the larger issues at play. You also see clearly the path that led you to your current job. A wonderful word in Eastern philosophy is *maya,* or *delusion.* Often people are unhappy with their jobs for reasons that have nothing to do with the actual set of circumstances they find themselves in. This week we part the veil of *maya* and face reality. And what would reality be without some magic? Reintroducing a long lost passion into your life can make your very soul sing. Next week we'll figure out the next step for changing your life. Are you excited?

WEEK TWO

Decide Where You Want to Be

This week, you can

- Set realistic career goals for yourself to accomplish this year . . . and beyond
- Break your goals down into the steps required to fulfill them

Time required: Ninety minutes

WE'VE ALL SEEN THE CHARACTER in movies or on TV who wakes up one day astonished that his life has flown by and he has not accomplished what he set out to do. It's so easy to identify with him. This week you're going to craft a plan for the coming year that will give more direction and meaning to your life, so you will never again be in danger of identifying with that archetype when you see him on screen or read about him in books. You'll be thinking: didn't he have any goals?

GETTING AHEAD

Let's look at the most mundane of examples. Most of us greet the New Year with at least five extra pounds. You don't have to get on a scale—you know the minute you can't zip up your pants that all those holiday treats have taken refuge on your hips and that you want to do something about it.

Goal: Lose five pounds.

Next, you'd set a target date. Say you want to get rid of these five pounds before a wedding two months away.

Goal with target date: Lose five pounds by March 1.

The key to weight loss is simple and as old as the hills: If you eat less and move more, you could lose one pound a week. After setting your goal, you'd probably research diet and exercise plans before deciding what diet you are going to follow and which exercise you feel you can enjoy. You know you need to stick with both programs to ensure success.

Goal with target date and plan: Lose five pounds by March 1 by following a low-carb diet every day and jogging three times per week.

Guess what? This simple sequence is the blueprint for achieving all your goals. Figure out what you want, ascertain the steps that will bring them to fruition, and then schedule these steps in a logical way. Grab your notebook and let's start making sense of your future. After all, that's what our goals carry us to . . . the future.

Getting Ahead: Your Current Job

Let's say you've been in your current job almost a year. You know your review is coming up in a few months and you want to ask for a raise or a promotion. This situation has two usual traps: self-doubt, and the feeling that if you were appreciated, you would be given a raise without asking. Instead of falling victim, why not plan to achieve your goal? Here's how your plan might look.

Goal with Target Date: A raise at the end of your performance review in two months.

The Plan: Now that you have a target date, you need to figure out what you will need to present to show that you have earned this raise:

What have I accomplished in the last year? More to the point, what have I accomplished that is above and beyond my job description? Be as specific as possible.

Why am I valuable to the company's bottom line? What are my unique contributions? A good sales rep's value to the company, for example, can more easily be judged in dollars and cents. But an executive may also be judged on the extra efforts she makes to promote the company's standing in the community. An assistant might be evaluated on her ability to keep herself as well as the executives she is assigned to well organized.

What can I do between now and my performance review to improve my position?

Are other people performing my job? Is my pay commensurate with theirs? If not, have they been here much longer than I have?

How does my salary compare to the salary range for my position in the industry?

Does the economy in general or the economic fortunes of my company or both indicate that money for a raise is within the company or corporate budget? For example, if a memo just went out canceling all raises and freezing new hires for the next fiscal year, it may not be the best time to ask for a raise. However, it would not be imprudent to document your contributions to the company. After all, these will have an affect on your ability to make more when the time is appropriate to ask.

What other kind of research can you do to improve your chances? The more homework you do, the stronger your presentation will be.

Getting Ahead: A New Job

Let's face it. Nothing is forever, not even your current job. I am not advocating that you leave your job on a whim, but at some point you will outgrow your current situation and need to challenge yourself.

Goal with Target Date: A new job in eight months.

The Plan: Securing a new job is similar to your plan for getting a raise. You have to ask some of the same questions about your achievements and abilities, except now your field has widened.

The big difference is that you will be reaching out to other entities for assistance. If you are devoted to the Internet, you might register at a site like Monster. com. If you have a high-level position and live in a major city, you might register with a headhunter. Perhaps you have family, friends, or colleagues in the area of business in which you'd like to work. It would be prudent to open those lines of communication.

You'd be wise to have all of your ducks in a row (I couldn't resist) before you go public with your search. If word gets back to your current employer, you may find yourself on the unemployment line before you find your new job. The key once again is preparedness. How current is your resume? Have you documented the contributions you've made to your company? We'll go into both areas in detail in a later chapter. For now, the watchword is simple: create a time frame to pull together all the items that show what a rising star you are!

Getting Ahead: A Career Change

Perhaps an examination of your lost passions in life may spark a desire to change professions altogether. Whatever the impetus, this requires a bit more research.

Goal with Target Date: Change careers in the next eighteen months.

The Plan: Your biggest challenge is to find out what credentials you need to enter this new field of endeavor. Do you already have them or will you need to head back to school? A client of mine is in the middle of just such a quest. She works in an office as an executive assistant, and makes good money, enjoys her colleagues, and has wonderful benefits. However, Fran wants to work with children because she feels that mentoring children will bring her far more satisfaction than helping to sell widgets. Her specific goal is to help the parents of children with disabilities so that they receive all the financial, educational, and psychological help to which they are entitled.

Fran has a bachelor's degree. Her research revealed that she needs a master's before she can enter the school system in California as a special education advocate. She is on a three-year plan of transition that includes taking part-time classes at the local community college.

Do you need a bachelor's degree, an advanced degree, or some specialized training? Do you know which colleges or universities in your area offer the classes you need? Would a move to another city make this career change easier? Can you count on your family to be supportive? They will need their own transition plan if this is the route you take.

Does research sound like a daunting task? Do you feel that you had best stick with your current job because you just don't have the time to do this extra work? Let's reframe the term *research* so it doesn't sound so scary. Instead of "doing research," why not say to yourself, "I am figuring out the details to make my dream a reality." Who would run from that task?

LOOKING AHEAD: ACHIEVEMENT IN LIFE

If you aren't sure what dream you want to chase for your life, here are some questions to help flesh out the reality that's hiding just beneath the surface of your conscious mind. Grab your notebook and have some fun. You're Indiana Jones on a mission. Cue music!

1. What do you most long to achieve in life? (If you have several things, list them in order of importance.)
2. Is this a realistic and achievable goal?
3. Have you done anything yet to make this goal a reality?

   If you have, what has stopped you in the past from going all the way to the end?
4. What steps would you need to take now to see this goal as part of the reality of your life rather than a dream?
5. What stands in your way?

Please be specific and detailed as you answer these questions.

Here's an example of how this exercise might look. Janet is a middle manager in a large corporation located in Manhattan.

What do you most long to achieve in life?
I'd like to be part of a company that is working toward transforming the planet, such as Greenpeace. I admire what they do for the environment. And when I was growing up, music was my passion. I'd like to find a way to incorporate it into my life and if possible my work.

Is this a realistic and achievable goal?
Transferring to a "conscious corporation" is a possibility, but it might come with a pay cut. I'm not sure I could make that work and continue to live here in Manhattan. I need to make some calls and research online and see the fiscal reality for positions with such companies. I'd also need to find the headquarters of the top five companies that appeal to me.

Have you done anything yet to make this a reality?
Nope. It has stayed in the dream phase, until now.

If you have, what has stopped you in the past from going all the way to the end?
My parents harp on my need to build my financial security. They don't support any organizations like this. Their charitable contributions go to medical research because diabetes runs in our family. My dad thinks global warming is a public relations campaign.

What steps would you need to take now to see this goal as part of the reality of your life rather than a dream?
As I noted, I have to check out company headquarters and see if I would enjoy living

in any of the cities involved. If I've never been to those cities, I might take some fact-finding weekend trips. In addition to salary and location, I'd need to see the typical available positions in this type of company. Would my current experience and skill set make for an easy transition? I might need some additional training, such as an advanced degree or some classes in law or accounting to boost my resume. In the meantime, I think I'll do some volunteer work. This will make me feel good about myself and I might snag some contacts!

As for music, I'm not sure. I think I need to work on my career transition first and foremost. I might take some piano lessons. Haven't done that in years! Or perhaps I could find a school nearby that would be open to my developing a music program as an after-school activity. I'm open to anything!

What stands in your way?
Fear of failure, I suppose, and the wrath of family and friends. Nobody likes change and this would really rock the boat. However, I also think that it wouldn't take too much time for everyone to see how much happier I would be. I'll do my investigating in secret for now. When I'm ready to make a change, I'll share my dream, my goal, and . . . my research!

FOCUS ON THE FUTURE, NOT THE PAST

Remember the old V8 commercials? Someone was always slapping their forehead and exclaiming: "Wow! I coulda' had a V8!" Well, you'll do a variation on this theme after this exercise. It's so easy and so human to resort to guilt, shame, and fear when we think about what might have been. Let's replace "I should have gotten my degree, traveled to Europe, owned a home, gotten married, . . . by now" with something more positive like "I didn't realize that my goal to be a social worker was postponed after I left college to get married. I can resume my studies. It may take a bit longer because I'll have to study nights and weekends, but at least I will reach my goal."

I have a client who came to me in desperation. Colleen had just been terminated from a job she felt was her true calling in life: director of fundraising for a charity devoted to helping battered women. Losing her job was devastating to her. We decided that in addition to getting her physical space in order, we would do some work to help her find another job, perhaps in a related field, one that would satisfy her need to be of service in the world.

Looking back over her childhood dreams and her experiences as an adult, Colleen did indeed find a new profession that would allow her to use her compassion and communication and the skills she had acquired thus far in life. There was one problem: The position required a master's degree in psychology and she had only a bachelor's.

So she made a plan. With a little creativity and a lot of faith, she found an interim job working as a weekend nanny. She was able to maintain her connection to children and at the same time prepare for her eventual career. Her position as a nanny to a wealthy family pays full-time pay for part-time hours. She enjoys the work and makes use of her free time by taking classes toward the degree she needs. It will take a few years to reach her goal, but in the meantime she is supporting herself and her family. It's win-win for everyone involved.

ONE GOAL AT A TIME

If you have multiple goals that are dear to you, remember not to get caught in the trap of becoming overwhelmed. You probably can't fulfill all your goals at once. See if you can group them by category. Start with the one whose fulfillment will send positive energy into all the others.

Of all the assignments this year, I think this week might be my favorite. You can waste a lot of time *dreaming about* rather than *working toward* fulfilling your goals. The rubber hits the road this week. Do you really want what you say you do or are you content to just dream? Either decision will change the course of your life. After this week, however, you will know how to break down a dream or wish into the steps that will bring it to you. By the way, be prepared to find that the fulfillment of your dream may not look exactly as you imagined. Different is very often better. Next week we're going to investigate a simple, often overlooked tool to help you in your quest for something more fulfilling in your life. Get some rest and enjoy a reward for all of your written preparation and research.

WEEK THREE

Keep a Calendar

This week, you can

- Invest in the right calendar
- Harness more time to serve you and your goals

Time required: Sixty minutes

I COULD DESCRIBE SYLVIA AS A HUMAN dynamo. She's an executive assistant who has a special gift for putting out fires. I was in awe of her capacity to keep her forward motion with such grace and humor. One day, the true situation revealed itself. Sylvia was indeed terrific at dealing with emergencies but had almost no ability to stay on top of projects and everyday matters.

Constantly reacting to last-minute (or past-due) deadlines has a certain level of drama. You live a life tempered by emergency and excitement. When you step in and save the day with that urgently needed report, you are perceived as a hero, aren't you? But this kind of work life is physically, mentally, and emotionally exhausting.

Sylvia needed to embrace the *extended* use of a calendar. Like many people, Sylvia had some things written on her calendar but depended on her memory to hold the balance. We worked out a system that recorded all of her appointments and project deadlines. Each day she had an agenda to accomplish no matter what fires erupted around her. With a little conscious planning, each day led her and her boss to the fulfillment of the big-picture goals they shared for the future of the company.

Life without conscious direction never changes. It is the very essence of "same old, same old." Moreover, when we see things written down, we are in a better position to judge the whole. We are no longer thinking in snippets of time; we're dealing with the macrocosm called our life. By the end of this week, you will understand exactly what I'm talking about. Let's get started.

YOUR NEW BEST FRIEND: A CALENDAR

First things first. Are you one of those people with a brain that retains all the details of your life? I can't tell you how many of my clients tell me they keep key details in their heads. This often includes their entire schedule, from their weekly 8 a.m. meeting with the boss on Tuesdays to their 12:30 p.m. lunch date on Thursday . . . or is that *next* Thursday? I assure them that one day the biology of their brain will change and it won't be possible to do this juggling act. In my youth I had a photographic memory; I too kept a lot in my head. Time passes, however, and one day this skill becomes a little rusty.

A calendar is your lifeline. It tells you in black and white where you are going and where you have been. (In fact it's a good item to save at year's end as proof of your work schedule should you itemize your deductions for the IRS.) If you want to become more successful, you'll want to consistently use some kind of calendar system to support your efforts and conserve your energies. Let's take a brief look at the major types of calendars you have to choose from.

Calendar Don'ts

Desk Pad Calendar: Many of my clients use a calendar on their desk that also serves as a desk pad. This is a highly inefficient idea. (The one exception is if your desk rarely has any paper on it.) If you have to move papers, reference books, or your lunch to check a date, reconsider!

Pocket Calendar: Another calendar I don't recommend is the type you carry with you that is so tiny you have to be a Lilliputian to use it. I realize these calendars fit nicely into a purse or suit pocket and that some are made by purveyors of fine luxury leather goods and cost a king's ransom. No matter how much you pay, if you have no room to write, well, reconsider.

Calendar Clutter: By the way, in late December and early January everyone will be handing you a calendar. The charity you donated money to will send you one with sweet animal faces or starving children peering back at you. Your dry cleaner will have one for you with photos of sweeping natural vistas or great works of art. And, of course, at least one friend or colleague will make a calendar for you showing the family kids or pets.

A simple "No, thank you" to your dry cleaner will suffice. Recycle or give the charity calendar to someone else. Take a moment to ooh and aah over the pics of the kids and the dogs and then . . . you guessed it, recycle or trash. These calendars are not useful. Except for the last example, they are inexpensive marketing tools. If you hold on to all of them because you feel guilty, you are creating clutter. I give you permission to let them go.

Calendar Do's

Paper Calendar System: At any large office supply store, you will find a vast array of paper calendar systems that you can tailor to suit your own needs. I use Day Runner, the Franklin Covey system is wildly popular, and Day Timer is another good system. Many of my clients who work in corporate America have been offered the Franklin Covey planners as well as free training in how to use the system. I find it complicated and it has too much cross-referencing for my taste. I do, however, admire the advice they offer: Don't adopt our system in total; adapt it to suit your needs and your personality. That's the key to success with any calendar system.

All paper calendar companies have holders for the pages and whatever other inserts you purchase. (A calendar insert is a type of document or product you might need for your planner, such as telephone and address pages, business card holders, and notepads.)

I use the Entrepreneur Edition of the Day Runner because of its large size, which gives me the most room. You might want a midsize calendar so that you can carry it with you to appointments. I protect my calendar by not taking it out of my home office. Every night, I consult my calendar and make a to-do list for the next day. It can be fulfilling to cross items off and watch the progress of your day unfold. Remember: Your schedule should be fluid. You aren't writing it on stone tablets!

Zippered leather (and mock leather) planners are also available. Some versions simply shut closed and others have a Velcro snap. You will be using your planner and its holder frequently; buy ones that are esthetically pleasing so you will enjoy using them.

If this is a new purchase, the holder will come with a few basic sheets. At the store, you can study the other reference materials the company offers, such as expense reports pages, a pouch for the front that can hold writing instruments, and blank or lined sheets for note taking. The choice of the calendar pages themselves, however, is perhaps the most important choice you have to make. Let's take a look.

Calendar Pages: If your schedule is unpredictable week-to-week or tends to get crazy, *month-at-a-glance* calendar pages can help you build some downtime into your life. Last weekend, for example, I worked Friday, Saturday, and Sunday with clients. In addition to standing on my feet each day for eight hours, I knew I'd then be spending three hours in traffic! It was important to me to have Monday blocked out as a day of rest. If I didn't use a calendar, I might be tempted to say "yes" to a social invitation without thinking that I would probably be too tired to enjoy the event.

If your days are frequently full of different meetings and events, you might prefer a *day-at-a-time* calendar system so you have more room to jot down notes and appointments. This page is in effect your to-do list. If you carry your book with you and make notes during the day with phone numbers and e-mail addresses, for example, log them into your main contact area (computer or hard copy) so you won't be using this year's planner as a reference book for years to come.

I rarely collect business cards unless I am truly interested in the person and his or her service. Keep a business card holder in your office and file new cards as soon as you return. If you take a minute to review the cards, you may find that you don't need to retain them after all. You'll find many such tasks become mechanical, take little time, and keep you organized. It's easier to take two minutes to log today's contacts than to sit for hours once every year because you weren't committed to the ongoing maintenance process.

The average client has a collection of business cards and slips of paper scattered about his desk. About once a year they get gathered and shoved into a container. Don't let this happen to you! This is not only inefficient but also bound to make you feel guilty. Let's create another good habit—log new contact information at the end of each day. You can keep a computer file and toss the card itself.

The *week-at-a-glance* calendar system is in many ways a nice compromise between the two previous systems and works well if you have a set schedule with little variation. You aren't concerned about balancing your energy expenditure with a month-at-a-glance system, and a week's worth of events can be less overwhelming to absorb than a month's worth.

Wall Calendar: The only way I see a wall calendar being of use in a work setting is if you simply want a quick visual reference point. If the staff meets in a command center or conference room on a regular basis and it's key to instantly know the whereabouts of team members or due dates for projects, a large calendar would serve you well.

There is a place for wall calendars. In the home where a busy mom and dad are trying to keep track of multiple after-school programs, parties, and social invitations, a large, centrally located wall calendar can be the best way to keep everyone abreast of the family schedule.

Electronic Calendar: An electronic calendar is a great tool whether you use a Mac, a PC, a handheld PDA, or a combination. If you work for a large company or corporation, you most likely use a PC and have Outlook as your calendar. The Mac calendar system is equally helpful. These electronic calendars automatically perform functions for you that would take a lot of work to cross-reference by hand. But the crux of the matter is the word *use.* No system is going to divine your schedule, your needs, or the way you like to function. You have *to do* something, and you have to do it regularly!

Online Calendar: You can find calendars online from providers such as AOL, Yahoo!, and Google. Check with your Internet provider to see what they offer. These calendars are usually creative and fun to use. If you are at a computer all day, you couldn't have a handier calendar.

MAKE A DATE, WRITE IT DOWN . . . EVERY SINGLE TIME

Any system, whether handwritten or electronic, requires that you maintain it. Let's look at the time involved for this task. Taking the time to keep going back to your calendar to jot down or modify appointments may seem like a waste at first if you're not used to doing it. But it takes no more than ten minutes a day to maintain and reference whatever system you choose.

Let me ask you this: How much of your time is spent in a frantic search for invitations? You know you have a social function to go to soon, but you don't know whether it's this weekend or next. Will you have time to shop for a gift? What about work assignments? Do you hit your head against the wall when you realize that you have less time than you remembered to turn in a proposal? These shocks to the system not only waste time but also drain you physically and emotionally.

If you agree to something, whether it's a meeting at work, attending your daughter's dance recital, or flying to Dallas on business, you must *immediately* enter that commitment on your calendar. This is a wonderful habit to cultivate. Have you ever noticed how happily married couples never say "yes" to an invitation? They always say something like, "I think that date is clear but I have to check with my spouse." You must first check with your calendar. It holds the key to your time—and that's the key to your future.

Commit your energies one hundred percent to the activities of the present moment. You can do this with ease when you consciously plan your life. When your schedule just seems to happen, it's more difficult to be in the present moment because there's a constant drama in your head. You wonder, "What's next on my agenda? Did I forget something? Should I be doing something else right now?" Getting organized using a calendar system takes time, but it requires far less time than the hit-or-miss, "I've got it all in my head" system. Give it a try. What have you got to lose but a lot of stress, aggravation, and oh yes, wasted time?

WEEK FOUR

Calm the Morning Rush

This week, you can

- Commit to going to bed earlier each night, eating breakfast, and exercising for a few minutes
- Clear the debris out of your morning rush as well as your kitchen
- Practice making decisions
- Create a morning routine

Time required: Thirty to ninety minutes

WE HAVE A TENDENCY TO COM-partmentalize our lives. We think of the work we do as something apart from the time we spend being with our family and friends, engaging in our hobbies, or practicing our spiritual beliefs. In the traditions of the East, all aspects of our life are seen as parts of the whole. Once again, my favorite Zen proverb to reference is, "The way a man does one thing is the way he does everything."

So this week, let's examine what's happening in your home in the morning. Do you leave the house exhausted before you even get to the office? If you are always getting up late, can't find your clothes for the day, don't have a chance to eat breakfast, and leave too late to be on time, I bet

you take that scattered energy into the workplace. Even more than that, I bet you recreate that crazed morning experience throughout your workday. You feel there's never enough hours, you can't find the information you need in a timely fashion, and the day begins with drama and continues in that vein. Does this ring true for your experience?

FROM MAYHEM TO MAJESTY

When it comes to meals, "breakfast is king." How would you describe your first meal? Or do you have one? This year is about change, so grab your shopping list and get ready for breakfast. Whether you are introducing new types of food or up-grading what you eat now, food is where the new morning ritual begins.

And I don't know about you, but being late and having to rush sends me into a panic—and it takes me hours to unwind. This week you'll organize an easier start to your day. We're going to consider all the elements: food as I noted, exercise, time wasters like e-mail, and of course that in-dispensable ingredient . . . sleep.

Food Is Fuel: Eat Breakfast

Proper nutrition is vital to our ability to think clearly, focus easily, and have the stamina to work well. If your typical break-fast is loaded with sugar, caffeine, white flour, and other empty calories—think cof-fee and doughnuts—or worse, if you're skipping breakfast, guess what? You aren't going to be a dynamo of energy in the morning. Your body is a machine and needs fuel; a quality breakfast is key to the success of your day. Whether you have a full, balanced meal or a fruit smoothie and a piece of whole grain toast, it should be something you can prepare quickly and easily. A health food bar, by the way, is *not* a meal, especially if eaten while you drive your car or sit on the train. (And check the ingredients on that health food bar. If high-fructose corn syrup is in the top three ingredients, you are really eating a candy bar.)

Take a few minutes to sit and plan your breakfast menu for the next week, and then add whatever ingredients you need to your shopping list. Try real food for one week and see if you don't feel the difference.

Exercise for Fifteen Minutes

It takes energy to boost your energy. In the morning, set aside fifteen minutes to exer-cise at home. During the times when I was unable to exercise, within a week or two I began to feel sluggish and exhausted.

You don't have to run a marathon. Be-gin slowly. If you live in an apartment building, take the stairs instead of the ele-vator. Or choose an exercise DVD and spend a few minutes getting in shape with the whole family in your living room. Not only will you get more energy for the start of your day, but your body will change, making you feel more self-confident. One good change feeds another!

Go to Bed Half an Hour Earlier

If you are working into the wee hours and getting up at the crack of dawn, you are go-ing to be exhausted. Your body needs rest to perform at optimal levels. Commit to going to bed a little earlier at night and getting up earlier each morning. It's the easiest way to break the cycle of chronic lateness.

Avoid snoozing by getting out of bed immediately after your alarm goes off. If you absolutely need more time to wake up, I suggest two alarm clocks *without* a snooze button. Set one to go off fifteen minutes before you need to get out of bed. This will give you a chance to wrap your mind around the need to rise and shine.

Eliminate Electronic Time Wasters

Checking Multiple E-Mail Accounts: Avoid checking e-mail first thing in the morning. If you are an international trav-

STILL EXHAUSTED? SEE YOUR DOCTOR

I had a client who could not get up for work. She was chronically late and on the verge of being fired. After seeing her physician, a blood test revealed she was anemic. A few weeks of iron supplements and she was up with the birds. You might be suffering from a health condition that's dragging you down. Low thyroid hormone levels is another common culprit for exhaustion. Don't neglect this opportunity to monitor your health. Make an appointment to see your physician for a physical, especially if it has been more than a year since your last visit.

eler, I understand that you might need to be kept abreast of overnight developments. A doctor might need to know the condition of a critically ill patient. For the average person, however, checking e-mail is a trap. It's amazing how creative we can be when we just don't want to face the day.

As you get ready for your day, don't stop to open personal e-mail. Don't open work e-mail. Don't check the sales. Don't make a purchase. You can do all these things later in the day. In fact, if you commute by mass transit, you have time for this built into your day.

It's tough to turn away from the computer, but you can do it. Why not devote the time you would waste to eating a good breakfast? If you feed your body, you're going to be a lot more attentive when you do read those e-mails.

Listening to Work Voice Mail Messages: Let's face it: In a true emergency your office knows how to reach you, but true emergencies are few and far between. Devote your morning to yourself and any family obligations you have. Let work wait its turn. Sometimes the need to check e-mail and voice mail are symptomatic of problems that do not arise from our work but certainly have an effect on it. Does feeling needed by colleagues 24/7 fill an emotional void? Are there problems at home with a spouse, parents, or children? You might be avoiding dealing with those issues by staying plugged into work.

Surfing the Internet: You say to yourself, "Wow! I got up early this morning so I have five minutes to surf online or resume that game I started." A half hour later you are now officially late for work. Follow the old antidrug slogan, just say "no." Schedule twenty minutes of Internet surfing or gaming as a reward later in the day. In the morning, keep the focus on *you*.

Time It! If you frequently spend your morning on any of the time wasters just listed and can't seem to break the habit, why not set a timer and see exactly how much time each of these take from you each morning? What if you spent that time another way? Let's say you find that you spend twenty minutes on the Internet. If you haven't been eating breakfast or exercising, could you spend your twenty minutes on that instead? Instead of getting up earlier, you could just shift your focus.

Organize Your Kitchen

For many people, the morning madness is exacerbated by a kitchen that is not organized and doesn't support any morning routine except ongoing chaos. Let's do a quick cleanup of this room. It will be good practice for next month, when we'll be sweeping through your work space eliminating the obvious debris. Are you ready?

Set a timer and spend twenty minutes moving through your kitchen from one cupboard to the next, from one drawer to the next, and checking under the sink. Remove whatever items you are not using. Do they need to go in the trash? Could they be donated to a charity? Is there a close friend who might like the item? Perhaps it's something like the turkey roaster that gets used only on Thanksgiving. Would it free up space if you moved it to the garage? You get the idea. And don't forget to check expiration dates when you get to the pantry. You'll be amazed how old some of your staples are!

Make your decisions quickly. If you have a very large kitchen, you might need an additional twenty minutes to complete this task. Before we move to the world of paper and projects, we're going to practice in this arena. And the by-product will be a room freed of clutter where you can more easily plot the beginning of each day.

Once your kitchen has been divested of extraneous items, you'll feel a change. We can't take the time now to completely reorganize your kitchen, but you can, however, take a look around and make a few additional key improvements. A few simple changes can help you work faster in the morning. Decide what you have to do and set the timer for thirty minutes. Here are your guideline queries:

Are your dishes, glasses, and mugs grouped in convenient areas or spread out in various cupboards? Dishes and glasses are usually stored on either side of the sink. If you have a coffeepot on the counter, put your mugs on a nearby shelf, preferably right above the pot. You can grab your mug while the coffee is brewing. "Geographical intelligence" can be applied to a room, not only driving around your neighborhood.

Is your food in one area and grouped by category? When you're looking for your morning cereal is it currently buried behind large cans of soup or chili?

Would you save time if your children could serve themselves? If you move their plates and cups to a low shelf, your children will be in a position to help themselves. This will save time and build their self-esteem.

Do you have older children who could pitch in and handle some chores? Setting and clearing the table; loading and unloading the dishwasher or washing the dishes by hand and putting them away; taking out the trash; walking the dog; feeding the dog or cat (or whatever other pets you might have); emptying the litter box; and last but not least, helping younger siblings.

What other activities do you have to tend to in the morning that lend themselves to becoming chores? No one person should be responsible for everything, especially a parent who works outside the home!

Plan Your Bathroom Time

Create a bathroom ritual to help you save time. For example, in the morning before I hop into the shower, I set out all the lotions and potions I need to use before I leave the house. As my makeup, deodorant, toothbrush, floss, and oral rinse return to their permanent locations, I can gauge how much progress I am making and how much time I need. Would this process help you?

The more people in your home vying for bathroom time, the hairier things can get. Why not call a family meeting and work out a set schedule? Who needs to shower first? How much time is fair to allot for bathroom use? Are things being done in the bathroom that could be done in a bedroom? Putting makeup on in the natural light of a bedroom window, for example, might give someone else more shower time. The larger the family, the more regimented the schedule becomes.

CREATE A MORNING ROUTINE

How could you make your morning flow more easily? Let's see if we can't create a sample routine that you can adjust to suit your situation. The great thing about a household routine or system, by the way,

is that it is composed of a series of good habits. You are in effect building your organizing skill set with this simple exercise.

The night before, do the following:

- Set the table for breakfast.
- Put cereals on a shelf in a low cabinet so the youngest members of the family can help themselves.
- Assign chores.
- Determine who will feed and walk the dog (or tend to whatever pets you have).
- Decide who will help with the younger children.
- Assign the task of taking out the garbage.
- Set your clothes out and be sure everything from clean underwear to your jewelry is in place.
- Teach your children how to plan their outfits to save time during the morning rush.

ENJOY YOUR BONUS TIME

As you introduce positive routines into your daily life, you get a little bonus: extra time. For example, I am very slow in the morning but I can't stand rushing. To have a peaceful morning, therefore, I have to rise exactly two hours before I exit my home. The first hour is devoted to meditation, taking the dog out, eating breakfast, and skimming the newspaper.

The second hour I take my shower, get dressed, and take the dog out one more

IN THE MORNING

Here's a sample routine for a single working mother of two school-age kids.

5:30 a.m.: Mom wakes up. She takes a quick shower and then enjoys five minutes of meditation.

5:45 a.m.: Mom does ten minutes of yoga postures or takes a brisk walk around the block with Fido. She flips the switch on the automatic coffeemaker (that was set up last night) as she starts her exercise.

6:00 a.m.: Mom wakes her oldest. While she spends fifteen minutes showering and getting dressed, mom is packing lunches for everyone. The menu for the week is set the previous week so there is no guesswork and all grocery supplies are in the pantry.

6:15 a.m.: Mom wakes her youngest. He has fifteen minutes to shower and get dressed. The oldest is helping mom set the table and make breakfast.

6:30 a.m.: Everyone sits down for a quick, nutritious breakfast. There is a review of schedules for any changes that must be logged into mom's Outlook calendar.

6:45 a.m.: While the children take out the garbage, give Fido his food and fresh water, and wash the breakfast dishes (or load the dishwasher), mom is double-checking all school backpacks (if applicable, depending on the age of the children) and her briefcase. Anyone with a cell phone remove it from cell phone its charger and places it in a backpack or purse.

7:00 a.m.: Everyone has twenty minutes to take care of last-minute grooming needs. The car rolls out of the driveway at 7:30. Ten emergency minutes are built into this system at this time. They can be applied to any needed segment and the entire routine can shift according to demand.

7:30 a.m.: Mom drops her oldest at the public transit station, then takes her youngest to school, and starts her commute around 7:50. She is at work by 8:30.

time. Anything I need in terms of organizing tools, such as my label maker or business papers, has been laid out the night before. If I need a briefcase, it's all packed and ready to go, as is my lunch. I've decided the night before what I'm going to wear. In the morning, everything is easy to grab.

If I do every task just a little bit faster than usual, I get a few minutes of bonus time to apply any way I like. Your routine is meant to serve you. Play with it and feel free to experiment.

Becoming more successful and leading a balanced life literally starts with each new morning. This week you are to be applauded for the work you have accomplished. (I am sure many of you were surprised to find that a book on increased work productivity has taken you into your kitchen.) To be truly successful, every aspect of our lives must work in concert with every other. As your morning goes, so goes the day . . . a little more sleep at night, better food in the morning, and some exercise will reap huge benefits. In about three weeks you won't remember living life any other way.

JANUARY SUMMARY

WEEK ONE

Is your work life in chaos or is the chaos a reflection of your unhappiness in life? The former can be solved with organizing techniques; the latter needs a reexamination of the direction you are taking in life. View it as a great opportunity, not a homework assignment!

WEEK TWO

Set a realistic career goal for the year into motion. Now your work has a direction.

WEEK THREE

Some tools are indispensable in the war against wasting time. Invest in the most important one of all, the humble calendar.

WEEK FOUR

Create your first routine of the year by making your morning a smooth transition into a busy day.

2. FEBRUARY

Make the Most of Your Office Space

A person works best when he or she works without motive,

neither for money, nor for fame, nor for anything else . . .

and out of such people will come the power to work

in such a manner as will transform the world.

—VIVEKANANDA

Now that you have a plan for your future in mind, let's roll up our sleeves this month and do some organizing. It's going to be easier to achieve your goals if the environment you're working in is in order. The way a physical space is set up can support your best efforts or sabotage you at every turn. When you can find your important papers easily, when you no longer have to search for a pen that writes, and if coworkers are always remarking how great your office looks, these are signs that you are being supported by your environment.

Removing debris is one of the first and most important things I do with my clients. Energy in a space can't be seen but we certainly experience it. Your office will literally *feel* different when it has less stuff. Tackling large clusters of clutter enables us to see immediate and dramatic results.

Your colleagues will immediately appreciate the clear path to your desk, and you'll be encouraged to continue your organizing journey when you can open a drawer with ease or have more surface space.

By the end of this month, with a little old-fashioned elbow grease, you'll be working in an environment that works for you—and stays that way! You will experience peace of mind whenever you enter your office.

FIGURE OUT HOW THIS CLUTTER HAPPENED

If you are swamped, you have probably allowed garden-variety clutter to pile up in your office or cubicle for one or more of the following reasons:

- You have an inability to make quick decisions. When we don't know what to do with something, it stays put. After last month's practice, you are well on your way to solving that issue.
- You have no idea what the fix might be. It would be great to get rid of those stacks, but where will they go? It's not difficult, but it can seem overwhelming if you don't know the steps and the tools.
- It takes time to set things right.

"How can I take the time to get organized when I need to devote every second to work?" Is that your lament? You are right. Getting organized does take some time. But let's consider the benefits.

If you were to add up the time you spend looking for things over the course of a year, it would be far greater than the time you are going to invest in getting organized now. A streamlined environment will continue to save time and you are free to apply it to your projects. How much more efficient is that?

You also cut down on your stress level when you eliminate clutter and the daily drama it creates. Constant stress can lead to or exacerbate health problems; an ordered environment contributes to peace and harmony. Next time you lose your keys or an important document, check your body after the drama passes. Is your heart racing? Did you break out into a sweat? Do you feel sick to your stomach? Taking time to get organized now will eliminate these reactions from your work experience.

Finally, when your environment is organized, you know what you have. For example, you won't be wasting money on office supplies you already own, nor will you be calling the Human Resources department for yet another copy of the company medical plan.

These are the most common benefits. What other benefits would you add to the list?

BREAK IT DOWN

While I prefer working in large blocks of time dedicated to getting organized, I realize you might not have that luxury without staying late or coming into the office on a weekend. With projects piled up and a busy home life adding demands to your day, the desire to get organized may be strong, but feeling overwhelmed will threaten to wipe out all your good intentions. You gain control when you break a project down into manageable chunks. Where possible throughout this book, I'll give you tasks that shouldn't take too long to complete. Commit a half hour or an hour each day this week. It's one desk drawer, one bookcase shelf, one piece of paper at a time until you are organized. Watch the results multiply! Each contribution builds toward the ultimate result you're working to achieve: a balanced life.

Okay. It's time to roll up our sleeves and apply some elbow grease. Are you ready? Your new workspace is waiting for you to claim it.

WORK HABIT OF THE MONTH: DRINK WATER

If you aren't a water drinker, I sympathize. I wasn't either until I had to go through chemotherapy. (You have to drink at least *eight* eight-ounce glasses of water a day to help flush your system of those toxic chemicals.) When the treatments ended, I decided to keep this as a habit. I have found that it helps relieve stress during a busy workday. Yes, it's true!

If you are used to drinking soda or coffee nonstop all day, here is your new habit: Place one 16-ounce bottle of water on your desk each morning. Take it with you to meetings. Take it in the car, the subway, or the train. Just be sure you consume it by day's end. On weekends, keep your trusty bottle with you at home and as you run errands. Use a refillable bottle, or stock up on cases of water at the start of the month. Of course, you're welcome to drink more, but sixteen ounces is the goal to start.

HOME HABIT OF THE MONTH: USE THESE QUICK BATHROOM FIXES

When we're in a rush, we often leave a room looking like a cyclone blew through it. We think we're saving time by not stopping to restore order. In fact, we're setting ourselves up for chaos. When we return to this room, the disarray is going to make us feel tired or, worse, like a failure. This month your habit centers on your bathroom, and it's a threefold action:

- Check your towel. Is it going to be rehung or go to the laundry? If it's the former, hang it up neatly on the towel bar (rather than throwing it on the floor!) or put it into a hamper.
- Wipe off the counter. Use a damp sponge or a surface cleaner wipe. In fact you can keep a dispenser under every sink in the house. Bathroom counters are magnets for sticky residue from hair products, toothpaste, and the like. Catch them before they harden.
- Empty the bathroom trash can as you exit.

WEEK ONE

Reclaim Your Office

This week, you can

- See your space as others do
- Make a space diagnosis to develop a plan
- Do a speed elimination to remove the most obvious debris

Time required: Two hours, though the time varies depending on the size of your work space and the amount of clutter

EVERY OFFICE WORKER FROM THE chairman of the board on down needs to have one thing: a functional space. Whether you're in a corner office or a cubicle, you need space to work and space to think. No matter the size, your office is a controlled area and the perfect place to begin to practice my mom's best advice: "There is a place for everything and everything should be in its place. Then the next time you need it or want it, you can find it."

The simple act of returning an item to its established home is the essence of maintenance. You're going to put everything down eventually, so why not in the same spot? The energy you expend is no different. It's the energy you *save* that's enormous. This month we're going to tear through your office, removing the extraneous and the useless. Then we can designate a home for every item that remains. Imagine never having to wonder, "Where did I put that folder or book or binder clip? It was just here!"

The whole of anything is overwhelming. This week you'll figure out specifically what's bothering you about your space.

FRESH EYES EXPERIMENT

This is a fun experiment to do after you've had some time away from your office. Maybe you can come in a few minutes early one morning or shorten your lunch break? You pick the optimum time.

CREATE A STREAMLINED SPACE

Walter is a well-known and highly respected attorney, a partner in his firm. When I entered his large office, I saw stacks of papers everywhere. "Huh, I suppose there are," he said. Walter no longer paid any attention to them.

Very often we create piles and promise ourselves we're going to deal with them later. And then life interrupts us and those piles become permanent fixtures. We don't really see them anymore; it's as if we redecorated with them! Walter had fallen victim to this common problem, but it wasn't just paper he had been ignoring.

Reference books he used frequently were littering the floor to the right of his desk. There was a large credenza in the office; Walter had the shelves decorated with career memorabilia and family photos. I asked what was stored inside. He didn't remember; he hadn't looked in years. Can you guess what we found? Dusty law school textbooks! This material, which didn't need to be used again, was a big space hog.

What else did a fresh perspective bring to our attention? The credenza had two small file drawers that were stuffed with miscellaneous items. Once again, Walter hadn't opened those drawers in years.

First we spent a few hours going through the stacks on Walter's desk and dividing the material by the legal cases they supported. He had completed his work on them and now they needed to reside with the rest of the documentation for each case. They vanished easily; a law clerk whisked the cases away to files housed outside his office. Walter was excited and ready to forge ahead.

We discovered he needed two additional small bookcases: one for the reference books he needed at his fingertips and one to house material for his law clerk. (By the way, you can't have too many bookends. They are inexpensive and will keep your books upright and easy to grab.) When papers were placed on the second bookcase, the clerk would know without asking that he was to clear off the shelf and take care of the next step in the legal process. Two simple pieces of furniture and Walter would never again see piles on the floor.

After we cleared out those old textbooks from the credenza, Walter had lots of room to store items that were part of his present, not his past. We then cleaned out the credenza file drawers and moved several categories of rarely accessed but necessary files to those drawers. This freed up additional space for current projects in the file drawers in Walter's desk. He got so into the process of elimination that we filled up every wastebasket in the vicinity and had to call the maintenance staff and get a small dumpster!

Walter's office was transformed from a storage facility and dumping ground to a streamlined legal machine in a matter of hours.

Pretend you have never been in your space before now. This will enable you to look at things with fresh eyes. Have you ever had a last-minute call from a relative or friend who wanted to drop by? Suddenly you survey your home and see it differently. Let's say it's a lazy Sunday and you've been enjoying the paper. You find it relaxing to toss all the newspaper sections about the couch and floor. Now you realize that while this scenario gave you a few minutes of relaxation, it will look untidy to your guests. This is exactly how I want you to view your office.

Here are some questions to help diagnose the state of your work area and the zones you might tackle first. You'll be able to guess what the correct response and desired state of affairs is without any prompting. Remember, we're pretending this is your first visit.

First, as far as the space itself is concerned, how would you answer these questions:

What do you *immediately* know about the occupant? Is this a tidy person or a human whirlwind? Do you feel this impression is a fair description of you in general?

Does the space appear organized or chaotic? Which of those words do people most often use to describe you?

Are you drawn into the space or does the desire to flee overtake you? If it's the latter, is it possible that this chaos is part of the reason you have trouble keeping up with assignments?

Does it appear the space is being well used or do you see countless miscellaneous items that belong at home or perhaps in the trash?

Is the floor space clear or are there so many piles you feel like you are negotiating an obstacle course every time you enter or leave?

Do you see items that reveal who this person is (such as wall art or personal photos) or is it a sterile environment that yields no clues about the occupant? Whatever your reaction, does it please you?

If there is a bookcase, is there any room for books or have miscellaneous items usurped the shelf space?

Next, let's turn our attention to that all-important fixture, your desk. How would you answer these questions?

Is your desk surface clear or a paper graveyard? Would you like to use your desk in a more functional manner but can't seem to find any space because photos, food, and gadgets occupy every square inch? Are your drawers organized or a jumble of miscellaneous items? Can you actually close them? Is your computer monitor covered in Post-it notes?

Finally, consider how you feel in your office. How would you describe it to others in light of these feelings? See if any of these nail it.

Are you energized the minute you enter or do you feel overwhelmed?

Do you laugh and tell colleagues it's a "black hole"? Or do you find that it is a workable space with a few "broken parts"?

Do unexpected visits from your boss or colleagues fill you with pride or shame? Do you find yourself saying things like, "Oh! I'm sorry about all the stuff on that chair. I was just about to clean up when you arrived."

How did you do? What are the top three things that bother you about your space? Are they covered in my list of questions or do you have something unusual? Don't fret if you found you were guilty of most or all of these common clutter traps. We're spending this month digging out. And guess what? The more work you have to do, the bigger your sense of accomplishment at month's end.

Are you patting yourself on the back and thinking, "Hey, I don't have too much to do here." Or are you shaking your head in disbelief? "Why didn't I see how this really looks and what I was doing to myself?" Remember, we are *fact finding*. This is not an exercise to make you feel guilty or ashamed; neither emotion has a place in Zen organizing. Now that you know what the problem is, we're going to get up and do another of my favorite exercises. Are you ready?

FIFTEEN-MINUTE SPEED ELIMINATION

Set a timer or the alarm on your cell phone and move as quickly as your feet will allow.

Have some sturdy garbage bags on hand or borrow some wastebaskets from nearby offices or cubicles. Concentrate on the obvious garbage, excess items, or objects that don't belong in your office. Don't worry about organizing all your drawers or filing stacks of papers. We'll be doing a speed elimination for those areas later. Keep a narrow focus.

In addition to tossing items, create a section for items that need to go home with you. This means today! I don't want you to create a new pile of stuff that will languish in a corner. We don't want you to emulate Walter before he became a Zen organizer! You can also include items that need to be returned to others. If these items need to go back to coworkers, you can deliver them with a thank-you note when you finish the elimination process.

What might you be tossing, taking home, or returning? Here is a short list to help direct you. I've created areas for you so that this task is less overwhelming.

First let's look at those wonderful staples from home that invade most offices—food and clothing:

- Toss old, stale food items, such as candy and energy bars. Check expiration dates on all food items.
- Throw away take-out food or beverage containers. I had a client who unwittingly let fruit rot under her desk. Out of sight, out of mind applied to her forgotten banana.
- Exercise clothes make going to the gym easier. A small workout *wardrobe* tucked into a drawer is too much.

- A gym bag is a great idea. If you haven't been to the gym in months, however, take it home until you are ready to resume. In addition, see if you can't do with a smaller bag.
- An extra pair of shoes for inclement weather is handy if you live in a four-season climate, but more than that is too many.
- One umbrella is great, but more is overkill.
- What about clothing items for every-day use? If your office tends to run cold, you may have a collection of sweaters stashed on a shelf or in a desk drawer meant for files. Why not wear one each day from home that's coordinated to your outfit? Or leave at the office one generic sweater in a basic black or beige that will go with any outfit when the air conditioning starts to blow.
- A clothes tree is a nice way to hang seasonal sweaters and coats and keep your drawers free for office matters. It can be tucked behind a door or placed in a corner.

Another category of clutter is office supplies and equipment. What is designed to serve us can inhibit us. Let's take a look:

- What about supplies you can't use? For example, did your company change area codes and provide new stationery and business cards? Recycle the old rather than let them languish on a shelf.
- Did your company go from legal- to letter-size folders? Perhaps you have several boxes of legal file supplies and know you aren't going to use them. If you can't return them to a central supply area in the company, pass them on to someone who can use them. Perhaps the office at your child's school or your local library? If you can't quickly think of any person or organization, recycle them. By the way, remember that you can use letter-size folders inside a legal hanging folder!
- Scan your office shelves and desktop for electronic gadgets you no longer use or never used. We're working to abandon the "some day I might use this" mentality.
- Consider the reference books you receive every year. Toss the ones they replace.

Now let's turn our attention to the things we bring in to make us feel more at home. See if you have too many of these in your work space:

- Dated photos should be taken home. (If your son just went off to college but his photo is from the first grade, it needs to go home.)
- If your office runs warm, don't have too many fans on hand or one that's big enough to cool the entire department. In tending to our creature comforts, we often go overboard. Put your space on a diet. This warning goes for space heaters as well. Do you really need more than one? When it's

off-season, take equipment you won't be using for months home with you.

- Are you a collector? Although one or two items can bring a touch of personality to your work area, five hundred Beanie Babies, turtles, frogs, or any other collectible is overkill. You know what I mean.

We're down to the last category: miscellaneous! What nonessential items would you add to this category?

- Let's look at that time-honored collector of dust: the office gift that you know you will never use. Somehow you feel guilty giving it away. What can I say? As your Zen organizer, I give you permission. You have several choices: give it to someone else at work (not of course if a colleague in *this* office gave it to you); let your child play with it; save it at home with your holiday decorations for next year's White Elephant gift exchange (see Chapter 12 for details); or (gulp!) toss it in the trash. It's important to appreciate the sentiment behind the gift but it isn't necessary to be held captive by something you don't like and will never use.
- Do you have items you meant to return to a store for credit or exchange? Check the receipt. If it's too late and

you really can't use the item at home, pass it on as an unexpected gift to someone. This is far superior to having the item clog your valuable, and I presume limited, work space.

When your timer goes off, remove the trash. Give borrowed items back to your coworkers. Put the home items in the trunk of your car or in a box for the trip home via public transit. And don't second-guess yourself! Remember, you want to build on the ability to make decisions, not the ability to question those decisions.

> What items did you find that were not on my list? I give every client a "you have more of this than anyone else" award. For example, I worked with a doctor who saved the stamps from return envelopes that came with business communications. He had the biggest stack of these I'd ever seen! He never used them, but collecting them was his hobby. He tore them off without any regard to their appearance. I cut the edges down so they were actually ready to be pasted onto envelopes and then I stashed them in a desk drawer inside one legal envelope.
>
> What award would I give you if we were doing this together?

WEEK TWO

Employ the Magic Formula

This week, you can

- Learn how the Magic Formula works by cleaning out your desk drawers

Time required: Thirty minutes to two hours is the average time commitment, but the time varies, depending on the state of your desk

WHEN I FIRST STARTED WORKING with clients, I was sure that any day someone was going to show me an organizing project that would stump me. This fear would keep me awake the night before I was to meet a new client. What would I say when this happened? After about three years, I relaxed. I noticed an amazing similarity among all the projects, no matter what the setting. From closets to file systems, from offices to garages, every area of chaos gave way to order by following the same three steps: I call these the Magic Formula.

I promise that once you understand and master these simple steps, you will be able to use them to organize anything. That's what's so magical about them. For our purposes, we're going to use the formula to help you clear your desk inside and out.

The Magic Formula:

1. Eliminate
2. Categorize
3. Organize

It's important to remember that the whole of anything is overwhelming. I can't say this often enough! You need to break down any project into manageable sections. You know the old joke, "How do you eat an elephant?" The answer is, "One bite at a time." Let's examine each step in turn.

Eliminate: Elimination isn't just about getting rid of trash (although I would bet you'll find lots of items from every area that you can toss with great abandon). This step actually can be creative because it's about removing anything you no longer need, use, or want to keep. It includes returning borrowed items to others, returning purchases to a store, recycling, or simply taking an item to the room where it is meant to be used. As you eliminate, the space begins to feel less congested and you will find it easier to think clearly. I know you experienced that last week when you did the speed elimination.

Categorize: Categories are the lifeblood of an organized system. You have such power when you know at a glance exactly how much you have of any item or what you're working with. At home, you might experience the power of categories in your kitchen by grouping food items. You automatically know, for example, when it's time to buy soup or pasta. You can do this type of sorting with everything from your office supplies to your paperwork! For example, if you gather your small supplies into one category, I guarantee you will be amazed how many boxes of staples, rolls of tape, or paper clips you have. Until they are all in one place, it's anyone's guess. Later we'll examine categorizing papers related to a project. It is the type of item that shifts, not the principles of getting organized.

Organize: Organizing your categories so that your finished project is beautiful to look at, functional, and easy to maintain is the last step in the Magic Formula. This week you're going to tackle your desk drawers. I'm going to walk you through the Magic Formula and introduce you to the products that will keep your drawers tidy forever. If your office doesn't have these supplies, make these inexpensive purchases. (When you leave this job, organizing tools you have bought go with you.) Organized drawers will make you more productive.

THIRTY-MINUTE SPEED ELIMINATION

You're an experienced speed eliminator by now, so let's set the timer for thirty minutes and dive into your drawers. I know that this is scary territory for everyone. If the average person can hide it, dump it, or shove it in a drawer, that's where every miscellaneous item or small office supply lands. So for thirty uninterrupted minutes, I want you to be brutal. If you don't use it, need it, or want it . . . toss it! If it can better serve you at home, make a take home pile. If it belongs to someone else or the central supply area, return it when the thirty minutes are up. I have one caveat: If you have a file drawer and it's filled with files, *let them sit until next month.* Do, however, go through any other non-paper-related material you have stashed in the drawer. Usually an area in the back of the drawer becomes a de facto dead zone. What do you have hidden there?

After your timer goes off, we're going to look at what's left and organize it all. Still feeling shy about what you should toss or save? Here are some guidelines. Remember for this round we're looking for quick toss items. If you aren't sure, the best question to ask yourself is this: When was the last time I used this? If it was a long time ago (or never) and you're saving this item "just in case," I suggest you let it go. Remember: speed elimination represents one way to practice the first step in the Magic Formula.

Toss Take-out Stuff: Is one of your desk drawers clogged with condiment samples from take-out meals? Do you have more chopsticks than the local Chinese restaurant? Napkins, utensils . . . remember that these items are given as a courtesy. You didn't purchase them; you bought the food. If you work in a large office, does the company kitchen need these items? Does a nearby school or shelter need these items? Otherwise, just throw them away.

If you have several menus, gather them together. Later, you can put them in either a binder or a folder, depending on how many menus you have and how often you use them. A receptionist, for example, often has a large stash of frequently used menus. Under circumstances like this, I like to put the menus in alphabetical order, pop them into top-loading, heavy-duty sheet protectors, and put these into a binder that any office member could grab from the front desk area. Label the spine Menus.

On the other hand, if you have just a few menus and rarely order in, keep them in a file folder. Remember too that most restaurants post their menus on the Internet, so you might be able to just toss the paper versions.

Eliminate Excess Supplies: Throw away any office supplies that don't work and set aside overflow items to return to the office supply room. For example, it's important to have extra staples for the day when your stapler runs out, but you don't need five boxes of staples crammed into your desk drawer. The same is true for paper clips, binder clips, and tape.

Take an honest look at how many pens you have. Toss the ones that have dried out and decide how many of the remaining ones you need. As for pencils, if you use automatic ones exclusively, for example, you might want to donate the old-fashioned kind you need to sharpen. What about other writing instruments? I love Sharpies and highlighters. But do you have too many? They dry out just like your pens.

One good sharp pair of scissors is a must. But how many pairs do you have? If these are your personal property, take them home. Otherwise, once again, return them to the main supply area for the company. The same is true for rulers and letter openers.

Calculators: Do you have too many calculators? You might not even need one if you use the calculator on your computer or on your phone when you have to deal with figures.

Notepaper: You will want to store your personal note cards, company note paper, legal pads, and business cards in your desk. Whittle everything down to a sane number. What constitutes a sane number? The answer depends on how often you use these items. Keep what you realistically need and will use within the next six months. For example, if you rarely use a legal pad, one would be sufficient. If you're passionate about legal pads and use them right down to the last page, keeping a dozen on hand isn't out of the question.

Writing personal notes is a lost art. Are you a practitioner? If so, by all means have a box of note cards in your desk. If you rarely drop anyone a handwritten note, be realistic and save the space. Your company probably has printed cards you can use for business thank-you notes. Keep a few in your desk, and let the company store the main stash in the supply area they maintain.

Business Cards: Business cards are a funny thing in the work world. For some reason, most of my clients hold onto cards from previous employers. I have no idea why. Perhaps it's an unconscious record of where they have been and what they once did. Do you have boxes hidden away from other jobs? Toss them. If you must have a memento, save a few of the old cards in a nice business card holder. If you have a file drawer in your desk, the dead space in the back is a great spot to store your business card box. And I do hope it's a single box! In fact, you can tuck a box of note cards there as well.

Your desk will no doubt yield treasures I can't imagine. Here's a list of a few more fairly common items. Ask yourself, "Do I *really* use this or is it from a time past when it was important to me?" Be honest as you go through this speed elimination process. Where appropriate, remember to check expiration dates:

Grooming aids: hair spray, brushes, combs, and gels

Vitamins, supplements, aspirin, and medications

Food: cans, bags of snacks, teas, sweeteners, and so on

Miscellaneous decorative items that were once on your desk or were intended for that area!

Feminine hygiene products

Cleaning products, especially spray cans for electronic products such as your computer

It's time to set the timer and spend an additional fifteen minutes eliminating items you know you don't use. If they are still good (for example, surplus grooming aids or supplements that have not expired), take them home. Be ruthless. I can't tell you how many times I've entered clients' offices and been pleasantly surprised by how tidy they looked until they opened a drawer. As they sat at their desk trying to do good work each day, they were surrounded by a miniature black hole. Don't do this to yourself. Remember, every area is important even if you are the only one who can see it. Aren't you the most important person in the equation? Zen organizing is about transforming the environment so it serves you. It is not about making your space pretty to impress others.

These guidelines will help you eliminate the clutter with great abandon, no matter

what type of clutter it is. Okay. Set that timer. I'll see you in about thirty-five minutes: that's thirty to exercise your trash-tossing and decision-making muscles and five to remove the debris from your space.

CATEGORIZE YOUR REMAINING SUPPLIES

As you survey your desk drawers, you have probably made them a bit more chaotic than when you started. Don't fret. This is normal. First, clear off a space to work. In some cases I use the floor rather than the desk surface. We're ready to introduce the second step of the Magic Formula: categories. Start with one drawer and take everything out, placing related items together; for example, staples, tape, rubber bands, binder clips, paper clips, and glue sticks are a category. Why? They all hold things together. It's nice to cluster them in one area so when you want to attach some items, you have an array of tools. Keep your stapler next to your staple remover. You get the idea.

There are usually two, sometimes three, small drawers for supplies. You want the ones on top to be your command center. When you need a tool, be sure it's at your fingertips. Take a minute to create your categories. Here are some common categories I use when I am organizing a series of desk drawers:

Tools that bind (staples, paper clips, and so on)

SURPRISE THEM!

If you have this book out on your desk or people see your frantic movements and hear the timer, they may stop by with comments—let me clarify: unwanted and uninvited comments. "Oh! *You* are getting organized? Call me in two weeks and we'll see if it lasts." "Oh boy, you sure are making a mess!" "Oh wow! You are getting organized? Good luck with that!" On and on it goes. When you hear the comment, smile sweetly, nod your head as if in agreement, and keep going. Don't stop to chat about your efforts or defend yourself. Be amused. Say to yourself, "Wow! Regina was right. Here you are. Well, won't you be surprised when this all works!" You have a choice. Surrender your power or keep it. Decide to be an example and show them with your *actions and results* what is possible.

Writing instruments (pens, pencils, Sharpies, highlighters, erasers, and so on)

Emergency food

Personal hygiene (deodorant, feminine products, hair care items, and perhaps a nail file)

Cancelled checks, check registers, and blank checks

Receipts

Miscellaneous (money, batteries, keys, rubber stamps, business cards, return address labels, ruler, and so on)

Post-its (various sizes, shapes, and
   colors)
Blank CDs or DVDs
Legal pads, scratch pads, note cards
Envelopes (various sizes)
Company letterhead and envelopes
Cleaning supplies

What categories will you add to my list? Once you have emptied your drawers and made your categories, you may find that you can toss a few more items. It's when we see everything grouped together instead of scattered about like bird seed that we realize we have more than we need of a particular office tool. Remember our mantra: Take home the excess if you purchased it, return it to the supply area if it's company issue, or share the items with colleagues. Recycle where possible and toss anything that's no longer viable.

Take a minute to wipe out your desk. It may be quite some time before you have everything out like this again. Now we're ready to move on to the last phase of the Magic Formula. We're going to organize our categories.

ORGANIZE WITH THE RIGHT TOOLS

I don't want you to spend a lot of money getting organized, but I recommend some items to make your drawers not only organized but easy to maintain. The first is drawer liner. I like the kind that is thick, looks like a paper towel, and is washable. You can find it in the kitchen section of any home store, at Bed, Bath & Beyond, or at The Container Store. It comes in a roll and it takes only a few seconds to cut it to the size of your drawers. The key to maintaining order will be your liner because it will anchor what you have created. Without it, one good shove and voila! Chaos returns.

While you're in the kitchen area of one of these stores, I also suggest that you pick up a few drawer organizers, small containers that will hold your supplies so they don't become a jumble in your drawer. They come in clear acrylic, white or black plastic, black mesh, and wood. I prefer the acrylic because you can easily wipe them out from time to time and keep your drawer looking pristine. These aren't expensive items, and when you leave your job they will serve you wherever you work. I would purchase an assortment of sizes and shapes. You can piece them together in your drawer like a jigsaw puzzle. Didn't I promise you that organizing was fun? But if you want to pass on the purchase of these organizers, that's okay.

Finally, your company probably gives out the standard office drawer organizer, a square with sections for everyday supplies. This is great for that skinny center drawer. The small wells provide enough space for an adequate supply of everyday items. If you are a person who feels comforted by a large stash of backup supplies, I suggest that you keep everything in something called a grid tote. These are square or rectangular plastic containers with handles. You can find them at The Container Store and frequently at your local home store or Bed, Bath & Beyond.

You will need a spot to park this container, however, and your desk isn't the place. If you have a credenza, that's the perfect solution. Otherwise, try the bottom shelf of a bookcase or the cabinet above your desk.

Here are some guidelines to help you organize your categories.

Put some pens, pencils, Sharpies, and whatever writing tools you use on a regular basis in a container on your desk the size of a coffee mug. I've had clients who had several large containers on their desk. This causes visual chaos and gives you a false sense of security. Pare down to what you can use in a day. You might pop your scissors into this container and your letter opener as well if you use both frequently. Otherwise keep them in the top drawer.

If you like a clear surface on your desk, don't have any writing tools out. You can put the basics in the top drawer and have your backups in something like a grid tote. I like the idea of a pencil box. I have a small, opaque box that sits on the top shelf of one of my three office bookcases to house my backup writing tools. It also serves as a bookend holding up some reference books I need to keep handy.

For the tools that bind, I use a standard office organizer in the top shallow drawer of the desk and generously fill the wells with paper clips, rubber bands, and a few small binder clips. You can use standard-issue paper clips or have a little fun because they now come in many different designs.

I wouldn't take staples out of their box because they fall apart too easily. One box of staples tucked neatly in the back of the top drawer should do for several months. I have one disposable tape dispenser on my desk and keep a small stash of two or three backup dispensers in a grid tote. Tape dries out, so don't overdo it with your backup stash.

Receipts get tossed, shoved, and stored in desk drawers with great abandon. Guess what? They don't belong there! You can do one of two things. Create a tab for one of your hanging file folders and label it Receipts. Inside have individual manila folders for the various categories of receipts you have. If you like the folder idea but have mostly small receipts, you can purchase special hanging folders with accordion sides that will keep everything contained. The second choice is to use clearly marked legal-size envelopes. (These should be in the area you set aside for supplies last month.)

Speaking of envelopes, although it's great to have a few on hand, most of my clients go overboard. Instead of keeping too many of these items in your desk drawers, why not use another hanging file folder and store your company letterhead and envelopes here? With that said, if you have project files that no longer fit in your file drawers, you aren't a candidate for housing any office supplies here. Get them as needed from the main supply area.

Who doesn't love a Post-it? Don't you wish you had invented them? Most people show their appreciation by keeping enough Post-its in varying sizes to supply an army. I would keep *one* humble packet out on your desk (they have dispensers just for this purpose) and store the rest. These will fit perfectly in one of those acrylic drawer organizers I mentioned. By the way, remove the Post-its from the clear wrap they arrived in. Why? You should eliminate packaging whenever possible because it wastes space and is an eyesore.

If you keep anything relating to personal banking in your office drawers, I would advise you to take those items home. In this world of identity theft, it's too easy a target to have accessible in unlocked drawers.

Some of my clients work in offices where little paper is generated or else their files are kept in larger cabinets outside their immediate work area. If this is your situation, by all means use your desk file drawer for personal hygiene items, emergency food, and any miscellaneous items you like to have close at hand. Be careful, however, not to turn it into a junk drawer.

You can probably best be served by having your personal hygiene items in one grid tote and your food in another. (Another word of caution: Be careful how you store food. You don't want to unwittingly be the culprit who starts feeding the creepy crawlies such as roaches, as well as the rats and mice that may live in any large building.)

Anything on the bottom of a pile is likely to be forgotten or difficult to reach. You want to see what you have and be able to grab it in an instant. Containers help you avoid piling items into a drawer. Use a few acrylic containers in a desk file drawer for storing small miscellaneous items. My preference, however, is to see the desk file drawer used as intended. It's invaluable to have key files at your fingertips (more on this next month). In the back, as I mentioned, there is always dead space. If you are a legal pad person, again they are a great category to store here.

And now we come to the ubiquitous computer CDs. You can keep used ones with material you need in a binder or a special holder made for this purpose. (The latter are easy to find at large office supply stores.) If you don't have a drawer deep enough to hold the stack of new discs, do you have shelf space on a bookcase or room in your credenza? As a last resort, if you need them frequently, tuck the container behind your monitor in a corner of your desk.

Finally, let's take a step back and look at the finished product. I have a feeling you will be amazed how organized desk drawers can make you feel calm and powerful because everything you need is just a fingertip away. And that means you are saving time!

WEEK THREE

Clear Your Desk

This week, you can

- Speed eliminate clutter, trash, and other items you no longer use.
- Decide which small supplies you really need to keep on your desktop.

Time required: At least one hour, but the time varies depending on your situation

I'M SURE YOUR NEWLY ORGANIZED drawers amaze you. This week we're going to attack the desktop. This area works in concert with your drawers. You need space to work on your projects. So often I meet clients who not only work in small cubicles, they make the space completely claustrophobic with too much stuff.

ASSESS YOUR WORK SPACE

As with all clutter, this surface debris comes chiefly from our inability to make decisions. "I'll just put this here for now" is the kiss of death for organizing. When you feel that thought coming up, stop it in its tracks. Take a minute to make the decision as to *exactly* where the item in your

hand goes. A key question to ask is, "What does this item relate to?" It will reveal itself as part of a larger category.

Before we do our speed elimination of extraneous materials from the top of your desk, take a minute to examine the situation. Not all offices or cubicles are created equal. Let's evaluate the work space you have. We need to know if you have a great situation and you don't use it well or if the space itself is next to impossible.

Is your desktop a large space with adequate room for computer work and writing? If it is and yet you are always cramped for space, I'm going to bet the culprit is too much miscellaneous stuff clogging the area. Taking a quick look, do you see some items you can return to the supply room, take home, or simply trash?

Do you use the main area of your desk for your computer and have a return (the classic L shape) where you do written work? This is a common setup in most offices. Sometimes the return becomes a dumping ground for every electronic gadget one can imagine, from printer to fax to scanner. Some of my clients have put in a stand so they have two levels for all their electronic helpers. If this is your situation, ask yourself if all these machines are needed. If so, could they be moved to an equally convenient spot nearby? You really do need to be able to spread out your project files.

Sit back for a minute and look at your situation with fresh eyes. Can you remember the space before you moved in? Have you maximized or minimized it? Do you have items such as a large clock when there's one on your computer, a watch on your wrist, and another on your cell phone? Fresh eyes will reveal more space wasters like these. Think about what you will eliminate from the desktop once we set the timer. I have some ground rules, but first I have a story to share.

SONIA'S CRAMPED CUBICLE

Sonia told me that she needed to get organized. She felt that the state of her cubicle was holding back her sales. When I walked into her cubicle, I was amazed. Sonia had stuff on every square inch of her cubicle. I didn't know how she or the two colleagues who shared the space with her could breathe, much less do quality work.

The desk surface was a nightmare, holding stacks of unrelated files and equally high stacks of miscellaneous papers. It was impossible to know what was important and what was junk.

I set a timer and asked Sonia to do a speed elimination of her desktop. She moved quickly. When I felt her start to slow down, I peppered her with questions about the items I saw. "When was the last time you used this?" "Why is this here?" "Do you need that?" After fifteen minutes, we actually saw the top of the desk! Sonia was hooked. She worked with me for two days. We took out so many bags of trash we had no idea how it had all fit in that small space.

We created a file system. We organized her desk drawers. We made the desk surface functional and clear. Can you guess what happened? She stopped being late to work because she no longer dreaded her office. She began to utilize her desk rather than seeing it as a place to park stuff. In short order, Sonia's sales went through the roof.

We're still in touch. She remembers that day her desk revealed itself as a tool in her success arsenal. Today is your day.

DESKTOP SPEED ELIMINATION

Here are some ideas for the kinds of things you might be able to toss, recycle, give away, or return. Read through this section, and then set your timer and go!

Put into the recycle bin papers you no longer need, such as old drafts of projects, invitations to seminars and classes now past, and flyers, menus, and other miscellaneous papers you may have brought in after lunch and simply dumped on your desktop. (Set aside papers you need to hold on to, whether newly completed or active work projects. When we get to the next steps, we'll figure out the best way to categorize and organize material that can be archived.)

Do you have paper coffee cups that can be tossed? What about mugs and dishes that should be returned to the kitchen?

You will probably find some items that belong to other people in your office. Set those aside to be returned to their rightful owners.

Are there items you will want to pop into your briefcase or purse for the trip home?

Are there books that need to be returned to a bookshelf?

Can file folders be closed up and put away?

You may find file folders for projects that are completed. This material should be set aside and archived.

Space Hogs

Photos: Is your desk cluttered with family photos? Why not go all digital and have photos rotate automatically on your computer desktop, or hang one photo on a wall, or put only the most recent framed family photo on display? I am always amused when I see many photos of someone's young children, only to learn they are now in college. You can't freeze time—keep moving in step with it. Did you avoid eliminating these earlier this month? Now you have a second chance!

Small Tools and Holders: Do you have more small tools or holders than you need on top of your desk? What are small tools? Here's a starter list: tape dispenser, stapler, stapler remover, and a pen and pencil holder. I've seen people who have multiples of each. Leave one out if you use it and give the other(s) to someone who needs one.

Electric Pencil Sharpener: Is an electric pencil sharpener taking up space? How often do you use it? Could this be moved to a communal area? You'll also be freeing up a plug.

Plants: Did you place plants on your desk? If they are fake, do they take up valuable real estate? And if they are alive, are they thriving? Is it time to repot them? (Pick up your pot and, if you see roots crawling out the bottom water drainage hole, your plant needs to move to a bigger pot.) Would your plant be better positioned on a bookcase shelf or a windowsill? Would it be more prudent to get a silk plant for the office and take the living one home?

File Stand: Most office workers need to have some files that stay within reach. These may relate to general office reference materials or one or two special projects. Several types of file stands are available. We're going to deal with this more next month, but let me say that my favorite is the one that keeps your files flat on the surface of the desktop. Graduated stands always pose the risk that your files will be knocked down, spilling their contents. (By the way, using a label maker or computer-generated labels will make the folders easier to find, whether the holder is flat or graduated.)

If you are an out of sight, out of mind worker, a file stand is probably a good fit for you. Just don't use one of these because your desk file drawer is full of miscellaneous items! Next month we'll set up a file system. At that time we'll clean out all existing files. What's the status of the ones on your desk? Are they old material you can toss, shred, or recycle? Could the files be cleaned out and streamlined? Do you keep everything in alphabetical order? Are there files here from closed projects that could be archived?

Rolodex: Finally, do you have a Rolodex on your desk? If cards are spilling out, you won't be able to clean this up during the speed elimination. This represents a project that requires a bit of time to streamline. After the speed round, why not devote about twenty minutes to your Rolodex? Quickly thumb through the cards and pull out anyone you can't identify or haven't contacted in over twelve months. In today's volatile market, these good folks have probably moved on to other jobs. Never underestimate the power of the Internet to help you track down someone. If you are wary of tossing this material, put it into an envelope and file it with other archival material.

Paperwork
As you work your way across (and through)

your desk, you will of course have papers to categorize. We're going to create an entire system for organizing paper next month. It's one of the biggest, most time-consuming projects for the year—but one of the most important. The end of paper chaos is in sight.

For now, gather all the papers into one pile. Go through the pile and create the following categories: toss (do immediately), shred, and to-do. Then create categories for specific projects you may have. (Next month we'll create Action files by taking the temporary to-do file you create today and breaking it down further. This will give you more control over the tasks you need to accomplish.) For today, however, gather your to-do items into one folder. It's a big first step. Check this folder in the morning to see what details you need to take care of that day or check it before you leave for the day so that your morning tasks are lined up for you.

Insert the papers you have for individual projects into the appropriate files previously set up for these projects. Haven't done that yet? No problem: You can gather all your project files and put them in alphabetical order. Now, depending on the size of each and the frequency you reference them, put them either in the file holder on your desk or in the file drawer in your desk. Next month we'll set up the individual projects; for now at least the scattered pieces have been brought to one file folder.

Until you create your official file setup or improve the one you're using, continue to add to these temporary folders. The days of allowing papers to gather on your desktop like fallen leaves are over. This may seem alien to you at first, but in twenty-one days you won't remember any other way to function.

Last week you created categories using physical tools. This week you are grouping related papers. As you will see, the principle is the same; what has changed are the items. You'll get really good at this next month when we work on your files. If creating a category seems like a daunting experience, take heart because with practice, it will become the most natural thing in the world.

DECIDE WHAT YOU REALLY NEED

Let's get back to your desktop. You've eliminated the miscellaneous clutter. It's time to ask the next question. What do you *really* need on your desk? It all depends on what you use all the time. Think about surgeons. They have a specific tray set up with the instruments they need for the procedure at hand. Can you imagine how ineffective they would be if they had to shuffle through all their instruments? You are just as ineffective if you have a surplus of tools on your desk "just in case" you need one of them one day.

Many of my clients use a matching set of tools consisting of a writing tools holder, stapler, and tape dispenser. Some even have a matching desk pad. If this arrangement appeals to you and you use those tools on a regular basis, I invite you to make use of a set that is esthetically ap-

LOOK AT YOUR DESKTOP

So many office supplies that make life easier are in the marketplace. However, no one needs them all! Here are the basic items for a desktop. Remember: Be prudent in your selection.

Computer monitor
Phone
Inbox and outbox
Lamp
Reference binder (see next month)
Small supplies (stapler, tape dispenser, and writing tools holder, which may include a pair of scissors and a letter opener)
File trays
File stand
Tissues
Post-it note holder
Legal pad
One personal item such as a photo or a plant, if you have the space

pealing. For my taste, this is too much clutter. I keep my stapler and some tape close by. On my desk I have my flat-panel monitor, a lamp, and a keyboard. And that's it! During the course of a typical work day, papers gather on my desk. I have a water bottle out until I've consumed my eight eight-ounce glasses.

Computer: I hope you have one of the flat-panel monitors—if not, see if you can request an upgrade.

Telephone: Are you left- or right-handed? Be sure your phone is accessible to the hand that most easily grabs the receiver. And be careful you aren't pulling the cord across your desk and taking the chance you will knock items over.

Desk Organizer: Are smaller items, such as packs of Post-it notes, rubber bands, binder clips, pens, pencils, Sharpies, and highlighters, scattered across your desk? Transfer them to your newly organized desk drawers. If you need to keep some on the desk itself, use a desk organizer or purchase containers to hold small supplies such as paper clips and pens.

Stacking Trays: These trays can serve as an inbox and outbox. We'll deal with the appropriate use of these boxes in detail next month. For now, remember that these boxes have a specific purpose. Don't allow them to become clutter traps. They are not gathering places for your unmade paper decisions! If you have multiple forms you use throughout the day, you might want to have a stack of trays on your desk for this purpose. You can reach in and grab at will whatever you need. Trays are useful also for someone who needs to print several drafts of a document. You can use different color paper and keep your supply handy.

Purchase good-quality trays. The inexpensive plastic units are flimsy and will be more of a hassle than a help with constant use.

File Box: Many people like the unit that holds active files on your desk in an ascending row. There are no sides to these units and I must say they don't work for me. If you're a bit of a klutz like I am, you may rue the day you trusted important files to this setup. Small items such as receipts, business cards, and the like can fly out and get lost. Why invite such drama? I prefer portable file boxes, which are available in utilitarian plastic or beautiful wood, and enable you to take your most frequently used files with you. If you work at home as I do, you have the freedom to work in your garden on a warm summer day. In a corporation, you can take material safely to a meeting.

At this point, you should have a handle on how to organize your desk and the area surrounding it. Your physical space is under control rather than littered with extraneous items. There is a designated place for every item that will remain and be of service to you. You know exactly what's in your office supply stash. In short, you control the space. Before this week, I bet you felt it was the other way around.

WEEK FOUR

Take Back Your Space

This week, you can

- Assess your office furniture
- Wrap up the organization of your physical space

Time required: Thirty to ninety minutes, depending on the size of your office and how much furniture you have

As we close out this month, it's important to wrap up loose ends. If we don't bring the entire office space to order, the chaos will creep back in and assert its dominance. Let's make a final assessment. By now your desk surface should be clear and the drawer contents kept to a minimum. Now it's time to go beyond the desk and look at the floor, the walls, and the furniture. Are you ready to wrap up this month in style?

WORK WITH THE SPACE YOU HAVE

Take a few minutes to honestly assess your situation. Here are some of the items I'd like you to note:

Your Desk: Is your desk too big or too small for the space and the work you need to accomplish? If you work for a company or large corporation, can you request a different size desk?

What's hidden under your desk? Were you hoping I wouldn't ask? Let me guess: a box or two of miscellaneous items you didn't take home, couldn't part with, or aren't sure about? Now is the time to make those decisions. Boxes of hidden clutter under your desk tell a story. What fear is holding you back from embracing change?

Your Chair: It's always important to have good back support but it's critical if you spend long hours at your computer. In the "Resources" section I have more information for you on this as well as one of my favorite stores specializing in ergonomically correct chairs and other furniture, Relax the Back. You also want to avoid injuries such as carpal tunnel, and neck strain, and eyestrain. Your body is a gift. Treat it well because it enables you to fulfill your life goals.

If your company issues only regulation chairs and you're on your own, remember there are relatively inexpensive products you can purchase that will enable you to have a more ergonomically correct experience, such as special pillows to sit on and for back support. You can transform your chair with these! If you are short, keep a footrest under your feet to release pressure on your back.

Is the chair you use on wheels? Is there a plastic runner under your chair so that you can easily slide around your space? If you are in a push-and-pull war just to get up and go to the bathroom or the printer, the day will feel longer and more frustrating. This kind of petty annoyance can cause an avalanche of pent-up emotions to come tumbling out onto a coworker at just the wrong time.

Computer: Is the computer monitor at the right angle to prevent neck strain and eyestrain? Also consider an ergonomically correct keyboard. They take some time getting used to but prevent wrist strain.

Guest Chairs: One culprit I frequently encounter is the presence of too many guest chairs. If your space is small, can you bring one in for a visitor on an as-needed basis? Can the company come and pick up the one(s) you don't need? If your chair has become a catchall and is rarely used for a visitor, eliminate it.

Shelving and Bookcases: Do you need shelving, a credenza, a bookcase, or a stand for electronic helpers such as your printer and fax machine? Or is it time to eliminate some of these pieces? If you want to remove some, is there a distribution person who will collect them? Investigate and follow company protocol.

Walls: As you are making your plan to improve your office, don't forget to check the walls. If they are bare, it will feel as if you have no relation to the space and just moved in. What is allowed in your office? If the walls have to remain bare, do you have space for something personal on your desk? Very often one or two items will help us feel that we have our own individual stamp on the space. If you like to have family photos around, remember you could put out a digital frame and have rotating photos to comfort you whenever you look in that direction. This one frame might replace five or six individual frames you now have.

On the other hand, if every available inch of wall space is covered with posters, photos, and memorabilia from trips, you will feel overwhelmed every time you walk in to work. If you feel sad at the idea of downsizing these items, try this solution: Leave a minimum number in your office and take the rest home. Rotate items from home on a monthly or seasonal basis.

When it comes to your wall art and the decorative items in your space, remember again that less is more. The goal is to feel more at home but not to literally recreate home! Take a look at the decorative style and solutions used in the offices of coworkers you admire. Follow the company culture.

Bulletin Board: Do you have a bulletin board near your desk littered with out-of-date memos? Clear it off as well. It's difficult to use a board artfully. They become catchalls like refrigerator doors.

Trash Can: Do you have an adequate trash can for your space, or is it too large?

Lighting: The type of lighting we use contributes to our ability to focus, think clearly, and be productive. And yet it is often overlooked. One of my favorite clients is a real estate office manager who has worked for several companies over the past fifteen years. Steve agrees with me that lighting is very important. Because overhead fluorescent lighting can be harsh, he uses a lamp instead. This works if you have permission from the company to bring in a personal light fixture. And of course you need available surface space on your desk. If you have the space and permission, I invite you to try a lamp instead of fluorescent lighting.

Your Predecessor's Things: If a former employee leaves files that he set up for his own convenience, don't hesitate to go through them. If you feel you can use them, do so. Perhaps this material will give you a clearer window into your duties. After you are familiar with your job, don't hesitate to toss the files that are of no use to you. By the way, if you are new to a job, remove leftover personal items from the previous occupant. You would be surprised how many of my clients surrender space to the possessions of someone who is destined never to return.

THE BIGGEST SPACE HOG: PAPER MACHINES

In most offices, the fax machine, the copier, the scanner, the printer, and paper supplies are in a centralized area. Every time you need to fax, copy, scan, or retrieve something from the printer, you have to walk across the room. Instead, why not establish a few times during the day for completing several paper tasks at once, rather than jumping up and down all day. Remember: saving steps automatically saves time!

However, if your office setup is such that you have these machines and paper reams on your desk, do they absolutely need to be there? Would your printer be better off on a stand by the side of your desk? Do you use your scanner enough to keep it in sight? Could your fax move to the stand with the printer and free up more space? I recently purchased an all-in-one so that my fax, scanner, and color printer are housed in one machine. They have come down in price and it's a great way to save space.

Be mindful too of not keeping too many paper supplies close at hand. If you have more than one or two reams of paper, you run the risk of losing space for things you actually use. Can you put your excess into a community supply closet or create a supply area in a corner of the office? An organized supply area is inviting visually. It's the office equivalent of a full pantry! If you work at home, an easy way to do that is to purchase an inexpensive bookcase and stick it in the closet, if the room has one.

Almost everyone opens a package of paper for the fax or copier or printer and lets it sit in the original paper package. Here's a simple idea to keep your paper handy and tidy: Place it in a legal- or letter-size paper tray. Keep your backup paper supply on your newly appointed supply bookcase or in a nearby cupboard.

Is a shredder at the ready to serve you? If you shred on an ongoing basis, the task won't become so daunting. If you run a home-based business, however, you may need a professional service to come out from time to time. Very often you can pay a fraction of the stated fee if you bring the material to them. It all depends on how much you have and how easily you can transport it.

If you work for a company that doesn't have a document shredding policy, see if you can convince the powers-that-be to start one. A locked, communal receptacle in a central location is ideal. I see this setup now in most of the real estate offices I visit. A professional shredding company that's licensed and bonded comes on a periodic basis to empty the bin. This eliminates hoarding paper in cubicles and offices because you don't have the time to deal with it appropriately. The increase in productivity usually offsets the expense to the company. And the security factor is priceless.

KEEP YOUR DESK ORGANIZED

When I teach my class, I begin with this statement, "I've got good news and bad news. The good news is that everyone is already organized. Not only are you organized, you have a system in place. And you work that system with the diligence of a religious zealot." People stare at me wide-eyed. I can hear them thinking, "Oh no! That's not me, Regina." But it is everyone in my audience. It's you as well. And that's the bad news in a nutshell: Some systems cause chaos and others foster a nurturing environment.

If you toss everything into your drawers, guess what? That's your *system*! I want you to replace it with a new system that says you will now consciously place items where you designated they belong, not drop them willy-nilly wherever they land.

Here are some ideas for maintenance routines that will help you to honor the hard work you've done to organize your space:

- The minute you are finished using a tool, return it to its designated area.
- Clean off your desk at day's end. As you enter the next morning, a feeling of peace, calm, and control will greet you. This will boost your productivity.
- When you start to feel out of control, take a minute to step back and look at your space with fresh eyes. Perhaps you have allowed too much to stray onto your desk? As you restore physical order, mental clarity will return.

Maintain the order, not the chaos. The choice is yours and it takes the same amount of time. Now, we all see our environments tumble into chaos from time to time. Don't panic. It's probably a sign that you may have been too busy with a special project to be as careful and consistent as you'd like. The beauty of a system—having a designated place for everything—is that you can restore order in a few minutes. This month, you decided where things should be stored. Now you have only to restore the system you created.

This month's work has laid the foundation for change. Next month you will create the all-important file system, which is the heart of your work setup. As this week ends and the month comes to a close, plan a reward to celebrate your progress!

FEBRUARY SUMMARY

WEEK ONE

Look at your office with fresh eyes to make an accurate diagnosis of your issues, needs, and wants for this space.

WEEK TWO

The power of the Magic Formula is introduced. With it, all chaos yields to order. Start with desk drawers.

WEEK THREE

Clear the surface debris off your desktop and begin to experience the beauty in an absence of clutter.

WEEK FOUR

Uncover and eliminate all underused, never used, or formerly used items that lurk in your office, from bulletin boards to scanners and everything in between.

3. MARCH

Stop Paper Pileups

I urge you not to throw away time,

for it's swift as an arrow, fast as a stream.

—YUNG-MING, "FIVE HOUSES OF ZEN"

Your work space is much like your physical body. It's what everyone sees on the outside. But every outside has an inside, and so does your office. It's the world of your files, binders, cupboards, and drawers. It's how you deal with paper in general. Last week you organized your desk and set stacks of loose papers aside. This week we need to find them a home.

Paper takes over your life for three major reasons. The most common reason is an inability to make a decision. I have organized executives in high places who were afraid of making a mistake. To avoid that mistake, they saved *everything*. Ironically, saving everything is a decision you make. You lose valuable space and feel cramped and unwelcome in your own office. You can't find anything easily. The chaos makes it difficult to think. Every quest for a report or invoice leaves you exhausted and feeling guilty. Lost papers leave you in a mild state of depression. There is a better way.

The second reason that paper piles up is that no logical system is in place to absorb it. You need a system that stores your incoming paper until you need it and relinquishes it with ease. It takes a time commitment to create such a system, but once it's done the rewards are invaluable:

- You save time. No more searching for paper.
- You have more space. With the congestion gone, you can use your work surface to do just that: work.
- You increase your productivity. As the paper disappears, you'll find you can think more clearly. Clutter has a type of noise about it, and when that noise is silenced, you are free to devote your energies to what you need to accomplish.
- You save money and resources. You

won't be printing multiple copies of documents because you can't find them. The trees of the world will be grateful.

Finally, the third reason paper accumulates is that you're too tired to deal with it. If you aren't getting enough sleep or exercise and don't eat nutritious food, you aren't feeding your brain and you can't think clearly. Soda, Twinkies, potato chips, skipped meals, and four hours of sleep a night won't cut it if you want to be productive. Adequate rest and proper nutrition are key factors in your ability to make quick decisions.

When I work with clients, about four hours into the organizing process, I see their eyes glaze over. Suddenly they've run out of steam and can't make a decision to save themselves. The cure is easy. Walk away for a few minutes and eat something. I'm a professional organizer and when my blood sugar dips, I'm not worth a dime. Take good care of yourself. You want to be around to enjoy the success all this increased productivity promises to bring you!

The papers you save should represent documents with information critical to your success. This month you're stepping into new territory. You are assuming control over the inner workings of your space. "As within, so without," said ancient yogis. Their wisdom wasn't directed at the modern office but the analogy holds true. We create in our physical space a picture of our thoughts. When you calm one, the other follows suit.

THE ART OF MAKING DECISIONS

Yes, making decisions is an art form. It's a skill. It's also your ticket to freedom, increased productivity, and power. You don't have to buy anything. You don't have to study. All you have to do is make a decision.

One day I worked with a client who stands out in my mind as the best student I've ever met when it comes to learning this skill. He's a medical doctor with a practice here in Los Angeles. When we sat down to work, I told the good doctor that we'd be going through one piece of paper at a time. He was free to move at his own pace.

The first piece of paper he picked up was one he told me without hesitation he didn't need. He placed it back on his desk, ready to make a new pile. I said gently, "If you don't need it, why would you save it?"

The doctor looked shocked. "What else would I do with that paper?" he asked. I said, "Toss it."

He blanched. He gulped. I believe for a nanosecond he stopped breathing. And then he tossed that paper.

I could feel him thinking, "What if I make a mistake? What if it turns out I really do need this?" But by the end of the day, he was a man possessed. We had filled multiple large garbage bags with unnecessary debris that was occupying space in his office. My client had caught what I call the organizing fever. When it happens to you, you'll know. And so will your colleagues. As mountains of trash exit your office, they will ask, "Where in the world were you keeping all that stuff?" You'll be thinking, "The real question is not where, but why on earth did I bother?"

Making decisions gets easier over time—and the amount of time is a few hours, not days or weeks.

WORK AND HOME HABIT OF THE MONTH: SAY NO

Every day, say no to at least one thing. Speech is a verbal action. Pressing the delete key on the computer is an action. You can tackle this challenge in many ways. Here are some ideas:

See an obvious e-mail pitch for something that doesn't interest you? Say no to its clogging up your inbox and press the delete key.

Receive a piece of junk mail? Toss it in the trash. And, yes, I mean without opening it and reading all the drivel that you know you don't care anything about.

Receive a voice mail from someone who keeps you on the phone too long when you call them back? Send a polite e-mail response in lieu of a return phone call. Say no to allowing them to waste your time.

From phone calls you'd rather not take to invitations for after-work drinks you'd rather not attend, life will offer you the opportunity to say no at least once each day. You may find that deleting e-mail is your strong suit and saying no to a human being puts your stomach in knots. That's okay: You have this year to practice.

And don't forget to practice this wonderful habit when you are at home. "No, Johnny, you can't stay up past your bedtime." "No, Mary, you may not go to a sleepover Friday night. You are still grounded." "Sorry, darling, I have to create my new file system this weekend. You'll have to visit your parents without me." There will be no shortage of opportunities.

WEEK ONE

Buried in Paper

This week, you can

- Organize reading materials and archive old projects

Time required: At least two hours; your situation may require extra time

THIS WEEK WE HOP ABOARD THE Decision-Making Train. You may have a slow start out of the station, but once you get up to speed, there will be no stopping you. At the end of this week, space in your file cabinet will emerge. And your file cabinet is critical to your success.

DECLUTTER MAGAZINES AND PERIODICALS

You have probably heard of the five-thousand-year-old philosophy called Feng Shui. The ancient Chinese believed that everything in the world was made of energy, or *chi*. If you blocked this energy flow, you caused problems. Feng Shui dictates that blockages in your space can prevent certain aspects of life from fully flowering. You remove the obstruction by taking away clutter. Isn't that amazing?

Over five thousand years ago, clutter was causing a problem!

Well, why not join the ancients and think of your work space as alive. Do you think it can function to its maximum potential with every nook and cranny groaning under the weight of unnecessary paper, magazines, newspapers, gadgets, and miscellaneous items?

Let's look at ways to stem the paper tide.

Organize Your Reading Material

Do you receive a large number of newspapers, magazines, periodicals, and newsletters? Let's be honest: If you were reading this material, it wouldn't be in piles all over your office, would it? Your good intentions are clogging up your space. As Dr. Phil likes to say, it's time to "get real."

Don't forget that you have the option to cancel your subscription. Later, if you see a magazine with an article you absolutely must read, purchase that issue or borrow it from a colleague.

Does your company subscribe to a particular publication? Is there a company library? Could you check out the publications at the receptionist's desk each month? If you see an article that's critical for you to have, you can photocopy it.

Why not see how many periodicals you can visit or subscribe to online? Create a *Reading Materials* bookmark folder in your Internet browser. Inside this master folder, create individual folders for all the categories of publications to which you want to subscribe. Within each of those submaster categories, create folders for each of your individual publications. For now, here is a visual for how your periodicals might look on the computer. Your hard-copy files will follow the same pattern. Grouping related items saves you time.

Reading Materials
- Magazines
  - *Newsweek*
  - *Scientific American*
  - *Time*
- Newspapers
  - *Los Angeles Times*
  - *Pittsburgh Gazette*
  - *New York Times*

Store Your Reading Material

Choose a way to neatly house the reading material you want to keep. You can find all types of magazine holders; my favorite is clear acrylic. Choose what works best with

WHEN MORE IS LESS

I had a client who was blessed with more file drawers than anyone I have ever worked with. Imagine my surprise when she told me they were too full to absorb any more material. That was why her current projects were in piles on the floor. I opened every drawer and saw that Cassandra was not exaggerating.

When I asked what this material was, I was shocked to learn that all of it represented her past. Completed projects had the place of honor in her office, and current projects languished like orphans on any available speck of floor space. I wondered how vested she was in these new projects.

We cleaned out all her file drawers and archived her files. We created a new file system and sorted her new projects. Now they were dynamic and ready to absorb additional material. She could actually find what she needed on demand! Cassandra stands out in my mind as the perfect example of the over-stuffed office file dynamic, which is the most frequent scenario I encounter as a professional organizer.

My mother used to say that some people talk and others act. You can wax poetic for hours about all the things you want to accomplish. If you have not honored these projects by giving them the space they need to grow, however, it will be difficult to achieve your goals. Nurture whatever is in your care, including your work projects.

your office décor. You want your support items to blend in rather than stand out. Purchase an adequate number of containers and stick with one type because an assortment will create visual chaos.

You will need shelf space for your containers. Check out your newly cleared bookshelf, credenza, or free-floating shelf. Avoid the floor. At last your magazines will be standing at attention ready to serve you rather than hiding at the bottom of a stack. When they are buried in a pile, they are of no use to anyone. Piles don't work!

Organize the issues in chronological order and decide how many to keep. Two months' worth or less is ideal. When a new issue arrives, toss the oldest even if you haven't read it.

If you receive newsletters or periodicals that you feel you must hold onto and they come three-hole-punched, house them in a binder. Again, you will need shelf space on a bookcase or in your credenza. Label the spine of the binder so you know at a glance what is inside. And of course decide how long to keep an issue.

When a file, binder, or folder isn't cleaned out regularly, it gets bloated. It becomes difficult to handle or to find anything. You stop using it and now you have clutter. I'm forever asking clients about abandoned file systems and bloated binders. "Oh! That was a system I started and deserted," is what I hear. What's the antidote? Maintenance.

You need to maintain everything, from your car to your body to your lawn and, yes, to your office files, magazines, and all other forms of paper paraphernalia.

Looked at this way, maintenance isn't something you need to struggle with inside your office. It's just a part of life.

ARCHIVE OLD FILES

Do you have a file system in place? If so, do you feel it's helpful or do you shy away from using it because the drawers are so full it's hard to maneuver? I'm going to make you a bet. If you look inside your drawers, you will find that a great deal of the material relates to completed projects that you haven't referenced again. If so, you don't have a file system; you have a cemetery! It's important to pull this material and archive it.

Your company may be large enough to send material to off-site storage for you. If not, speak to a supervisor and ask for guidance in dealing with this material. It's highly unlikely that you are the only employee who needs archival storage space.

And now it's time to tackle the assignment for the week. I'd like you to set aside some time to clean out the files in your file cabinet, desk drawer, and desktop file holder. Don't be concerned about organizing or perhaps reorganizing the system you are using. We'll do that next week. When we get to that stage, we need to know that all excess materials have been removed. What you have left is what you'll turn into your working file system.

Work with one file at a time. Examine one piece of paper at a time. Your entire file cabinet and all its contents is an overwhelming project to tackle. One piece of paper at a time is very doable. If you find that an entire file is no longer needed, remove it. If your folders are worn, torn, frayed, or dirty, ditch them and start over. Although it's important to be conscious of the environment and recycle, it's demoralizing to see your new projects in these old, worn-out holders. Would you dress in such clothing? Give your projects and papers the same respect.

The first time you tackle the task of archiving material, it can be time consuming. But this won't be such a daunting task in the future if you take the time to archive material as soon as a project closes.

Sometimes these files may contain reference material that you feel you might need in the future. The key question to ask is: "What will I *realistically* use?" Remember that this material will be archived, not sent to Siberia.

If you feel you need to keep some names and numbers, add them to your Rolodex or contact file on your computer before you send the files away.

In some professions, archival material needs to be kept close by for a set amount of time. Be sure you know the rules for your company as well as the specific guidelines of your profession. For example, I have a large number of clients who are real estate agents. They tend to keep closed escrows handy for a year, and then move them to archived status.

Will you need to have electronic copies of material created on the computer or sent via e-mail included with the material the company wants archived? Check company policy.

Finally, be sure to keep a list of the projects you are sending off to storage. Don't rely on the office to catalog your material. Let them be your backup.

If you organize your subscriptions this week and archive your old project files, you will have taken a giant step toward taming paper clutter in your office. This accomplishment plus last month's speed elimination will really make you feel different in and about your space!

WEEK TWO

Learn the Secrets of a Working File System

This week, you can

- Understand what does and doesn't need to be filed
- Continue to clear out your existing file space
- Discover more organizing tools at your disposal

Time required: Two and a half hours

Let's get down to brass tacks this week. I want you to understand *why* I am suggesting that you spend time revamping or recreating your file system. I'm never one to encourage busy work.

Let's say that I have promised to buy you a new car. It's going to be custom-built for you. The catch is I'm sending it piece by piece. You will have to decide with each delivery if you have received panels, tires, or nuts and bolts that are part of my gift. I'll also be sending red herrings, other miscellaneous packages along the way that are clearly not car parts. If you save a delivery you don't need, you forfeit the car. I bet you'd be hypervigilant with each package, wouldn't you?

Guess what? Paper is pretty much the same as it enters your life. If you save unimportant and unnecessary paper, you don't forfeit a car. However, you do lose valuable space on your desk and in your file cabinet, ultimately forfeiting the prize: the ability to accomplish your work with ease.

Let's take a quick look at the most common types of paper I encounter in an office situation. See how many of these pertain to you:

- Some paper we encounter offers information that requires **follow up** regarding general company business.
- Other paper, thank goodness, can be **tossed**, recycled, or shredded the minute you have read the contents.
- And then there's that wonderful group that immediately gets **forwarded** to a colleague!
- But most of the paperwork crossing

your desk probably adds information to projects you are responsible for and should be **filed**.

Follow up, toss, forward, or file. The heart of the matter is clear: You need to make one of these decisions.

WHY FILE? Q&A

I am presenting the reasons for filing in a question-and-answer format. I've been organizing clients for over twenty years, and I could probably count on one hand those who have said they had a *functioning* file system when we met. Once you do, you will wonder how you lived without it. Our focus will be on the files you create in your office. For dealing with company files and shared systems, see page 79.

1. Why do I need a new file system anyway? No matter how bad my desk looks, I can put my hand on whatever I need.

I had a client who was extremely successful. When Jim called me in to organize his office, I was surprised to find he didn't have a single file folder. He operated using the pile system or, as I like to call it, the "It's in here somewhere system." Jim assured me he knew where everything was located. I knew better. Only Superman with his x-ray vision could possibly know what lurked on the bottom of so many piles.

In a so-called system like this, the most frequently used papers are scattered across the desk. There are usually piles, and the top layer (about five or ten sheets deep) holds other frequently accessed paper. The rest of the stacks are a combination of trash and material that should be archived. Jim assured me I was wrong. I made him a promise: If he allowed me to create a file system and he didn't like it, I would restore the piles and not charge him. It was an offer he could not refuse.

Long before the new system was in place, Jim was won over. I think it was about the fifteenth time he discovered a piece of paper he had forgotten. He would exclaim: "I forgot all about this!" or "I didn't know I still had this!" or " I was looking for this just the other day!" He finally said: "I guess I don't know what's in all these stacks!" As you might guess, his day-to-day affairs were run by a crackerjack assistant. I created a file system for Jim using the techniques I'm going to teach you. Now he really does know where everything is!

You may indeed know what's in the piles closest to you on the surface of your desk, the top of your credenza, the bookcase, and even on the floor. But this is not efficient! And it's an exhausting atmosphere in which to try and do quality work.

A file system is a logical collection of pertinent material. It is important because it makes you powerful. Whatever you need is at your fingertips. You save time and energy, which are commodities that can be squandered but never recovered.

2. How can I predict if I will ever need a particular piece of paper again? Isn't it better to save everything?

Whenever I hear the phrase "better safe than sorry" regarding saving paper, I know the person is speaking from fear, most often fear of making a mistake. I have a friend who was nominated for an Emmy. The department secretary was to send the episode selected for consideration to the Television Academy for viewing by its voting membership. The night of the award telecast, brief clips from the nominated shows were shown to the television audience. As the tape rolled, my friend was surprised to see that another episode from her show had accidentally been submitted! Everyone who worked on the selected show was denied the once-in-a-lifetime chance for this prestigious award.

The secretary in charge of submitting the episode inverted two of the ID numbers when she requested the episode copy. She didn't check the numbers on the tape when it was delivered to her. She sent it directly to the Academy.

When you look back over your career, did you ever make a big mistake like this? Has it made you gun-shy about office routines? Do you want to save every document "just in case," so you won't get in trouble? It's important to learn from our experiences, not be bound to the results.

When you have to make a decision and you feel fear rise up in you and start to hear all those excuses inside your head exhorting you to make no decision, stop yourself. Breathe into the fear. Be in the present moment. Remember that today is a different time and this is a new set of circumstances. You need to make a decision, not allow a retreat into fear.

3. I know I need to save this document. Now what do I do with it?

First, recognize that you are operating in a finite universe at work. You don't have ten million possibilities for each piece of paper; you probably have less than ten. We'll get into file categories next week in detail. Here are some questions to ask yourself with each piece of paper whose fate is uncertain:

- Is this part of a project I am currently working on? If the project is new, there should be at least one file with that project's name on it. Later you will break the project into different areas and have folders for each facet, such as financial information, schedules, and vendors.
- Is this information I need to keep? Here are some possible reasons to keep a paper other than its being part of an ongoing project: It has information you will need to reference again; it has legal significance and you should retain it as part of a paper trail should a problem arise; it indicates work that must be completed by you and it may relate to your personal affiliation with this company (for example, health benefits, 401Ks, and human resource department communications).
- If you decide this paper is in fact not needed, how will you dispose of it? Will it be tossed into the trash? Does your company recycle? Or should it be shredded for security purposes?
- Are you new to this company? If you

have been here less than a year, you may encounter paper whose fate you can't fathom. If you're going through a stack, set these questionable papers aside. Find a colleague who can guide you. Before you meet, do some sorting. For example, if you have ten communications about one project, clip them together. Ask your colleague if he knows about this specific project. If he does, you can blast through everything related to it at one time. When you're dealing with a lot of paper it's confusing to be constantly shifting from one subject to another.

4. I've had a filing system before but it didn't work for me.

"If my files are in a drawer, I can't see them and therefore I won't use them (out of sight, out of mind)." Your file cabinet won't open magically for you and present what you need when you need it. You will see those files if you open the drawer and look for them!

I'm going to bet one of four things was at play with the file system that didn't work for you. One, perhaps it was a system that you inherited from the person who had your job before you. Because you didn't create it, you had no sense of ownership or control. It wasn't a pleasure to use so you abandoned it. Two, if you did create the system, it may not have been compatible with the way you think and deal with paper. No system will work on its own; it has to be used.

Three, perhaps you were like some of my clients, who used bits and pieces of different organizing systems. Nothing worked as a whole. Make a commitment to one system.

Four, you might have given up on the system too soon. You need to work with a system *for at least twenty-one days*. Give yourself time to see if this is the one for you.

Again for the "out of sight, out of mind" reader I have some alternatives, as well as a surefire way to have a file system and be able to see its contents at a glance—without ever opening the file drawer. That is part of next week's lesson.

5. What about paper that needs my immediate attention?

"Even if information relates to a specific project, I don't want to file it because I may forget to look in the project file. Can I let these papers pile up on my desk?"

The short answer is no! Paper on your desk can easily get lost. You want your papers standing at attention just like your magazines and business periodicals. Next week we're going to create a section in your files called Action files. Paper that needs your attention will be placed in a To-Do folder in your Action files section. This theme has variations, depending on how busy you are. For example, you might have a To-Do/ASAP or To-Do/High Priority folder and then a To-Do/General or To-Do/Low Priority folder for things that are not as time sensitive.

If you have a lot of projects, you could have a Projects section in your Action folder area at the front of your file drawer.

Every project could have its own To-Do folder. When you are ready to work on a project, you won't have to search for what you need to accomplish.

Now a word to the wise: People say to me, "I hope I remember to look at my *Action* files." It's as if they have no control over this process! Establish a time each day when you check your *Action* files. This is a great habit to cultivate. Set an alarm on your computer to remind you. Looking inside a file is much easier than scanning the paper debris on your desk.

6. Is there any way to keep files on my desk?

For those who love to have their most frequently accessed files on their desk, you can use a holder for this purpose. Again, I don't like the ones that are graduated in height because I'm a klutz and would knock those files over. Can I share that often enough? These are called metal incline desktop file sorters, should you wish to check them out at your stationary supply store.

I prefer a horizontal sturdy holder. You might think that the graduated height makes it easier to see the labels, but I have found that as long as the files are in alphabetical order, have printed rather than handwritten labels, and remain few in number, you will find them almost by touch.

A small portable file holder called a "file caddy" gives you extra protection because the sides are closed. Nothing can escape and get lost on your desktop. If you have nothing but 8½-by-11 sheets inside your folders and no small receipt-size items, you are probably safe without a caddy.

I have only one request: Please don't clutter your desktop with several holders instead of creating a file system. "Oh! I don't need a file system. I have everything I need at my fingertips." That's a little like saying you don't need a closet because all your clothes are tossed on your bed ready for you to grab.

7. Colleagues never know where to leave things for me in my office. What could I use to streamline this process?

A great tool for handling not only incoming mail and interoffice deliveries but the material you are ready to send to coworkers and beyond is a simple inbox/outbox. This is usually two stacking trays placed in a corner on your desk. Be sure to label which is which. Also be sure your assistant or colleagues know that you now have this in place.

Don't fall into the trap of using these trays to stack papers that you don't know what to do with. Didn't think I knew about that trick, did you? Just about all of my clients do that before we work together. Keep them *strictly* for incoming and outgoing materials. This method of communicating without words saves so much time.

If you have no room on your desk for these trays, try using holders on the wall. The official name is a "wall pocket unit." If people have a tendency to come into your office to leave something and then stay to chat, this little tool short-circuits that. All they have to do is stick a hand in and drop off the material. They never have to cross your threshold.

8. My files are always bulging at the seams. What is the cause and what can I do about it?

Let's talk about how to use a file first. You have a choice of putting the most recent material in the front or in the back. It doesn't make any difference as long as you always know where to look for the most recent addition. Be consistent.

With that said, I have to wonder if you are filing everything related to this subject without any decision making. Are you filing items that can be tossed, shredded, or recycled? Filing seems like a clever way to circumvent the decision-making process and never make a mistake, but it is guaranteed to clutter up your files!

Remember too that files are meant to hold active information. Periodically leaf through and remove what has been handled or replaced with more current information. We all enjoy crossing things off our to-do list. Periodically culling your files should bring you the same feeling of satisfaction.

When you see the impending paper explosion, stop and make an appointment with yourself to remedy the situation. It's a small act that demonstrates respect for yourself and the material/project.

9. I don't have enough file space. What should I do?

In all likelihood, you are not using the available space to its maximum potential. After this week, the last of the debris should have exited your office or cubicle.

You'll probably find that you do indeed have adequate file storage. Very often material that can be tossed or archived is robbing you of much needed space for current business.

When you cleaned out your desk's file drawer last week, for example, did you discover that it was filled with a previous employee's files? Or were you using it to store food and grooming items? This drawer is meant to be used for the files you are using daily. In addition, it may house files of a personal nature. You'd want your performance review file here, for example.

If you have cleaned out your files and your desk file drawer is housing frequently used and personal files rather than miscellaneous ones and you still come up short, it's time to talk to your supervisor. Very often my clients will be given a drawer in another cabinet. Even if it's just outside their office, at least they've acquired more real estate. Infrequently used but must-keep files should be housed here. When you create your master file list during the last week this month, you won't miss them. The list will be in the reference binder on your desk. Yes, it's true: You can let your fingers do the walking and find what you are looking for at a glance.

DEAL WITH SHARED OFFICE FILES

The information presented in this chapter is meant to assist you in creating a personal file system. Large companies and corporations generally also have shared

INSTITUTE OFFICE CLEAN-OUT DAY

They say that misery loves company. There you are ready to tear your office apart and create a new file system. You'd like to have others take this journey with you. Why not propose an official "Office Clean-Out Day?" Here are some guidelines to help you get started:

- Choose a day when business is traditionally slow.
- Be sure you have extra trash or recycle containers ready. (You might want to alert the cleanup crew and the trash pickup service).
- Ask your supervisor if extra office supplies (file folders, hanging file folders, tabs, and so on) might be made available to everyone who participates.
- Have a sign-up sheet so you will know what supplies to purchase.

- Make it fun and offer a contest. Have silly prizes for the first one to finish, the prettiest files, the neatest office, the one who threw out the most. You get the idea.
- Be sure you have water and healthy snacks such as fruit and cheese. You'll want to feed those decision-making brains!

If you work in a friendly, supportive environment, this could be an empowering day. If it's successful, it might become an annual event. I suggest, however, that you make participation optional. At least one person will be terrified at the very idea of tossing a single piece of paper. Inspire this person with your collective example. And let him or her know you'd be happy to help in any way possible.

office files. Whatever system is in place should be respected and maintained. Unless you are in charge of maintaining these files, be circumspect when it comes to offering your opinion about how they could be improved. In an effort to do some good, you might alienate the person who has been in charge for years. In lieu of something positive, unsolicited advice often comes across as judgment. You don't want your well-intentioned gesture to backfire!

If you are in charge of shared files, be sure and poll your fellow employees before you implement the changes indicated here. What do they like about the current system? What would they like to see change? Do they have specific ways to effect that change? Asking people for their input *before* you change a system they are comfortable with will make the transition easier. No matter how broken the system is, for some it's easier to hold onto it and complain than try something new. Be respectful and do whatever is best for the greater good of the company.

FILE SUPPLIES THAT MAKE A DIFFERENCE

Next week we will be ready to take the next and final step in creating a new and improved file system. Following is a list of supplies you may need. Be sure and ask if your company has them or could order them for you. Resist the temptation to purchase items you don't need.

Box-bottom hanging legal or letter file folders: One box of twenty-five of these is usually sufficient; two inches wide is my favorite. This type of folder is a wonderful tool for streamlining any file system. They latch onto the sides of the file drawer in a desk or onto rails in a file cabinet. Measure your drawer and purchase the rails at your local stationery supply store, if needed.

You'll also want some **regular hanging legal or letter file folders** (whatever your drawer holds). Box-bottom folders are an adjunct to these and keep large categories together; they are not a replacement for regular hanging file folders!

Your hanging file folders are one of the key ingredients in the creation of your new file system, but they aren't the only tools you'll want to have on hand. Here are some additional supplies I use with all my clients:

- Legal- or letter-size folders, manila or color or both
- Label maker with extra cartridges. I use the Brother P Touch. (If you prefer to use your computer to generate labels, have label sheets on hand).
- File tabs (get the long ones)
- Post-it notes

Every so often a client will tell me that lines are drawn on their hanging file folders. They presume that if they bend along these lines, they can create a substitute for a box-bottom folder and save some money. The lines you see are for decoration. If you fold along them, you will indeed create a flat bottom but you will also shorten the file folder. Now your papers will stick so far out that you will most likely not be able to close the drawer! In addition, there will be nothing to keep that folder flat in the drawer. Box-bottoms come with cardboard inserts made for this purpose. Accept no substitutes. (Be sure and check your box before you leave the store to be sure no one filched your inserts.) If you have large categories and it would behoove you to keep material in one area, treat yourself to a box of these special hanging file folders.

SET YOURSELF UP TO WIN!

Over the years I have noticed that my clients will do small things that make their organizing life more difficult. Here are a few tips to remember:

You probably find that tossing items is stressful. Be sure your garbage can or recycle bin is close by. I have seen clients put these containers in places that only a contortionist could reach.

Open all of your supplies at the start. You don't want to waste time when you are in the thick of the decision-making process to open a pack of Post-it notes or a container holding a cartridge for your label maker.

Have plenty of water at the ready. Eat a good meal before you start and have healthy snacks nearby. Feed that brain of yours! It's going to be working overtime.

Cleaning out files isn't fun, but oh, the rewards! Next week you're going to be grateful you did this prep work. I've tried to spread out the file system creation process so that you don't have to spend too much extra time at your office. Notice and appreciate the changes as you go along. Like a person losing weight, your space should be getting lighter by the day. "It isn't the destination that counts, it's the journey." You are establishing new habits that will change your work life forever.

WEEK THREE

From Piles to Files

This week, you can

- Create a working file system

Time required: Two to five hours, depending on the complexity of your work and the volume of paper that accompanies it

AT THIS JUNCTURE ALL YOU SHOULD have before you are the papers that need a permanent home (if you have some remaining stacks, you may still find hidden papers to be discarded). When I get to this point with a client, I am always eager to find the connection points for all the material they have. What is a *connection point*? It's a fancy way of saying a *category*. I'm going to show you how to find yours this week.

My clients enter the process thinking they have a broad spectrum of information that can't possibly be contained. But no matter how many interests you have, how many projects, or how complicated the company you work for, we'll be able to boil this information down to a group of main areas.

Roll up your sleeves and have a few large garbage bags, healthy snacks, and wa-

ter on hand. This will be an intense week, but when it's over, you will have a truly working file system. Please be sure you read this week through to the end *before* you begin work. This setup is easy and logical once you get the hang of it. But read the week through once to squash any latent fears about change that may rise up.

CREATE A WORKING FILE SYSTEM

Most of my clients face the task of creating a new file system with as much glee as facing a root canal without anesthetic. The result, however, fills them with pride and they can't wait to use the new system. Aside from being completely functional, the system is beautiful to look at. On crazy busy days, you'll be calmed the minute you open your file drawer. And I have more good news. Are you ready?

We've been using a four-week month as our model. This month is the last in the first quarter of this year. You have a bonus week coming up because there are thirteen weeks rather than twelve in every quarter. Use that week to get caught up, if you need it. Isn't that a nice surprise? And if you are up-to-date, practice using and maintaining your new system next week. After all, it's meant to work with you, not be a museum piece!

Step One: Review

You have been working the first step of The Magic Formula (eliminate) for the past two weeks. Here is where you should be

- Completed projects that must be saved are in archival storage.
- Existing files have been purged of extraneous paper or tossed if the material is no longer pertinent.
- Magazines, periodicals, newsletters, and such have been pared down, eliminated, and organized.
- Drawers have been divested of their bloated contents and are organized.
- Surface or storage areas such as bookcases and credenzas have been cleaned out and organized.

Step Two: Eliminate Distractions

One of the most important factors in your success is setting aside time to do the work

> Don't forget to shred any information that shows your social security number, active bank or investment accounts, and any other vital personal information. If you have little material in this category, shred as you go; otherwise save it to be done later. Be just as cautious with private company materials.

of creating your file system. I suggest you either stay after work or come in over the weekend. Eliminate as many distractions as possible. Phone calls, e-mail messages, chatty colleagues, and other forms of disruption will take you away from your goal. One minute you'll be organizing and the next you will be enmeshed in a work-related issue. The more you can focus, the faster you will finish.

The most difficult situation is working in a cubicle you share with others. When I have to work with a client in this situation during business hours, we warn the others in the space what we will be doing, tell them when we will be doing it, and we project how many hours it will take. If they can, they make themselves scarce. After all, we are a big distraction in their workday. If you have cube-mates, be sure you find out their schedule the day you plan to get organized.

You're also going to need a workstation. You want a clear area to sort through your piles as you turn them into the new file system. This is another great reason for working when no one else is around. You can spread out material on the floor of your office or, in a shared space, use other people's desks as a staging area.

Take a minute to work out the details for your project. When you have chosen the right day and time, schedule it on your calendar as you would any business appointment. If you are working on a weekend and are part of a family, remember to share your plans with everyone at home. You don't want to wake up on Saturday ready to work and discover that little Emily is competing in a soccer match later this afternoon. Make a solid plan!

Step Three: Begin the Conversion

Have your supplies set out and ready to grab as you need them. If you can clear off your desk, you might set your supplies in front of you. Start with the loose papers on your desk. You gathered them into a file two weeks ago when you were clearing off your desk. As you go through everything today, you may be in a ruthless mood and be willing to eliminate more material. This is wonderful! Just be sure you are focused on making careful decisions. You don't want to be caught up in a "toss everything" frenzy.

Remember always that the whole of anything is overwhelming. You achieve success when you break projects down into manageable chunks. Take a stack of papers no more than three inches thick. Work one piece of paper at a time. Your goal is to create your main file categories. No matter how vast the scope of your work, it will have only a few main areas.

CREATING CATEGORIES

Frank called me in desperation. His office was drowning in paper. His assistant was overwhelmed. During the interview, I uncovered the big sources of confusion: Every time Frank hired a new assistant, he or she made use of a file system they were comfortable with from a previous place of employment, but there were two problems. One, no one ever converted all the files to the new system. The result was a mishmash of ideas masquerading as a company file system. Frank couldn't find anything because there was no rhyme or reason to his files.

The second problem was that no assistants ever explained to Frank how they worked with files. He wanted results, and as long as he got what he wanted, he felt he didn't need to know how they were achieved. When an assistant moved on, Frank had no clue how to find anything. He in turn had his own system for the files closest to him.

The good news was that the company was growing by leaps and bounds. The bad news was that it was growing by leaps and bounds! But it gets worse. Frank had a large office with two desks, side by side. He ran part of his business from one computer and part of it on the second. Frank hopped from one desk to the other all day.

Papers didn't have a home so they were everywhere. I couldn't see a surface that wasn't covered. I realized immediately that categories were key to his survival.

Frank is a real estate developer with various facets to his business: He owns apartment buildings that he rents; he is restoring several historic homes; he invested in some high-rise buildings; and he is deeply involved in historic preservation in the genteel Southern city he calls home. Every file, no matter which facet it related to, was mixed together in his filing cabinets. Even with alphabetical order, it was a nightmare.

As you read through this section, take special note of the way all the material Frank had amassed was broken down into related *topics* of information. We started with what I call *master categories* and then organized each of those topics into the information that made up the whole.

Here is a sampling of how we broke down his business for the files. I will return to Frank's files later this week. At this point, don't worry about mastering the *physical* setup; instead, understand the concepts that drive the setup. Before the week ends, I'll teach you the mechanics.

Category One: Rental Properties. I asked Frank what he needed to know about his rental properties. They all had common aspects, and these became the parts that made up the category. For example, they all had

- Managers
- Repair history
- Tenants
- Vendors:
    Gardener

Handyman
Plumber

Rental Properties became a master category. Once I had the preceding figured out, I made files with those names for *each* rental property Frank owned. Fortunately each rental property had a name. These were large multiple dwelling units, so you can imagine how much paper each one generated. This was the perfect place to employ box-bottom hanging file folders. (Again be sure you check your box at the store. You don't want to come home and find that the cardboard inserts were filched by someone else. And, yes, it happened to me!)

I further assigned a different color to each of Frank's master categories. His everyday business was kept in manila folders. If you have a lot of files, I suggest this for you as well. If you don't want to purchase colored folders, attach a large colored dot to designate a category.

Frank had so many file drawers that we were able to assign two long lateral file drawers to *Rental Properties.* If Frank was looking for something related to a rental property or a particular unit, he had only to look in one of the two file drawers assigned to Rental Properties. We put a label on the outside of the drawer to make life easier. Incidentally, I use only black letters on a white background with my label maker because colors can be difficult to read.

Category Two: Restoration Properties. Frank loves real estate and history.

When he can marry those interests, he is in heaven. Frank had so many lateral file cabinets we could keep his master categories in separate drawers. This is a rare luxury. Even if they had been in the same drawer, however, *Historical Restoration Properties* (his second master category) and *Rental Properties* were different colors and therefore easy to identify.

Once again, we gave each historical property he was restoring its own section in a file drawer, just as we did with the rentals. Each of these buildings had a name as well, so it was easy to identify.

Our files here had a slightly different twist. Here are some of the main categories we created within the master category of Historical Restoration Properties:

Contractors
Finance
Historical material
Legal
Renters

These files were voluminous. Once again, as previously noted, we secured two lateral file drawers for the Historical Restoration Properties material and put a label on the drawers.

Category Three: Investment Properties. The most complicated area of Frank's file system was the third master category, Investment Properties. There were legal files because he had to document the purchase. Anyone who has ever dealt with an attorney knows that an avalanche of paper is headed your way! These are not docu-

ments you want to search for; they need to be handy.

Frank also had partnerships with other business entities to finance the purchase of these buildings. We had a "Financial" section in the file cabinet where those documents were kept.

With large-scale investment properties, you are not likely to have a file on every renter. The buildings are run by management companies. Frank had a file on these entities as well.

As with his rental properties, we tried to streamline the type of file so they recurred for each building. Every building had a Financial, Legal, and Management section. And again these were in a different color from the other two master categories.

Category Four: Historical Preservation. Frank sat on the board of several preservation societies, each of which generated a lot of paper. He received historical data and invitations to meetings, classes, and fundraisers from each one. We needed only one lateral file drawer for this material.

Category Five: Reference. Everyone has reference material. It's the information about your business that can be applied to many areas and categories. For example, Frank had specific vendors he used for each of his buildings. They were reliable, local to the property, and the price was right.

He was smart to realize that from time to time, he might need to replace someone or use a new vendor in a pinch when his regular person wasn't available. Frank had a file called Vendors in his reference section. In an emergency, he checked here. As you go through your papers, be on the lookout for the material of this category!

The Bottom Line. Every time Frank wanted a piece of information, he needed to ask himself a single question: "What is this a part of?" Once he had his category, he had to search only one or two drawers for the item he needed. And the same question would let him know which area of the files would house the information he needed or wanted to file. Colored files further helped him effortlessly pinpoint information and location. The piles vanished and Frank's office became a pleasure to work in. The question "What is this a part of?" is your ticket to order and control as well.

Name That Category!

Now I'd like you to make a list of the master categories for *your* files. When you are finished, study your list for a few minutes. Don't make everything a master category; be sure you understand the difference between the parts and the whole. Rental Properties was a master category for Frank, while Tenants was one of the parts that fleshed out Rental Properties. Got it?

See if you relate to these common office categories. Feel free to use them in your system:

Company Information
  Interoffice communication guidelines

  Phone list/Roster
  Shipping instructions
  Voice mail system instructions
Contracts
Correspondence
Employee Information
  Employee handbook
  Holiday schedules
  HR materials
  Investment plans
  Legal information
  Parking instructions
Forms
  Fax cover sheets
  Letterhead (blank)
  Second sheets (to accompany letterhead)
  Work forms
Projects (current)

You can keep ongoing projects you are working on (like Frank's historic home renovations) as well as ones that are periodic, such as the office holiday party, in your file cabinet. Frank's projects were large in scope, so we had to break the material to be included into subcategories. He would have wasted time looking for the latest bill from the contractor, for example, if he had to sift through legal documents to find it.

Don't create more categories than you really need. An office party's support material can usually be kept in one single folder. For example, if you had a separate folder for flowers, caterers, entertainment, and so on for a party for twenty people, that would be organizing overkill!

DIAGNOSIS NEEDED

Madeline works as an office manager for a large medical practice in the Bay area. She keeps the multiphysician practice as a whole running smoothly. A large section in the office is just for patient files, all of which are kept in alphabetical order. Here is how we broke down some of the key aspects of the practice that serviced everyone.

Billing
    Direct (for patients with no
        insurance)
    Insurance
        Electronic Submissions
        Paper Submissions
Claims
    Accepted
    Denied
    Pending
Marketing
    Newspaper Ads
    Radio
Office Business
    General
        Conferences and Symposiums
        Holiday Party
        Parking Passes/Regulations
    Personnel
        401K Information
        Individual Staff Folders
        Medical Coverage (Staff)
    Purchasing
        Office Supplies
        Medical Supplies
    Reference Materials

Find Your Categories Step-by-Step

If you still can't seem to make a list of your categories, here are step-by-step instructions to help you make them appear. They are there, I promise you. It's just a matter of recognizing them.

1. Take one piece of paper at a time from the stack you've chosen. Designate a specific location for it in your soon-to-be-created file system. Don't put it down and say something like: "I'll decide later." Before you know it, you'll have transferred the material from one mystery pile to another!

2. As soon as you know the category, write that name on a Post-it note. Place the Post-it on your clear work surface. Place the paper just below or above the Post-it so you can start a stack. Remember: One piece of paper does not make a category, nor does it deserve an entire file. Let me give you an example.

Let's say you are in charge of the holiday party this year. It's June and you want to start collecting information. September feels like the right time to implement a plan. The company wants you to find an outside venue, hire a band, secure a caterer, and get a decorating committee. As you go through your papers, you find a flyer from a restaurant with a room for private parties. This would be the ideal first piece of paper in a file that is going to grow and be dynamic. The logical and easy label for this file might be: Holiday Party/2009.

Or let's say you find a piece of paper with information about plants that survive in low light. You've been thinking about

EASY ACCESS

When items are easy to access, you are more apt to use them. You don't want a project to suffer because its support papers are inconveniently placed. Who would do this? Almost everyone! We make unconscious choices that sabotage our work. Sometimes a left-handed person like me will use a file desk drawer on the right side rather than the left for their most frequently accessed folders. All that twisting and turning is frustrating!

I had a client who had two desk drawers. The left side was easy as pie to open. She used it for rarely used files. The right side opened only halfway because a support beam was in the way. She had her *most* frequently used papers here. When she wanted to get into the back of the drawer, she had to turn into a contortionist! It had not occurred to her to flip the material.

Is there anything like that in your work environment?

getting a plant for your office when you get organized. If you know the chances of buying a plant are slim to none, toss the information. This is the type of material you can Google any day of the week. If you have interest but it's low because you have some other office ideas to implement first, create a Miscellaneous file. And, if you are anxious to introduce a plant, put it in your To-Do file when you create it.

3. Speaking of your To-Do folder(s), don't forget to make a pile for items that fall into the Action area I promised we would create. This is a section at the front of the file drawer you access most frequently. Your desk file drawer would be the ideal place. You would probably have the following:

> Pending
> To-Do/High Priority
> To-Do/Low Priority
> To File
> To Read

I and some of my clients like to separate To-Call from To-Do. When I am taking care of details from my To-Do folder, sometimes I want a change of pace. I will switch to my To-Call file and spend about twenty minutes taking care of business on the phone.

Do whatever makes sense to you. I don't want you to micromanage yourself into paralysis. I'm trying to prevent you from having a folder that is so fat you are depressed every time you look at it! Be sure you understand the difference.

Pending is probably the favorite file in my system. When you work on something, often there is a pause in the action. Someone has to get back to you and, while you are waiting, what are you going to do with the paper(s) that prompted your action? Most people return the paper to their To-Do file. Wrong! You've dealt with the issue for now. These items are in process and should go into Pending. I check my Pending folder every Friday to see who I need to goose the following week. When an item is handled, I either file the paper(s) for reference or I toss them if I need no record of the matter.

Having a Pending folder also ensures that your To-Do folder won't be overloaded. When my business is slow, I check To-Do/High Priority every day. When it's jumping in my world of organizing, I check it on Friday to plan what items I will be able to handle the following week. I check To-Do/Low Priority once a week. You will come up with a schedule that suits your personality, the amount of work that crosses your desk, and your level of responsibility. Remember the Franklin Planner advice: adapt, don't adopt.

A word of caution: Don't overuse the reminders on your calendar. Be sure when a reminder pops up that you are going to pay attention to it. If you have a huge block of items set as reminders, you will accomplish nothing because you will be overwhelmed. Here's a good idea: Set a reminder for every morning at 9 to check your To-Do/ High Priority folder until that is an ingrained habit. Reminders are a great calendar tool if you use them judiciously.

4. If you decide to add a paper to a category, just before you plop that paper down by the Post-it, ask yourself a second question, "Do I *really* need this?" An acceptable answer is not, "I don't know." You do know. Make a decision. It gets easier as you go along.

If you weren't able to sketch out a file system when you started, you will probably be inspired by the time you get through sorting your loose papers. If you can sketch your entire file system, you are ahead of the game. However, few people can do that at this point.

5. Next we need to look at any existing files you have been using.

Once the loose papers are sorted, it's time to look at existing files in light of today's discoveries. Here are some questions to ask:

- Do you have any existing files that you can use in the new system?
- Do you see any material that should be sorted differently?

For example, let's consider your holiday party planning. Suppose you had made separate files for Caterers, Entertainment, and Venues, in alphabetical order in the main system. But now you realize that this information will never take up a lot of room and could all be contained in one file folder. Look at the room you can save in your file cabinet. You have one folder instead of three, plus only one hanging file folder to house that file instead of three.

Take a look at your existing files and see if you can save some space. You may be amazed at the new way you are beginning to view information. Making categories means finding the relatedness among the vast storehouse of material you have. Long after your new file system is in place, it will continue to support this kind of thinking. How? Let's say I ask you how much the company has spent so far on the XYZ project. You go to your files and check the financial file you created for this project. But while you are looking into the financial folder, all of the other material for this project is at your fingertips. Seeing it together may inspire you to gather other

Let's say that the ABC project relates to re-modeling at your place of business. You'd have all manner of files, including the following:

Office Remodel
Construction
Design
Research

Furthermore, suppose the Research section has brochures, letters of introduction, and samples from all the vendors you contacted before the project was given the green light. This information is the perfect candidate for a box-bottom hanging file folder. You will be able to keep the various files related to this topic in one section rather than having a se-ries of smaller hanging file folders, which re-ally eat up space.

When the project is finished and you are ready to archive the material, you can proba-bly toss most of the research. Why? Because the only reference material you might need in the future is from the suppliers you did busi-ness with. Your research will become obsolete in about six months, because businesses shut down and new ones open. No point holding onto it, right?

previous steps, you can easily see the size of your existing categories. Finally we'll be ready for the last step as we start organiz-ing the individual categories. At that point the parts that make up the whole will re-veal themselves and you will see your file system reveal itself in its totality.

You want the material you use all the time to be the closest to you physically. It should move away from you in direct pro-portion to how often you have to access it on a daily basis. I have one caveat to add to these instructions: If you have any per-sonal files such as your 401K, your last performance review, or your medical cov-erage, keep that close to you or keep it where you can lock it at night.

We are now ready to turn our categories into a beautiful, perfectly functioning file system that's always ready to absorb addi-tional information. Have you taken any breaks? Now would be a great time. The hard mental work is pretty much over; the tedious part of the process is about to be-gin. Congratulations on all your hard work.

CREATE A PROJECT SECTION IN YOUR FILE DRAWER

We always have projects in our lives, don't we? One ends and before we can catch our breath, another begins. Some are ongoing, some are brief, some are easy, and others befuddle us every step of the way. When we're ready to work on any given project,

information to present to me at the same time. The more you are able to see the link between the parts, the greater your vision of the whole of any project will be.

6. Now let's look at available drawer space and decide which categories live in what area. By the time you have completed the

we need to have all the information pertaining to that project in one easy-to-find place. Whether that place is a single file folder or a full drawer in a file cabinet, we have to be able to put our hands on what we need at a moment's notice. And so you shall!

Step One: First consider how much material you have for this project. Will you need a single hanging file folder, a box-bottom hanging file folder, or both? Not sure? Here are some guidelines. If you have a few thin folders (that is, you don't have a lot of material inside), you can put two or three file folders inside one hanging folder. This means a small project is now contained in one area. On the other hand, you may be a project manager who organizes several large projects at once. You have stacks of papers for each project. This is where a box-bottom hanging file folder will save you lots of space in your drawer. (I never use ones wider than two inches because wider means heavier and the folder is apt to fall apart quickly).

You can use box-bottom hanging folders with single hanging file folders. It isn't a matter of one or the other. The size of a category determines the optimum tool for you to use. Let's say I fill one two-inch box bottom for my XYZ project but I have two small files left over. They can go into a regular-size hanging file holder right behind the box bottom. A box bottom has to be full to work. Otherwise it pops up in the drawer.

Step Two: Decide if you are going to use manila folders, colored folders, or colored dots.

Step Three: File tabs are markers in your drawer. They are like road signs on the freeway, alerting you when a new project is beginning. They can also tell you which files are support files. Write the name of the project on the tab and insert the tab on the hanging file folder. Use a consistent system for naming your files.

Feel free to use your computer to print labels. Again, I prefer to make mine on a Brother P Touch label maker. If you watch for specials, you can get a low-end machine for about $15.00 plus the cost of batteries and cartridges.

I place a tab on the left side of every hanging file that begins a new category. As I look into the file drawer, I see all my categories on the left. I keep my tabs in a straight line instead of stagger them because they are easier to read that way. (Plus, if a file needs to be eliminated, a stagger pattern has not been disrupted.) On the right side of the hanging file, I put a tab that announces subdivisions in that category, if necessary.

ORGANIZE A FILE DRAWER

Most people have file drawers that are positively scary when I peer inside. The folders are dog-eared and often dirty. No alphabetical order is in sight. Handwritten file tabs are almost impossible to read. And the plastic file tabs are attached to the hanging file folders without rhyme or reason. It's no wonder these files aren't used!

We're going to give as much attention and respect to the setup within the drawer as we did to the assembly of the papers the drawers will house. Let's create a system that's as beautiful as it is efficient. You're on the home stretch now!

Alphabetize! Whatever material is in your file drawer, it needs to be kept in strict alphabetical order. This applies as much to a row of single files as it does to a series of files in a box-bottom hanging file folder.

When you use your desk file drawer, be sure the files face you. I can't tell you how many people push back their chair so they can see into the drawer. This is a waste of time and energy.

Buy a file frame if you can't get one from the company's supply and drop it into the drawer. Now when you open the drawer your files will be facing you and ready to serve.

If you are using lateral files, can you easily stand at the side of the cabinet and look down a row of files? Or are you sharing a cubicle and will your posterior be in some other worker's personal space as you bend over the file drawer? Convert your file drawer so when you open it you see your files in two rows, facing you!

If you have a file drawer that's frequently in use, add a marker to indicate when a file has been removed. One of my clients uses yellow construction paper. It's a visual clue that a file is missing and a quick way to restore order when the day is done.

If all you use is letter-size paper but your file drawers can't be adjusted from legal to letter, use letter-size files with your legal-size hanging holders.

YOU HAVE A SYSTEM!

You'll find that the actual assembly of your material in the file drawer moves quickly and you will enjoy it—after all, you are watching the new system come alive before your eyes! If your system is large or complicated or both, take a break when you have completed this phase before you create your master file list. I have that scheduled for next week. Many of you will want to move on quickly and have your master file list handy for reference. However, it is best to wait a few days so you can work with your system and see whether it should be tweaked before you commit it to paper. If you'd like to see what a master file list looks like, feel free to peek into next week's material.

It's a good idea to keep a single hanging file holder in the back of each drawer with a few blank files in it. You don't want to have to stop, walk over to a credenza or bookcase, grab a file box, take what you need, and have to return it every time you need to make a new file. By the way, stand your boxes of files and hanging file folders from the stationery store on their sides so you can pull them out easily. If you stack them, it will inevitably be the one on the bottom that you need. You would be surprised how little things yield big benefits.

Take a few days to live with your system before you create your master file list. This gives you a chance to move things around, if you feel you could streamline even further by doing so. When you prepare your master file list, you will probably make a few additional changes, and then you will be set.

WEEK FOUR

Maintain Your File System

This week, you can

- Create a master file list
- Understand the importance of maintenance
- Find out how binders and project boxes can augment your file system

Time required: Ninety minutes or more, depending on the number of files you have

Now that you have a file system, and especially if it's fairly extensive or complex or both, I suggest typing up the names of your project files on your computer and printing a copy. I call this the master file list. Whenever you are in a panic about where a new piece of paper should go or where a particular file is located, you can whip out your reference binder and check your master file list. It's one of the best examples of "let your fingers do the walking" that I have ever encountered.

Steve Mathis works for a prominent real estate brokerage in Beverly Hills. Here is what he had to say about the master file list we created for his files: "The menu of documents saves time and increases my effi-

ciency. It also makes my files more accessible to my assistant and associates as well as easier to update and manage."

Steve has generously allowed me to share a portion of his current master file list. You will note that I have indicated the location of each category of files. What you can't see in this black-and-white format is that each category is printed in the color dot I used on the files in that section or category of information. I also place a dot on the file drawers. In other offices I have used colored files, but as I indicated earlier, this can get expensive if you have a lot of projects or categories. Dots save you money!

Every file system I create has certain things in common, but I also allow my client's personal style and creativity to be part of the process. If I try and pour them into a one-size-fits-all system, it will be abandoned in short order. Some key questions I ask are, "What is this material a part of? Where would you look for it? What should we call this file folder?"

In the list that follows, you may see some file names that mean nothing to you. They might be part of the world of real estate or a reflection of Steve's relationship to the material. For example, the phrase "Office Systems" is unique to Steve and indicates all the material that helps him run the office. You might use a different phrase.

I am sharing this list as another example of master categories and subcategories at work. It is meant to inspire you. It isn't meant to be a template that you slavishly follow. Recognize and honor your personal style, creativity, and relationship to the material you need to organize.

A MASTER FILE LIST EXAMPLE

The first file drawer holds two master categories: Risk Management and Special Language. Risk Management contains a long series of file folders in alphabetical order. Special Language is a large collection of papers that pertain to the topic. They are not sorted but fill three folders.

The second file drawer has two master categories: Office Systems and Personal. The Office Systems master category has two subcategories, Broker Correspondence and General Files. When we assembled the General Files category, we noticed that it contained several natural subcategories. This means that a topic under General Files had more information than could be housed in one folder. So we made subsubcategories to make retrieval easier: Financials, Marketing & Advertising, Office Environment, Special Projects, and Supplies.

Please note in the following list that text in bold represents a category, not an actual file folder.

This list was created on 15 December 2007.

It was updated in June 2008 and September 2008.

Risk Management

Agent License Info.
Conflict Resolution
Contract & Disclosure
E & O
Joint Venture
Marketing Phrases
MLS Benefits
MLS Rules & Regulations
Multiple Spread Sheets/Multiple
   Offers
Multiple Offer
Mold Prevention/Global
Newsworthy Articles
Procuring Cause
Probate
REO/Foreclosures
Short Sales
Special Assessment
Tech Support
1031 Tax Deferred

Special Language
Office Systems
  Broker Correspondence
  General Files
    Biz Plan/Current
    Commission Concessions
    Commission Schedules
    Correspondence/Personal
    Desk Cost
    Display Board
    License & MLS Information
    Office Floor Plan/Seating Chart
    Office Policy
    Office Roster
    Parking Options
    Parking Valet Proposal
    Realty Rescue/Signage Service
    Referrals
    Reimbursement Forms
    Sales Assistants Information
    Sales Meeting Topics
    Sales Meeting Notes
    Vendor List
    Voice mail
    Website Information
  Financials
    Financials/Agent Earnings
    Financials/Office Dollar
    Financials/Pending Sales
  Marketing & Advertising
    Advertising Venues
    Agent Advantages
    Agent Marketing Materials
    Client Benefits
  Office Environment
    Focus Groups
  Special Projects
    Montecito Property
    NBC Property Awards

    Office Remodel
    Relias & Chateaux
    Transaction Coordinator
  Supplies
    Envelopes
    Labels
    Stationery, Pages 1 and 2

Personal
  Contacts/Personal
  NAR Membership
  Real Estate License Renewal

Once you create your own master file list, you will have to maintain it. When a file is eliminated for whatever reason, it gets crossed off the list. When a new one is created, it is added. Generate an up-to-date hard copy, put it in sheet protectors, and keep it in a half-inch or one-inch reference binder.

You can keep in this binder other frequently referenced material as well, such as interoffice phone lists, instructions for your office phone system, hours for different departments, and a cheat sheet for your computer's functions. I like a binder much better than a bulletin board. It is almost impossible to keep a bulletin board from descending into hopeless chaos. Things go up and almost never come down!

MAINTAIN YOUR FILE SYSTEM

When I first moved to California, I discovered that it was true what they said about cars in L.A. You really did need one. Growing up in New York, I was a subway

We're all inundated by paper. Make good decisions as you go along and you can truly keep the Paper Monster at bay. Here's a cheat sheet to help you stay focused and maintain your new system. You might want to make a copy and keep it handy. Is there a laminator in your office?

Incoming documents from colleagues → Inbox (check every day).

Documents you need to follow up on → Action file (check every day).

Documents that you're waiting for someone or something else before acting on → Pending file (check once a week).

Documents you need to forward to a colleague or mail → Outbox (check every day or ask your assistant to remove the contents by day's end).

Documents you don't need → Trash can or shred.

Documents you need to save → Consult master file list and choose the appropriate project file folder, create a new file if you are starting a new project, or hold in To-File folder (file once a week or as appropriate for your situation).

Periodicals and articles → To-Read file (check once a week), magazine holder, or trash can.

girl. My first car was used. A few months after the purchase, I went to a mechanic for something. He looked under the hood and asked me what I thought was a strange question: "Regina, do you want to keep this car?" I thought he was crazy. "Of course I do!" I replied innocently. "Why do you ask?" "Well," he said, "you are supposed to change the oil every three thousand miles. Yours hasn't been done in twelve thousand." This was the first time I ever heard you had to change the oil in a car!

The moral of the story is this: All things need to be maintained. Don't be resentful about having to keep up your office organization. It's just another part of the system that operates the world. And you don't have to expend more energy or add tasks to your already overwrought schedule. You just have to shift your focus and energies and do a series of *different* things. Here are a few examples.

Instead of tossing magazines, periodicals, newsletters, and newspapers just anywhere on your desk or in your office place them in their designated homes. If this takes a minute longer, you are still ahead of the game because you won't expend energy later trying to find them. Nor will you ever again be heard to say: "Oh gosh! I meant to read that article."

Instead of stuffing papers into stacking trays or already bulging files and saying that you'll deal with them later, place each piece of paper in the appropriate folder. Then when the moment arrives for you to do the work involved, the paper is waiting for you, not hiding in a forgotten pile. Over the course of a year, you will save considerable time.

ACCESS FREQUENTLY REFERENCED PAPERS EASILY

One common lament is the fear that once a paper goes into a file folder, it will be forgotten. Are you vigorously nodding your head in agreement? Take heart. This week I have two ideas for the one or two active projects you're referencing multiple times a day. I would use these *in addition* to your files. Put everyday information in the files in your desk drawer and file cabinet. You simply have to make use of this invaluable real estate to function at a high level of productivity. Take Steve's master file list as an example. He isn't going to be in and out of his real estate reference material on a daily basis. Nor will he need to access his personal files regularly. But he needs to have the location of this information handy. Trust yourself to use the master file list when you need to track down some needed information.

Binders

Binders have come a long way since I was in school. They now come in an array of colors, styles, and materials. Remember the box-bottom hanging file? This two-inch-wide folder enables you to keep several related manila (or colored) file folders in one area. We can create the same effect using a binder and some divider tabs. The difference is that your material can now sit on a bookshelf and be at arm's reach.

After your papers have been separated into categories, evaluate which ones you will be referencing frequently enough to keep in binders. When you look at the individual stacks of papers, how big a binder will you need for each category? Be careful not to go too big. If your binder weighs a ton, you won't be inclined to use it! It is better to divide the material into multiple binders. You can three-hole-punch your papers (or put them into sheet protectors), and then place them into your binder. Use a tab sheet to divide each section.

Just as you color-coded files for certain projects, you can use different color binders to designate a specific category. For example, when Steve sees a green dot in his files, he knows the material is part of Training. You might use a red binder (an easy-to-spot color) for your reference binder, blue binders for your XYZ project, and green for the ABC project. You would be surprised how easy it is to identify and locate active projects when you use color. And whether it's a colored file folder, a colored binder, or a color dot on a manila folder, it all works to make you more productive.

Two words of caution: You need to have a place for your binders, and that place can't be your desk. Unless you have a huge desk, you'll be crowded out by your binders. Wherever they land, if you need them frequently, be sure you can reach them easily. And be sure that when the first gets full, you start volume two. When a binder is so full that you can't turn a page easily, your productivity tool becomes a productivity hindrance.

Project Boxes

A few years ago, I began to see project boxes. You can find them at exposures online.com or at stores such as the Container Store. You can place a related category of papers in each box.

Now before you go crazy and purchase a wall of boxes, note that these are not for everyday files and fast-moving projects. They are a storage solution for related materials for a few specific projects with a small amount of material. When papers lie flat they become a pile, in this instance a neatly enclosed one. Items in a pile are difficult to access (we always need the one on the bottom, don't we?), and it's hard to keep papers separated unless you use paper clips or staples.

You can use a project box to hold a complete project, but it's also a good tool to use in addition to your files or binders. For example, let's say your office is being remodeled. You have been given the opportunity to choose the paint and rug color. Paint chips and rug swatches are wonderful tools. They are also easy to lose in a busy office— unless you place them in a project box.

You can get these boxes in a variety of colors, so once again you are free to assign a color to each project. They also have a place to affix a label. You could have a project that breaks down into several parts. Let's say the XYZ project has the following: Contracts, Correspondence, and Expense Reports/Receipts. You could have three blue project boxes stacked on a shelf. The color announces the project and each label designates the contents.

I'm not promoting project boxes as replacements for files. I'm suggesting them as an adjunct for the person with a true aversion to the traditional format of a file cabinet, like my wonderful client Craig.

Craig headed a large organization in Los Angeles with literally thousands of members. He hated file folders and wouldn't use them. Craig had a secretary and an assistant so his day-to-day affairs were handled by this team. They were the keepers of his files. When he needed one, it magically appeared. Lucky guy, wasn't he? Craig's aversion to files, however, didn't mean that he did not have to keep track of projects. In his private conference room, we had a credenza installed that had locked cupboards. During meetings, no one knew what was inside. When he wanted to work on a project, Craig would open the cupboards and take out the papers he needed.

How did he find them? The shelves were adjustable and had dividers. You could make a project area as wide and as deep as you wanted. We also had a place to attach labels. Those areas were like free-floating project boxes. This is an expensive solution for those who don't favor files, but there is always a way to honor the way your brain works!

Congratulations—the biggest month is behind you. You have laid the foundation for the rest of the year. I hope you are as proud of yourself as I am of you. Did somebody say "major reward"?

MARCH SUMMARY

WEEK ONE

Learn to make on-the-spot decisions. Begin the process of decluttering your space of unnecessary papers starting with magazines and periodicals. Archive completed projects.

WEEK TWO

Deal with shared office files. Encourage the entire office to clean out their files!

WEEK THREE

Create a working file system.

WEEK FOUR

Understand how to maintain your new system. Save time and steps with the master file system. Introduce project boxes and binders, if necessary.

4. APRIL

Break Your Worst Time-Wasting Habits

An ounce of practice is worth more than tons of preaching.

—GANDHI

TIME IS AN EQUAL OPPORTUNITY employer, isn't it? That is, time is an impartial, unemotional commodity, and everyone gets the same deal. It's our perceptions that change. When we're having fun, time flies. When we can't bear what we're doing, time seems to drag. And in a given week, we come up with creative ways to spend it.

But no matter what, lost time is never recaptured. Let's see if this month you can begin to understand the sources of procrastination: how you currently use and lose your time. Then we'll look at some tricks to make it work for you, rather than the other way around.

WORK HABIT OF THE MONTH: PRACTICE COMPLETION

This month we're really going to focus on learning how to instantly recognize an en-

vironment that's a swirling bastion of chaos. Set a timer for five minutes and devote this time to straightening up your office. Do so at the start or the end of the day, whenever you are at your peak. What are you looking for? Anything out of place is the simple answer.

For example, do you need to return files to a central file bank? Did you take a section of the newspaper or a magazine and set it aside for a specific article? Cut the article out and pop it into your To-Read file. Is your trash can overflowing? Are there items that belong to others or to other parts of the office? Return them when your timer goes off.

Keep this habit going over the weekend by spending this time either in your home office or whatever area you prefer to handle the paper you bring home as well as the paper that arrives each day in the mail. Your ability to tolerate chaos will lessen as this habit develops.

HOME HABIT OF THE MONTH: KITCHEN CLARITY IN TWO EASY STEPS

The kitchen is an important room in the home. Feeding our bodies is a sacred responsibility. Let's keep this room tidy this month. No dirty dishes in the sink; no clean dishes on the drainboard. If you use a dishwasher, load it the minute you dirty a dish and unload it when the dishes are dry. You are cultivating two habits at once.

WEEK ONE

Understand Procrastination

This week, you can

- See how procrastination and perfection keep you a prisoner of mediocrity
- Begin to free yourself from the need to put things off
- Understand the origins of procrastinating in your life
- Learn what your payoff has been for delaying the inevitable

Time required: Thirty to ninety minutes

I HAVE A SECRET TO SHARE. EVERY-body procrastinates. Yes, even professional organizers do so from time to time. It's called being human. The *chronic* procrastinator, however, has a rough road to travel. He is late for appointments, has difficulty turning in reports on time, and dreams constantly about the day he finally stops putting things off. Are *you* a chronic procrastinator? This month we do the work that moves you from a procrastinator to a doer. This is such a critical phase of our year that we're devoting the entire month of April to stopping procrastination.

First we need to uncover its origins in our lives. Armed with this information, we will understand why we act the way we do even when it causes us so much stress. The next step will be to replace delaying tactics with work habits and systems that release us from the bonds of all those last-minute dramas. Who would you be if you completed projects on time? How would you spend the time you save? You're going to find out.

This week we're taking a look at some creative ways that people procrastinate.

THE MANY PERSONALITIES OF PROCRASTINATION

When it comes to procrastinating, there isn't a one-size-fits-all description. We may fall into one category or embrace many depending on what we're trying to avoid. See if you find yourself in any of the following scenarios.

"I can't face this." You come up against a project you don't want to face. In your heart you've already decided it's going to be a bear to tackle. What happens? You wait till the last minute. You start around 9:30 the night before it's due when you could have completed the assignment weeks ago. And don't you just want to slap yourself when the project turns out to be *easy*?

"Now I'm going to be up all night." Sometimes a project is indeed as difficult as you thought. Now the inner negative arias begin. "Why didn't I do this earlier?" "I'm never going to finish this on time." "I'll be up all night!" "Why do I always do this to myself?" It's better than a night at the Metropolitan Opera. The opportunity to feel like a failure has presented itself right on cue. It's almost a self-fulfilling prophecy, isn't it? You're exhausted, sleep deprived, and as your coworkers will attest, cranky when you arrive at work for your presentation. "Someday, I'll stop this from happening to me," you vow as you nod off at your desk later in the day.

"Mommy, please don't go!" Let's say that you have a child who misses you terribly when you travel. Johnny is only five and he finds it difficult to lose his mommy. He has no concept of business travel. You assure him you will be home in X number of days. You give him a calendar so he can follow along with your trip. You circle the date you are due home. You promise to call every night to wish him "sweet dreams." It's all to no avail. He's five, after all.

You have to travel for business. A funny thing starts to happen the night before you leave. You've been so enmeshed with Johnny and your guilt that you haven't prepared for your trip! It's almost a form of magical thinking: Somehow it's all going to come together even if you don't participate. Your papers are all organized but you haven't packed as much as a toothbrush. As you bustle about the house, you notice a million little things that need to be taken care of. Gosh, the cat's litter box is a mess. Doesn't anybody else in this house take out the trash?

By the time you're ready to pack your suitcase, it's time to go to bed. "That's okay," you think, "because I know just what I want to take with me." And indeed you do. The problem of course is that you forgot that your grey business suit is still at the cleaners and that the crisp white blouse you always wear with it got a ketchup stain in Stockholm last month. Near dawn, as the bleary-eyed version of you piles your suitcase, laptop, and purse into the car to drive to the airport, you wonder, "Why do I always do this to myself?"

"Procrastinating is the only way I can finally get motivated." Procrastination is a serious issue when it becomes the way you live your life. Does an adrenalin burst make you feel so alive that you live from burst to burst? Do you think the rest of your life seems like a bore by comparison? Have you in fact noticed strange reactions at your weekly meetings when it comes time for you to report on your current projects? Are thumbs twirling? Perhaps you see eyes rolling? Or maybe some folks start texting wildly under the table? Is it possible they all know what's coming? Could it be a long-winded story describing *your* trials and tribulations as you endeavor to keep your project on track? Is your theme that old blues song, "Nobody Knows the Trouble I Seen?"

Perhaps no one at work wants you to have any important assignments because they know you can't deliver the goods on time. Or maybe you do deliver on time, but the drama your colleagues must endure along the way makes it undesirable. And this drama spills over into your home. You certainly are the center of attention, but might there be an easier way?

"I have to make it exactly right." A perfectionist lives in a world where every move he makes, every job he undertakes, every promise he makes binds him to yet another quest to be perfect. He is filled with pride about his high standards. His disdain for those with lower standards is well known. The perfectionist is a tough taskmaster.

This quest can color every facet of his work. Reports are late because the research may not have been adequate. Never mind that the report is longer than *War and Peace*, surely *something* is missing! Like Don Quixote, the perfectionist dreams the impossible dream. His efforts are often hampered as he waits for the perfect set of circumstances. In reality, there is no perfection in life. The challenge for the perfectionist is to shift perspective and strive instead to do his personal best. There is a subtle difference.

As you move through life and gain experience, you will bring the wisdom acquired in this book to bear on everything you do, including the way you maintain your office and the quality of your work. Your know-how can only get better over time. If you're always trying to be perfect, where will the joy be in life? What will there be to learn? And who is going to befriend a perfectionist? Who could live up to those standards? The quest for perfection is the quest to fail. You can never measure up. We're going to endeavor to give up all forms of procrastination this month, especially the procrastination that comes from trying to be perfect.

RECOGNIZE HOW YOU BENEFIT FROM PROCRASTINATION

It helps to examine your past to find the root cause for all your delaying techniques. One thing I have observed over the years is that the person who struggles on a grand scale due to procrastination may be enjoying the process as well as the outcome. How is this possible? Well here are some of the (albeit cockeyed) benefits:

You are the center of attention as you bluster about the office complaining about all the work you have to do on this project.

If your work is less than stellar, you have an excuse: You put everything off until the last minute. You didn't have time to do your best. Maybe you are unconsciously relieved because now you won't be asked to do any more big projects.

When your work is turned in, it knocks everyone's socks off. It was worth waiting for! Now you're the star of the show twice: during preparation and at the end. It can be heady.

In your childhood, one or both parents were consistently late with work. You learned by example that this is the way it's done. You unconsciously feel like a grown-up when you act this way.

Very often parents unwittingly teach their children by example or with their words that the best work is done with the most effort. The more difficult it is for you to meet a deadline, the better it is. You go out of your way to make your work experience much more difficult than it has to be.

Have these helped you understand how you personally benefit from procrastination? Here are some questions for you to answer. I hope you have one of those light-bulb moments when it suddenly all becomes clear. Have your notebook handy so you can jot down your answers:

1. Have you always been a procrastinator?
2. If your answer is "yes," how did this trait first affect your life? How did arriving late at school or social functions make you feel? Or were you just late handing in assignments? Did you feel special? Ashamed? Or did you have a sense of entitlement: "This is who I am, take me or leave me?"
3. If you answered "no," to the first question, when did procrastination begin for you? Was it in school? If so, what grade were you in? Why do you think that grade made such a difference in your behavior? If you became a procrastinator later in your schooling (such as college or grad school), again why do you think this happened? Or perhaps you were Johnny-on-the-spot until you entered the work force. Were you a star on the athletic field or in the drama department? An entry-level job in a large corporation is going to be quite a comedown.
4. Do you have extenuating circumstances that cause you to need extra time? For example, do you suffer from depression? Do you have a chronic condition such as MS? Is there someone in your home to whom you must give special attention? If so, have you ever considered that you might be so mentally, emotionally, and spiritually exhausted that it causes you to be reluctant to take on more? Is this how you view assignments for work? Just one more burden? Can you take something off your plate or get help to manage it all?
5. Looking at your current job with a critical eye, is something going on at your place of employment that makes you procrastinate? For example, do you

have a highly critical supervisor who denigrates everything you do? (Who would be eager to submit their work to such a person?) Or perhaps there is fierce competition among the employees in your division and you are not a competitive person? Turning in reports late gives you an unconscious chance to remove yourself from the pack.

6. Do you call yourself a perfectionist with pride? Are other peoples' standards of work lower than yours? Do you feel justified in procrastinating because it's for a lofty goal, whether you achieve it or not?

7. Do you get enough sleep and exercise and adequate nutrition every day? Are you procrastinating because your body isn't up to the demands that you and your job place on it?

8. As you race around the office getting everything ready at the last minute, does a rush of adrenaline fill you with excitement? Do you feel especially alive in those moments? Is that a guilty pleasure?

9. Do you think the pressure of working at the last minute helps you because it allows you to hyperfocus? Consider making changes to eliminate the attendant stress, because this harms your body in the long run.

10. A common cause of procrastination is ADD (attention deficit disorder) and ADHD (attention deficit hyperactivity disorder), which can cause havoc in both your home and work life. You are easily distracted, have difficulty completing assignments, and have impulse control issues. Many of my clients struggle with ADD, but they are also among the most successful and creative individuals on my client list. What separates them from the pack is their willingness to learn about ADD and find the best ways to manage it in their lives. If you suspect ADD is your issue, check with a professional. He or she will direct you to the resources available in your community. There are books to read, classes to take, and professionals to consult with. The "Resources" section can help get you started.

Questions like these help you unlock the links to the birth of procrastination in your life. Did I miss the cause that brought about your need to procrastinate? Whether it's indicated here or you found it on your own, why not take your notebook and do a bit of writing about your discovery? Understanding is the first step toward creating a new experience.

Once you feel you understand where and how your issues with procrastination started, I have some sentences for you to complete. These will clarify the steps you are going to take to change this pattern:

1. I now realize that the main reason I procrastinate is _____.

2. The so-called benefits I get from procrastinating (such as, I get to be the center of attention; I get to avoid assignments that frighten me) are _____.

3. The physical acts I now do to improve my work performance and avoid procrastinating (such as better diet, more exercise, and additional sleep) are _____.

4. The emotional changes I am willing to make (for example, when I feel fear or panic, I'll literally breathe into those emotions) include _____.

5. Five concrete rewards I would earn by eliminating procrastination from my life (such as reduction of stress) include _____.

Will letting go of procrastination be as easy as making a decision? No! This behavior is ingrained and will require vigilance, determination, and focus to change. Doesn't every worthwhile endeavor require a commitment? Accept the challenge with relish. Just think: By the end of the year procrastinating could be behind you. Right now you are taking steps to make life more difficult and a lot more stressful than it needs to be. Instead, take one step at a time toward success.

WEEK TWO

Let Go of Perfection

This week, you can

- Understand that achieving perfection is impossible
- See the relationship between fear of success and fear of failure
- Uncover how you have used procrastination in your life

Time required: Thirty to ninety minutes

ARE YOU SO CLUTCHED BY FEAR OF not getting things done perfectly that you don't do them at all? At work, attempting perfection often results in paralyzing procrastination because every activity from the simplest phone call or e-mail to the most complicated, multilayered project is laced with the need to do it perfectly.

Let's take a look at how this issue manifests in your life and think about some antidotes. I know a lot about the quest to be perfect. In an effort to teach me to always do my best, my mother assured me time and again that perfection was not only the goal but the only accepted result in our household. As you can imagine, this set me up for a lot of heartache and, ironically, failure. As an adult I have learned the power of doing the very best I can versus attempting to be perfect. Being perfect is an unachievable goal.

To learn this lesson, I decided to study something I knew I could never master. I would do my best knowing that everyone else in the class would surpass me. I studied the martial art form created by Bruce Lee called Jeet Kune Do. I was so ineffectual that for the first year many of the guys asked me why I continued to come back to class each week. There was no adequate way to explain. I wanted the experience of doing the best I could. What did that feel like? I left after two years, having pretty much expunged from my psyche the desire to be perfect.

RELEASE THE EVIL TWINS: FEAR OF SUCCESS AND FEAR OF FAILURE

The quest for perfection really lets us off the hook. "Oh! I'd love to get my office files organized, but I don't have the time to do it perfectly so it has to wait." We in essence embrace the status quo while sounding so noble. Underlying the desire to do things perfectly is fear: fear of failure. "What if I try this and it doesn't turn out as I hoped? What will people say?" It's better not to try. We aren't conscious that fear drives us. We think we're at the head of the class. We care about what we accomplish.

Fear of failure appears at work under other guises as well. Often a superior will give you an assignment. You become clutched by fear. The inner dialogue goes something like this: "John seems to think I can do this but what if I can't? Will I lose my job? What will my coworkers think? I like John and I just know I am going to fail him." Have you ever been given an assignment and been terrified? What was your inner dialogue? What happened in the end?

The companion to fear of failure is its ugly twin: fear of success. We see this played out in the tabloids. Someone achieves great success and their life implodes in direct proportion to the level of success achieved. The unconscious fear in a work situation may be that a successful assignment will backfire. Now even more work will be heaped on our plate. Or

worse, we fear our success to date has been nothing more than a fluke. What happens when everyone finds out? Have you ever felt anxiety about succeeding? How did that manifest? Did you forge ahead or did you give in?

President Franklin Delano Roosevelt said, "Do the thing you fear and the death of fear is certain." He was taking the United States through war, but the wisdom of those words holds true for all the fears we face. I'm not recommending that you sally forth without adequate preparation. I am suggesting that your performance fears will subside as you build your successes. Life can be a great teacher.

For example, when it's time for you to give a presentation for the boss at the weekly staff meeting, are you clutched with fear? Is it compounded by the desire to be not only perfect but the best presenter in the company? Nothing is quite as exhausting as matching up the quest for perfection with the need to compete! Have you ever been so worked up emotionally that you had to call in sick? Do you envy those who can stand up and command the room with only a moment's notice? Guess what? You may never turn into David Letterman, but you can become more comfortable in front of a group. The usual antidotes to fear are knowledge and practice.

Why not decide today that you are no longer going to be a fear-based person? Your goal, no matter what type of fear has you in its grip, is to shift your focus away from the fear toward the *solution*. And, if the solution is unknown to you, researching how others master this fear is far more productive than continuing to embrace it.

For example, if public speaking is your demon, you could join Toastmasters. What about volunteering your services where you will have to speak but the stakes aren't as high? A speech before a volunteer organization isn't as critical as one before your boss, but it may be the dress rehearsal you need. And, if all else fails, you can practice that time-honored antidote to fear of public speaking: picture everyone in his or her underwear.

DON'T PUT THIS OFF!

Please take out your notebook. List two specific times when procrastination has caused a problem in your job. Feel free to use one example from the past as well as a recent one.

1. As you searched your memory, was it easy to find examples or did you have to rack your brain to remember?
2. What happened in each incident in terms of the outcome? Did your procrastination create a drama? Is it possible that on some level your delaying tactics help to make you the center of attention?
3. By delaying, did the project move to someone else's care?
4. Do you think you use procrastination as a way of avoiding tasks that bore you? Seem too challenging to deal with? Frighten you?

5. In the examples you listed, do you see a common denominator? Please be as specific as you can. Can you recall when procrastination became part of your life? For example, did you learn it from one of your parents or did it enter your life after a specific event?
6. As you peel back the layers of discovery, do you think you might be ready to abandon procrastinating? How would this positively affect your life?

WHAT SIDE OF THE COIN FACES YOU?

Somewhere along the way, were you told that you would probably fail or that it was impossible to succeed? This message gets internalized in many ways. It can come from well-intentioned but shame-based parents. It can come from a relationship with a person who is secretly terrified of your potential. Often it comes from coworkers. We all know people who seem to be driven by an unseen force to spew out negative comments. If the person who shares your cubicle, the supervisor who is in charge of your workload, or the boss who directs your career is one of these people, you can be in for a rough ride.

Remember that it isn't what happens to you but your *reaction* that counts. And you always have a choice. You are consciously creating positive habits every month in an effort to streamline and control your physical environment. You can do the same with your inner environment: the world of your thoughts, feelings, and reactions. Whether you listen to a barrage of negative comments from your coworker or get hit by an occasional zinger, stop yourself and say, "I don't have to respond to this comment." Feel compassion for a person so mired in personal misery that he has to attack those around him.

Martin Luther King and Gandhi taught nonviolence. Although it is obvious how we can practice nonviolence to others, the concept (called *ahimsa*) as it originated in Eastern philosophy includes nonviolence to one's self. Don't buy into your coworker's emotional baggage. If a comment from someone else kicks off a stream of inner negative chatter, stop the process cold. The minute you abandon your reaction, I can guarantee your coworker will move on to someone else. Silently declare, "Game over." And indeed it will be.

What fears do you need to face? Do you have performance anxiety? Are you a perfectionist or a procrastinator? It's time to take concrete steps to alter your perception of yourself. Begin slowly and take small steps. Build patiently on your successes. How will you do that in your work and professional life starting today?

Wherever and however you became a procrastinator, it's not going to vanish in a week. But in that time span you can set into motion a new way of relating to work assignments and handling the everyday details of life. Next week we're adding to our understanding of time. Do you *really* know where it goes or how you spend it? You are about to find out! Next week the Mystery of the Vanishing Minutes will be no more.

WEEK THREE

Find Where the Time Goes

This week, you can

- Discover how you sabotage your work projects from the get-go
- Uncover your work time wasters

Time required: Thirty to sixty minutes

WHEN I AM EXCITED ABOUT A PROJ-ect, wild horses can't drag me away. I eat, sleep, and drink the material. I can't wait to rise in the morning and sleep feels like a waste of time. It's like being in love. It's all I can think about. And then there are those projects that just make me quite literally tired. When I feel this reaction rise up in me, I ask myself what is really going on. Why don't I want to work on this?

Here are some of the issues we may face as human beings. See if you can identify with any of these statements:

I've done a project like this many times before and a sense of "been there/done that" pervades my office. In truth, I am not energized but bored by the prospect of spending time on this material.

Something about this project reminds me of one I did in the past. That project didn't fare well and I fear that this will be a repeat.

If I do well with this project, I know the company will ask me to do more like it. I am already overworked. I don't want more work piled on my desk.

My boss thinks this project is a good fit for me. What if I fail? I will be so embarrassed! I'll let down the entire department.

I'm not feeling well. I wake up tired and drag myself through the day. How can I possibly handle this workload?

If you were to add to my list, what would you say are some of the reasons why a project makes you want to drag your feet instead of inspiring you? This week I have an exercise for you to do. It's an adjunct to the notes you are going to make regarding the preceding questions. We must get down to the nitty-gritty reasons for your personal style of procrastination. Are you ready?

FIGURE OUT WHERE YOUR DAY GOES

I want you to devote one typical day at the office to the following exercise. It's going to be brutal from the standpoint that you have to be vigilant about monitoring yourself. And it's going to be uncomfortable. It's one thing to wax poetic about our procrastinating. It's another to see in black and white where and how we fritter away our time.

For this exercise you'll need your notebook and a timer. You're going to be keeping track of exactly how much time you spend on each task at work, how many minutes you really spend on the Internet, and how many times a day you stop doing one thing to start another. I don't want you to do anything out of the ordinary. Just keep your notebook, a pen, and a timer handy. The clock on the computer or your watch will do nicely. Keep your format simple; I don't want you to create an official time-tracking document in Excel!

If you view this as a homework assignment, it's going to be a long day. If you feel guilt every time you jot down the time spent, you're going to throw this book across the room by noon. Remember: Zen organizing has no place for guilt, shame, or any other negative emotion. Today we're on a fact-finding mission.

I did this exercise myself recently. I wanted to find out how many ways I could delay working on a presentation I have to give next month. I work at home, so my opportunities for avoidance might be different than yours. The big discovery I made was that all my time-wasting activities were for a "good cause."

For example, here are three of my favorite personal home-office time wasters:

- I have three large bird cages in my office. Ordinarily I change the cages every Monday after I complete work for the day. But if I want to waste time, all I have to do is decide that my birds need a little treat and I've got to change the cage *today*. There goes twenty minutes!
- I might go to the bathroom and notice that the trash can is getting full. If I'm going to empty that trash can, why not check the ones in the master bathroom, the guest bath, my office, and the kitchen? Bang! Ten valuable minutes goes right out the window.
- The Internet is a great time sucker, isn't it? This day I stopped and researched airline prices and car rental fees for a personal trip I'm taking later this summer. This activity ate another twenty minutes. Did it have to be done? Yes. But this too could have been accomplished after work and on Wednesday, the day many airlines post specials.

On the plus side, my birds were tidy, the rooms were free of trash, and my vacation details were set. On the downside, I tossed fifty work minutes right out the window!

Keep track of your time wasting "skills" this week. I think you will be amused by your creativity and appalled by the time lost. The big benefit from all this work will be that you will have identified your tactics. The next time you go to the bathroom and decide en route to pop into the company kitchen to make a pot of afternoon coffee for everyone, you will stop yourself automatically and ask, "Am I avoiding something?" If you are, head back to your desk. If not, be a Good Samaritan and make that coffee.

COMMON TIME WASTERS

The human mind has no shortage of creativity when it comes to wasting precious minutes or even hours on any given day. We could all win an Olympic gold at one time or another. If you have a friend or colleague who is working this program along with you, compare notes at the end of the day. You will be fascinated by the commonalities and the differences.

Are you ready? Set one day aside as your official tracking day. Keep your list handy for the rest of the week and see if any new time wasters present themselves. If they do, note them and the time they stole from you.

1. Do you make or return nonessential or personal calls during work time? If so, you are frittering away time that belongs to your high-priority projects. Some-times a quick e-mail will suffice and save you time.

2. Are you texting or sending instant messages when you could be talking face-to-face with a colleague? I have a client who is driven insane by a colleague who works in the office next door but constantly sends her instant messages. Although my client wouldn't want to see her colleague at her door every five minutes, there's a balance to be struck. What do you know about this colleague without meeting her? That's right: She doesn't have a clue how to prioritize information dissemination. If it's on her desk or computer screen, she ricochets it to her coworkers the same instant she receives it. This wouldn't be you, would it?

3. Do you waste time researching nonessential information on the Internet? It's so easy to be on a legitimate quest for information only to go off on a tangent. It's the cyberequivalent of following a shiny object!

4. What about playing computer games between assignments? If you get lost in games (even one as benign as solitaire), you won't reach your goals frittering away time.

5. Are you blessed with family and friends who feel that you need to be available to them at all hours, including while you're at work? Do you constantly fend off their calls and e-mails?

Don't presume that you know all your time-wasting activities. Sometimes uncovering them takes a bit of sleuthing. Once you identify them, however, you can stop yourself as you begin to practice one and say to yourself: "Look at what I was about to do! Instead of delaying the inevitable, I'm going to work on what matters." My clients will often say: "I *hope* I can do this." It's as if someone else is inside their heads directing their actions. Do you feel that way now? You are not powerless. Make change a priority, make a commitment, and watch the transformation unfold.

WEEK FOUR

Improve Your Focus

This week, you can

- Identify the benefits you reap as procrastination is eliminated
- Discover the role of the brain in the repeatable negative patterns you have embraced
- Learn how to break your projects down into manageable chunks and avoid being overwhelmed

Time required: Thirty to sixty minutes

ONE OF THE TOOLS I SUGGESTED IN the Introduction is meditation. Have you added this ancient practice to your day? Even five short minutes will help you improve your focus and clear the extraneous thoughts that constantly chatter in your head. The sharper your mental focus, the easier it is to avoid procrastinating because you can zero in on the important tasks with greater ease. Drinking water and exercising will also help clear that mental clutter. You'll reap the benefits throughout the day. Earlier this month, we looked at the so-called benefits you may be deriving out of putting things off. But when you do your work and avoid procrastinating, you reap many far greater

benefits. Here are a few I consider the most important:

Working on a project allows you to have a "real time" experience. Removed from your day-to-day life are the what-if fears: What if I fail? What if I can't make the deadline? What if I'm doing this incorrectly? And on it goes. Eliminating procrastination, however, silences the what-if fears as we concentrate our energy on the "right now" reality.

The absence of added stress protects your body from being flooded with adrenaline. At appropriate times adrenaline can save your life. It's the fight-or-flight hormone. When stress is pushing it into your system on a constant basis, you're literally wearing your system out. Exhaustion is your reward.

As you work in a logical and organized manner, you begin to develop a natural feel for how long it takes you to perform certain tasks. Instead of fretting over the general size of a project, you automatically begin to break it into sections, understanding exactly how long each segment will take you. Few projects that are assigned will represent a brand new experience; they are composed of tasks or actions we have performed countless times before. In fact, this expertise is at the heart of the reason we have been assigned this work!

The larger the company, the more projects there are to be assigned. Very few are anomalies. In general, company projects are working in tandem to build the expertise and knowledge of the company as a whole. You are working on one cog in the wheel. When you do your work in a timely fashion, you benefit the entire organization. Consistent work like this will be remembered during your yearly review.

What would you add to the list?

RETRAIN YOUR BRAIN

This is the fourth month that you have been cultivating new habits. By now you might feel as though you have been doing them forever. We can hardwire good behavior into our brains as easily as we do negative. Once again, change isn't about making a huge, difficult shift in our lives. It's about switching one behavior for another. So when you are sitting in fear and embracing being overwhelmed, all that is required is that you change your reaction to the situation. Are you feeling that sense of dread rise in your system that signals the need to tidy your desk, empty the trash, visit all your colleagues, and make everyone afternoon coffee? Why not acknowledge the fear and decide to do a new series of actions. Let's look at two factors that will help you understand the mechanics involved.

If you are familiar with the amygdala and what it does, please go to the head of the class. I just recently learned about this fascinating part of the brain. The amygdala is the fight or flight center of your brain. Let's look to our cavemen ancestors. Walking through the jungle, our ancestors might have heard a rustle in the bushes. "Is it a bird and nothing to fear? Or is that a huge tiger that will pounce on me for lunch? I had best get ready to run like a bat out of hell." The amygdala freezes you in place for a few seconds so you can take in all the data and make a wise decision.

But then the amygdala takes another step to protect us. It registers the event so that the next time you hear a rustle in the bushes, you can identify even more rapidly what that sound is and know almost automatically if you need to flee. Guess what? Your office is the modern jungle.

Every time you procrastinate your way through a project (or even a regular day at work), your brain registers the event. The message is clear: Some of the things that occur here and some of the demands are just not safe. It is best to flee into the safety of instant messaging, or surfing the Internet, calling a colleague, or whatever your procrastination prompts you to do. At all costs, flee that work!

Our job as modern cavemen and cavewomen is to retrain our brains. Procrastination isn't a matter of being lazy or lacking the necessary intelligence. You've been caught up in biology, usually the biology of fear. You need to substitute a new reaction to the old stimulus.

Here's a sample scenario. Your boss stops by and asks about your progress on the XYZ project. You tell her you are working on the research phase and will have some concrete information in a day or two. "It's under control," you mutter as she leaves. As her footsteps fade down the hall, you break into a sweat. You are way behind on this project. If you don't hustle today and tomorrow, you'll be pulling all-nighters over the weekend—and your family has plans.

Now your stomach is in knots. You feel the need to send an instant message to a colleague down the hall. He commiserates with your dilemma. You're still tied up in knots. If you jump into the project right this minute, you could make some headway, but a strong cup of coffee would *really* help so you trot down to the kitchen. Does it matter, you wonder, that this is your third cup of coffee today and it's only

10 a.m.? You feel you're within the safety zone. Sound familiar? I'm sure you have your own unique spin on the Procrastination Ball.

STOP PROCRASTINATION

Now that you are a Zen organizer, let's see how you would handle the scenario presented in the preceding section. As your boss leaves your office, you feel the fear. Only now you take a minute to literally breathe into it. You quiet your mind and become conscious of how the fear is manifesting in your body. You tell yourself this isn't necessary. You are more than capable of succeeding at this project. Now is a great time to recite positive affirmations or meditate for five minutes.

You take out a piece of paper and open your calendar. Then you do the following:

1. Note the (drop-dead) due date on your calendar. This is the date beyond which there is no wiggle room. For safety, you give yourself a due date a few days before the real one. This is your personal target date.

2. You decide based on past experience with similar projects what the stages are for the XYZ project. For example, you might have research, financial overview, and written report.

3. You create due dates on your calendar for each phase.

4. You look at the due date for each phase. If research has to be completed in two weeks, what exactly must you do to

achieve your goal regarding this date? What forms of research are required? Do you have interviews to schedule? Is a trip to the library in your future or is everything on the Internet? How long will it take to write your conclusions? As you might imagine, you schedule each piece of research on your calendar.

5. Not only are you narrowing your focus with mini due dates, you also schedule the time you will spend on research for any given day. For example, the words *Research XYZ project* on your calendar for today are a wonderful indication of what work your day needs to include. However, it's even more powerful to say it this way: *Research XYZ project: 2 hours required,* or *Research XYZ project: 10 am to noon.* With each step you narrow your focus and take control.

At the beginning of the year, I told you that the whole of anything is overwhelming. When your boss sticks her head in your office and asks about the XYZ project, you automatically see all the demands of the project in your head. Who wouldn't be overwhelmed? But now, as a Zen organizer, you realize that the only facet of this project that is on your desk is research. And in *x* number of days, you will be free to move on.

This method takes a bit of practice, I admit. But one day, you will find that it's how you tackle everything in life. I can't help myself. I break everything down into the smallest segment I can. And then I build on my success. You don't need more time if you follow these guidelines. Instead of procrastinating and fretting, you use that time to make a plan and soar.

ASK YOURSELF IF YOU ARE AVOIDING SOMETHING

The short answer to the question, "Are you avoiding something?" is yes! We all avoid deadlines, commitments, and assignments from time to time. We're human. What if you have a big project due at work the month before you get married, welcome your first child, or leave on your yearly family vacation? Your mind is going to wander, isn't it? What we're after this month is squashing the perennial, destructive habit of *chronic* procrastination. Let's review some of the weapons in our anti-procrastination arsenal:

- Practice daily meditation to improve your ability to focus.
- Exercise regularly and drink water throughout the day to relieve stress.
- Identify the time wasters you habitually use to avoid assignments and deadlines.
- Know your ultimate goal for each project. When the time wasters tempt you, keep your focus on achieving your goal . . . not to mention savoring a reward!
- Throughout the day, ask yourself, "Am I avoiding my real work?" Drop the time waster and return to your critical assignments ASAP.

Whether mental or physical, every action that we repeat becomes a habit. Throughout the year we'll be working hard to add positive new habits to our lives. Without conscious intention, we have been adding negative habits throughout our lives. Repeat critical comments about yourself often enough and you will come to accept them as your reality. If one of those negative habits is a total embrace of procrastination, now is the time to set that habit aside. You needn't continue to be a procrastinator. You can instead become a high achiever, and you can do so with a level of ease and grace that may shock you.

There is no time like the present to jettison procrastination, the quest to be perfect, or your fears of success and failure. You've organized your physical space to achieve your business and personal goals. Why put off doing the work your environment is now set up to support?

No one can make your unique contribution. You were hired because someone believed in you and what you have to offer. It's time you believed in yourself. It's only April, after all, and I have eight more months of tips and tricks to help you work more effectively.

APRIL SUMMARY

WEEK ONE

Demystify the procrastination monster. How does it manifest in your life? When did it start? What do you get out of it?

WEEK TWO

Release yourself from the vise grip of procrastination, perfection, and the fears of success and failure.

WEEK THREE

Identify your personal time wasters so you can let them go forever.

WEEK FOUR

Learn how to manage your assignments so that procrastination doesn't rear its ugly head and attempt to manage you!

5. MAY

Set Priorities

To accomplish great things we must not only act, but also dream;

not only plan, but also believe.

— ANATOLE FRANCE

A FEW YEARS AGO A CLIENT CAME TO me in desperate need of organization for her fledgling business. She was in a difficult situation. As a small business owner, Pamela made the product she sold, marketed it, and did the shipping. You can imagine the drain on her physical, mental, and emotional energies. If you're a one-person band, you know exactly how she felt. Overwhelming, isn't it?

Her business needed space to grow. When you are mired in exhaustion, true growth isn't possible. First we worked on getting her physical space in order. This entailed organizing both her office proper and the small work area where the product was made. We brainstormed ways she might get outside help. She realized she had access to volunteers through a local church. I felt this could help lighten her load.

And then I made her an offer: I would coach her for free for six months. She was to call or write me via e-mail once a week; I would give her a new assignment and review her progress with the old one. We'd be building on her successes and adding new skill sets. The ultimate goal was to find ways of putting systems in place that would make life easier. At first, Pamela was excited. But can you guess what happened?

She never responded to my first e-mail assignment. It was one more to-do item added to her already bloated list. Pamela was doing what many people do: She was expressing in words what she felt she should do while being out of touch with the fact that emotionally she didn't want to achieve her stated goal. Within six months, Pamela closed her business.

What is the moral of the story? We don't always want what we *say* we want! Very often that's the key to understanding why we're at a loss as to how to prioritize. Subconsciously Pamela felt that success in her business meant a complete loss of all her time and freedom. She was recently married and wondered when she would see her husband if the business took off. She loved her work but didn't want it to consume her.

This month we go on a journey into the world of priorities, whether long-term or short-term. Prioritizing is dedicating yourself to making your goals a reality. All we need to do is ... say it with me ... make *decisions* about which goals we truly want to achieve. Once you embrace your priorities, you'll need to schedule the steps that make your goals a reality.

WORK HABIT OF THE MONTH: TAKE THREE!

Each day, I'd like you to note three positive actions you took to make your work life easier. Keep this log in your notebook. Big actions are certainly laudable and valid to note. But take extra care to acknowledge the little things you are doing each day. This kind of daily review is traditionally done in the evening just before bed. But you may want to do it each morning as you review the previous day. Don't be afraid to learn from your mistakes. If you note something in your mental review that was a negative action on your part, do the op-

posite tomorrow. Making a mistake is human. Learning from it is divine!

HOME HABIT OF THE MONTH: PUT THINGS IN THEIR PLACE

Are you a morning person or a night person? When do you feel you do your best work and are most alert? Carve out five minutes during your favorite time and walk through your home looking for anything that's out of place.

Carry a trash bag with you and set a timer. If you see old magazines, newspapers, or junk mail, toss them or recycle. If you spot items that belong in other parts of the house, gather them and, when your timer goes off, return them to their proper place. Is the blanket that lives on the couch tossed on the floor? Fold it neatly. Are CDs and DVDs languishing on the coffee table? Pop them back into their holders. You get the idea.

By the end of the month, you won't be able to enter or leave a room without noticing its true state. Never again will you turn a blind eye to piles, jumbles, and messes. If you can't do the entire house in five minutes, do one or two rooms with attention to detail. You'll gain speed with time.

WEEK ONE

Discover Why You Are in This Pickle

This week, you can

- Uncover the hidden reasons for your inability to prioritize goals and work assignments

Time required: One hour to ninety minutes during the week for journal writing

I HAVE A WONDERFUL CLIENT WHO heads the marketing division of a large corporation. Bill is recognized as a genius in his field. The fly in the ointment is his seeming inability to say no to whatever draws his attention at the moment. Running off to a critical meeting, Bill might notice that you have a cold and spend five minutes telling you what natural remedies you need to purchase. Or perhaps you pop your head into his office just to say hello and the next thing you know you're watching slides from his safari in Botswana. He'll be late to his meeting, of course. Once Bill arrives in the room, he knows he has to do his best to win favor with all those present who resent his tardiness. This pressure helps him rise to the occasion. After another stellar performance, Bill has been forgiven and praised to the sky.

As you might imagine, Bill was exhausted most of the time. He ran himself ragged going from early in the morning until late at night. We began our first work session, for example, after 5 when the office had closed. Imagine my surprise when Bill announced we had to stop at 8 because he had to get to his nightly spinning class at the gym. Bill's eyes were glazed with exhaustion. I wondered how he would keep from falling asleep on the bike.

Bill had big goals for himself and his company. Unconsciously, however, he threw roadblocks into his life at every turn, in the form of both overscheduling himself and getting sidetracked. It was difficult for him to get his day-to-day work accomplished. Do you see yourself in Bill? Do you have so much going on that only a bionic human could do it all? Let's see if we can use this week to see what's really important to you.

SEARCH FOR CLUES

An inability to establish priorities may be due to a number of factors. If you understand why, it's going to be easier to change. Here are some questions you can answer in your notebook.

1. What kind of example did your parents set when it came to establishing priorities? Did you witness them setting goals and then achieving them? Or did you observe that they were more dreamers than action-oriented? Were they both the same, or was one a dreamer and one an achiever? Have you unconsciously aligned with one or the other?
2. When you were in school, what experience did you have with homework assignments? Did you manage to study for all your classes with ease? Were papers turned in on time or did you flounder?
3. Do you experience the same challenge or difficulty in just about every job you've had? Or is this job experience different? If there is a difference, what would you attribute it to? Is it your boss, your coworkers, the number of assignments, or your situation at home?

Do these questions lead you to any realizations about how the past is affecting your present inability to set priorities? Let's take a look at Bill and Pamela and see whether you see yourself in the way they responded to today's work challenges.

My client Bill loves to have a good time. When he stops by someone's desk to offer advice, he truly seeks to be of service. He wants everyone to be happy. When I tried to get him to focus on his office, I noticed he preferred to launch into detailed stories about his past. It was a rich past, to be sure, but I had to keep him on track. When someone wants to show me their treasures or tell me stories, I know the work at hand frightens them in some way. I also know I have to keep them moving; otherwise we'll get to the end of our five-hour session with little accomplished. I have to stick to my priorities for the session!

As I got to know him, Bill shared something I felt might be one of the keys to understanding his current behavior. Bill is one of eight children. He told me he was always doing *something* to get his mother's attention. Do you come from a large family? (It certainly is a different experience than mine as an only child. I had too much of my mother's attention!) In addition, Bill was used to dealing with several people at once. The problem is that at work, you want to get your boss's attention and earn the respect of your coworkers. The dynamic at work isn't the same as it was in your family of origin. You might need to consciously alter the patterns you have when it comes to dealing with others.

Bill also shared that his family was close knit and outgoing. Bill wasn't bored growing up. When it was time to close his door at the office and spend some quiet time working, he realized he sometimes felt lost because he liked commotion. He found it by keeping his office door open and inviting anyone who passed by the chance to see his photos from Africa, pictures of the new furniture he had just purchased for his condo, or . . . well, you get the idea. Eventually, Bill learned to establish priorities and, when he felt the desire to give in to distractions, was able to say no to the impulse. You will too! But first, let's revisit the woman who opened this chapter.

Pamela wanted to be successful but subconsciously feared that the success she was working hard to achieve would rob her of her private life. Can you relate to Pamela's story? I know I can. As a small business owner, I spend far more hours at work than I ever did when I was employed by others. Balance is tricky. How do you do it? You have priorities! You can free yourself of obligations you don't want to assume in many ways. Here are a few common consequences when we are overwhelmed and are looking for an out: You get fired or your business simply fails, you get sick or suffer from clinical depression, your spouse or partner decides to leave. Wake-up calls come in all sizes and shapes.

TO SYNC OR NOT TO SYNC, THAT IS THE QUESTION

Do you see yourself in Pamela or Bill? Busy execs like these can sink or swim based on their ability and willingness to integrate a calendar into their lives. Here's a tip that can help you use your calendar with greater efficiency. Integrate your calendar with your address book and sync it to your PDA. You can schedule appointments and add a comment to help identify the activity or meeting for tax purposes. Let me give you our first real-world example.

A friend of mine is a multiple Emmy Award–winning television writer. Here's how he keeps track of business appointments for tax purposes.

> Say I met with an exec last year regarding a project entitled *Kingdom*. I can't remember the exec's name. I can search for *Kingdom* and it will come up in my calendar with all associated info, including the exec's name. . . . I can schedule a flight online, grab all the flight info, and copy it to my calendar. When I sync that to my Palm Pilot, I can open it at the airport with all my flight info right there in front of me. I never have to write it down. The idea is that once the data is captured you should never have to enter it again.

My friend is considering buying an iPhone, which will make his Palm Pilot a tool of the past. Technology is moving at lighting speed. Check with your IT person before you upgrade. By the time this book is published, who knows what the latest and the greatest will be in the world of communication and business?

When we attempt change before we understand how the current situation came to be, we aren't as powerful as we might be. Every day on every level of our busy lives, we experience the effects of the causes we have set in motion. This week's exercise will give you the key to the change you seek to make in the world of prioritizing. If you discover that experiences from the past, the needs of others, or simple mental confusion have ruled your days, take heart. Now that you have identified the culprit, you can consciously put yourself in the driver's seat. That's what the rest of this month is all about!

WEEK TWO

Stop Negative Thinking

This week, you can

- Recognize and avoid negative thinking
- Learn how long tasks really take

Time required: One hour

JUST ABOUT EVERYONE TELLS ME THAT they can't learn how to meditate because their minds are too busy. This is said with a combination of shame and pride. I assure everyone that this is the human condition. Everyone struggles to calm the inner dialogue of uncontrolled, unmonitored thoughts and feelings to get to the quiet, powerful, focused mind that awaits us. This week we're going to examine that "wild mind" to see what's going on. You need to be in charge in there whether or not you ever decide to meditate.

FROM SCARY MOVIE TO G-RATED

How would you like to go to a movie? Yes, that's right. I did suggest a movie. Or perhaps you're a music buff? Would you like to listen to some songs now? Whether you are a visual or an aural person, I'd like you to tune in all week long. Where? Into your mind. There you are, trying to figure out how to set your priorities, and guess what? There's a movie playing in your head. You're the star. It's called: *Suzie Fails Again.* Or perhaps you hear that old song, "Watch Bob the Dork Attempt the Impossible!"

We all play these absurd failure anthems in our head from time to time. It's only human. This week, I want you to watch for them. Carry your notebook with you and make quick entries when you can. How often do they pop into your consciousness? Is it always the same theme? And perhaps more importantly, who first planted these ideas? Have others tended this destructive garden? Let's uncover the seeds so we can let them go.

As you begin to look for negative thoughts, you'll be amazed how creative they are. They can shift in subtle ways, making us feel the thoughts actually belong to us. Be on the lookout for statements like "I can't do this," "I'll never be able to finish this," or "This will never work." What specific thoughts stop you or distract you?

How are you going to replace negative entertainments? With something positive. When an old destructive movie or song comes into your head, stop it immediately. Say to yourself: "This is a false idea of who I really am and what I am capable of accomplishing. I release these images/words and recognize my ability to succeed."

If you began this program with the material for January, you have developed several new habits. Remind yourself of this accomplishment. You are now drinking more water, enjoying healthy snacks, and exercising at least five minutes a day. These all contribute to your ability to think more clearly and plan how to reach your goals with ease. You have an organized office and a great file setup. You're straightening your office at the end of each day. Consider your successes when you are dismissing the negative. One day soon it will be these positive images and words that pop into your head.

KNOW HOW LONG THINGS REALLY TAKE

Sometimes the simplest actions yield the most powerful results. Whether or not you are a person with negative mental chatter, I'd like you to keep track of something else this week. How long does it take you to accomplish the daily recurring tasks in your business life? Here are some key items to track:

- Dealing with daily mail
- Answering e-mail, voice mail, text messages, and instant messages
- Creating e-mail, voice mail, text messages, and instant messages
- Attending meetings
- Working on projects
- Dealing directly with clients
- Dealing with coworkers

What other tasks would you add to this list to make it yours?

You'll make use of the data next week when you work on your to-do list. Your list is the engine that keeps you moving forward with your priorities in order.

You can read all the books on business productivity ever published and do all the suggested exercises and not achieve success if the inner dialogue in your head is negative and remains unchecked. What we do and how we do it are key factors in our success. But how we think and feel about our efforts are of equal importance. This week we strive to support our efforts in the physical world with the unspoken thoughts and feelings that live in our minds and hearts. We might call this the holistic approach to business productivity, where body, mind, and soul are working in sync.

You are busily prioritizing your workload and poof! If you haven't been backing up your work on your computer, it can vanish in a heartbeat. Here are some ways to be safe rather than sorry if you don't work for a large corporation with an IT division that automatically monitors these things for you.

The Mac: For about $100 a year you can subscribe to Mobile Me. One of its features is several gigs of storage on Apple's computers through iDisk. Here's how a composer friend of mine makes use of it in his career:

> I can transfer all my sheet music files for my musical . . . to a hard disk out there in space somewhere and I can access it from any computer in the world. Say I'm in rehearsal . . . with my musical and I need a print of one of the songs and I don't have my computer. I can go to any computer, log on to Mobile Me, and look at or download any files there!

The PC: The time-honored way to backup files was to regularly copy your files onto a disc. You can set a reminder in Outlook and do this at scheduled intervals. If you're in a small office with modest activity, this may indeed be the way to go. However, technology has advanced, and whether you're a PC or Mac person, backup can be automatic. You are in control of how often the backup occurs and where it is stored.

If the backup is on the same hard disk drive as the original, it won't help you in the event of a crash. It's best to change the location of your backup files to a private folder on a network or to a separate hard disk drive. The prices of hard drives have come down radically, making security an easily achievable goal.

WEEK THREE

Create a To-Do Plan

This week, you can

- Craft a realistic to-do list and a to-do action plan
- Organize your priorities by applying the Magic Formula

Time required: Sixty to ninety minutes

ONE OF THE MOST COMMON LAMENTS I hear from my clients goes something like this: "Regina, I always make a to-do list but at least half the stuff never gets done. I'm forever rewriting the same tasks over and over again." Does that sound familiar? I call this the shotgun approach to getting things done. The logic is something like this: If I write down every single thing I can think of that I have to do, something might get accomplished. This approach gives you an out. What do I mean? When your spouse asks if you picked up the dry cleaning or a colleague asks if you completed the proposal that the boss has been screaming for, you can say: "No, I didn't get to it, but I have it on my list."

A to-do list, however, is just that: a list. What you need is a *plan*. Frequently human beings unwittingly engage in "magi-cal thinking." In this case, using a list to jot down things that you want or need to accomplish is a step in the right direction and can bring clarity. However, it won't take care of itself. And that's where the magic comes in. We somehow believe that the act of recording the task carries with it the completion. It doesn't. You have to take more steps. And that's what this week will clarify for you.

FROM TO-DO TO DONE

Many productivity experts encourage a kitchen sink approach to making lists: write down everything you need to accomplish. I find this method counterproductive and overwhelming, so I've devised a variation: I note everything I have to do in my calendar on the appropriate day it can be accomplished. This is my version of a master to-do list. The night before a new day, I examine my calendar and make any adjustments to the self-imposed deadlines I have created as well as deadlines given to me by others. From this examination, I create the to-do plan for the next day. Here's the critical piece of the puzzle: You need to experiment to see what works best for you and then *stick to that formula*!

Here's a mock-up of a master to-do list for a busy working mother. As you will see, it's all over the place in terms of work, home, personal, and family obligations. How does it make you feel when you reach the end? Do you think, "Wow! That's so great, she has everything written down. Nothing fell through the cracks"? Or are you inclined to be overwhelmed? Take heart. We'll use the Magic Formula to get control.

> Shop for groceries
> Work on college applications with Allie
> Complete report for Mitchell project: due Friday
> Do laundry
> Write mom
> Buy gift for dad's birthday
> Schedule a massage
> Clean kitchen and all bathrooms
> Call plumber regarding leak in upstairs bathroom
> Send invitations for Don's birthday party
> Make travel arrangements for the holidays
> Schedule lunch with clients from the ABC Company

> Prepare for performance review/ask for a raise
> Clean out e-mail to-do folder
> Update calendar for staff

I could go on and make this list as long as I like. The bottom line is that it begins to resemble stream of consciousness writing rather than a document that will help me get organized. If I were new to organizing my time, I would make a kitchen-sink master list like this one. It would give me an opportunity to see what's on my plate at this time in my life.

However, I think you will be far more effective if you transfer the items on your list to your calendar. The master file list is your periodic tool to be used when you feel overwhelmed. Your calendar is your trusty, everyday companion. From it you can create your daily to-do plan. In the following sections I offer a few tips to help make your master list more effective. Find the Magic Formula at work here.

Create Your Master List in Excel
If you use Excel to create your master list, you will have an easy-to-edit, flexible format. After you are done, take a moment to review. Are there some items you can eliminate now because you realize they are never going to happen?

Are there items you could schedule on your calendar for the future? If it's March and you're already thinking ahead to Christmas travel while you're in the middle of tax preparation, you might want to note "make travel arrangements" sometime after June 15. Don't even look at that note until you are ready to deal with it at an appropriate time. This is a variation on the elimination theme.

Divide Your List into Categories

The second tip is to divide your list into categories. This is a matter of cut-and-paste whether you are using Excel or Word. That's the magic of the computer instead of handwritten lists. The woman in our example has tasks in the following areas: Work, Family/Children, Home, and Personal. Separating items gives you an opportunity to deal with one category at a time. Moreover, you can prioritize your categories and deal with them in order of importance.

Here is the same list categorized and streamlined. See how this list affects you in a different way from our original:

Work
Complete report for Mitchell project: due Friday
Schedule lunch with clients from the ABC Company
Prepare for performance review/ask for a raise
Clean out e-mail to-do folder
Update calendar for staff

Personal
Schedule a massage

Family/Children
Work on college applications with Allie
Write mom
Buy gift for dad's birthday

Send invitations for Don's birthday party
Make travel arrangements for the holidays

Home
Shop for groceries
Do laundry
Clean kitchen and all bathrooms
Call plumber regarding leak in upstairs bathroom

As I read over this list now, I have a sense of calm. I can choose one category at a time and schedule the items or break them down into the steps that will bring them to fruition. Here are some observations I might make.

The Personal category: This category is woefully inadequate. If all my energy goes out to others and the fulfillment of tasks, I'm not replenishing myself. You can only give to others if you first give to yourself. What would you add to this category? Do you like massages or would that be eliminated in favor of a night at the movies or a hot bath? Whatever you put on the list needs to be scheduled on your calendar. "Massage" floating on a master list is meaningless. If you write on your calendar for this coming Tuesday, "Book Masseuse for Saturday night," it becomes part of a literal plan.

The Home category: In the Home category, one item calls for immediate action, taking care of the bathroom leak. The other items are part of a maintenance routine, aren't they? They should be automatically performed on specific days.

Moreover, if children are in the home, some things such as doing the laundry make perfect chore assignments. I have "Do laundry" and "Shop for groceries" assigned to specific days on my calendar. The day changes if I have to do something like travel, work on an assignment that runs late, or entertain out-of-town guests. For the most part, however, these items are static. There is something comforting about performing tasks like these almost by rote. They become touchstones during weeks when life is anything but routine.

The Work category: I saved the Work category for last so we can spend the most time considering our options. Let's take each item in turn and see if we can't gain some mastery over what needs to be accomplished.

Two items—"Schedule lunch with clients from the ABC Company" and "Update calendar for staff"—are straightforward action items. I would schedule them on my calendar, choosing the day I feel works best. These items could also be given to an assistant if you have one.

"Clean out e-mail to-do folder" is something we all have to do, don't we? I'll address this task in detail in a later chapter. The key is daily maintenance. E-mail makes doing business easier, but it is also a time-wasting trap if you aren't vigilant.

Performance reviews are scheduled for specific times of the year. Rather than seeing this task every day for weeks or months before I need to prepare for it, I would make a note on my calendar on an appropriate day. Why clutter your mind with tasks that don't need to be considered at the present moment?

Whenever you schedule a task, ask yourself if there is a related item you might take care of at the same time. Your mind will be in the correct mind set, so why not take care of several similar items at once? If it is indeed time for my review, I would jot down "Prepare for performance review/ask for a raise" on my upcoming calendar week on the most appropriate day for me to take care of this action item. The night before I would check my calendar for the schedule I need to follow the next day. When I see "Prepare for performance review," I would add the action items that will enable me to do this preparation. Not sure what I mean? We will get into this in detail shortly.

We need to consider one other item: "Complete report for Mitchell project: due Friday." Let's see how we can marry our calendar and a to-do plan to achieve success with ease. The way we handle the Mitchell project is how we'll tackle the performance review. It's how you will deal with all your projects. The individual tasks will change from project to project, but the modus operandi will be the same. With a little practice, you'll be in control of your work life. Right now it's probably controlling you.

Back in January I introduced the importance of choosing and using a calendar. This month, you're going to build on your use of a calendar, which is a written guide to how you're using your time. Efficient use of time is what makes setting priorities possible! Let's go step by step.

PLAN YOUR SCHEDULE

Take out your notebook and open it so you have two blank pages facing you. Divide the left page into two columns. In the first column, list all the tasks you deal with at work on a regular basis. You created this last week, so it's just a matter of copying it. Next to each task, indicate how much time that task regularly takes you to complete. It should look like this:

Deal with daily mail/Thirty minutes

At the top of the second column, list all your special assignments or projects. What demands your attention for work at this moment? Let's take one of these projects and break it down.

Suppose that the Mitchell project from our sample master list is due June 15. In your calendar, make a note on that date.

On your to-do list, you might have written "Complete ABC project." Looking at that major due date on your list may feel overwhelming. Now, what are the *action steps* that will bring it to completion? For example, do you have to do some research? Will it be exclusively Internet-based or will you also have to call or write your contacts for further information? Do you need to interview anyone? Will you

need to write and turn in a proposal, or will you be required to make a verbal presentation? If the latter, will you need to write up notes and prepare? List the steps in the logical order they must occur in your notebook. Then assess how much time each will realistically take and schedule them in your calendar. For example:

Monday 5/15   Mitchell project report due Friday: complete Internet research

Tuesday 5/16   MP: complete all phone interviews; collect all data.

Wednesday 5/17   MP: write first draft of report

Thursday 5/18   MP: polish and finalize report

Friday 5/19   Submit Mitchell project

Each calendar note is meant to alert me to the work to be performed that day on the Mitchell project. The night before as I write out my to-do plan, I go into as much detail as I need to be sure I stay on target and move quickly the next day. Here is what Tuesday's notes might look like regarding the report for the Mitchell project:

1. Phone Doug Jones and Selma Proctor for final interviews re: Mitchell.
2. Ask Mandy (my assistant) to pull all existing data for this report and have it on my desk by 2 p.m.
3. Do a final review of all Mitchell material to be sure it is complete.

If people are helping you, which steps will be assigned to others? Make a note of the person's name next to the step he will be required to accomplish. Now figure out exactly when you must receive this information from your colleague or employee. Ask for it about two days early. The date you give allows you to have some wiggle room in case of illness or a flaky response. Your real due date is the drop-dead date. If you are using a computer, schedule an automatic reminder in addition to the note in your calendar.

Now let's be creative and look at this from another angle. I want you to have choices when it comes to tackling your work life issues. Create a week-at-a-glance page in your notebook or print a calendar page from Outlook or any other program with a calendar and paste it here. If you have projects due now, write in the assignments you want to cover this coming week. Note how much time you think each task will take.

Next, add the daily tasks you must accomplish along with the amount of time each requires. When you add the total time commitment (including what you hope to spend on your projects), is your work day adequate? Do you need to streamline some of your daily tasks so they don't take as long? Could something be eliminated? Keep in mind that this is only your workday. You have a life outside work and demands there as well. Do you have the physical, mental, and emotional strength to do it all?

When you look at your scheduled tasks and action steps, which ones are the most important to accomplish the next day? This week? The next month? Which of your tasks, for example, would be a do-or-die assignment? Which are necessary but flexible as to when they can be accomplished? And which should be set aside for when you have more time?

Your calendar is the macro universe, your template upon which you craft your schedule. Your to-do action plan is the "micro universe." You want to create the former once a week and the latter each night in preparation for the next day. Remember to ask yourself this question whenever you look at your weekly schedule or your daily to-do plan: Is this realistic? I can't use that word often enough.

Remember too that the Magic Formula is ready to serve you. Can you eliminate or delegate a task? Could you reschedule a task this week because it isn't due until next month? These strategies will help organize your day.

DECIDE WHAT TO DO FIRST

With this kind of detail work, you will find that most days go as you have predicted. However, a few difficulties or challenges may occur along the way and you will be tempted to toss the baby out with the bathwater. Please don't! Here are three concepts I'd like you to embrace.

Your day isn't written in stone: Just as you planned the original schedule, you can adjust it to accommodate changes that present themselves and demand your attention. The trick is to understand the difference between a true emergency and a subconscious excuse to jettison your plans and sabotage yourself.

Have realistic plans and learn to say no: If you plan your day carefully and then walk into your office and toss everything up in the air so you can serve whatever demands present themselves, either your plans are not realistic or you are allowing yourself to get caught up in the moment. Examine your plans to be sure they are realistic and honor your commitments to yourself by learning to say no.

Create routines: As much as possible, create rituals or routines ("If it's 11 o'clock, it must be time for me to . . ."). These will help you navigate through your day. Routines are also at the heart of maintenance.

Here are some additional tips and tricks to help you.

When a colleague pops in with an urgent request, make sure it's as urgent for you as it is for him! You don't necessarily have to say yes and jettison your plans to help someone else. If it's a true emergency (or a request from a supervisor), of course you'll need to reschedule your day. If the request is a reflection of someone else's needs or wants, graciously tell your coworker that you'll get to it as soon as you can.

Every day you will have miscellaneous tasks to do that require little time and almost no mental effort. Take care of these between the big items. It will give your brain a needed break. It will also keep your forward momentum going and feed your sense of accomplishment. Don't begin your day with nonessential items or give them too much time.

Keep your eye on the assignments that will increase your income or your prestige or both. Answering Aunt Maggie's e-mails may make you Niece of the Year but won't get you a promotion or earn a down payment on a new home or car!

Identify the daily essential items that present a trap for you. At the top of the list is e-mail. We're all pretty much addicts at this point in time, aren't we? You'll want to navigate this arena in a way that plays to your strengths. For example, I enjoy deleting as much e-mail as possible at the start of my day. I find great psychological relief in saying no to items that don't need or deserve my attention. If you are not yet comfortable with quickly deleting nonessential e-mail, you might want to check e-mail around 11 a.m. This will give you a chance to pursue your top priorities when you are fresh.

The phone is another trap, isn't it? When you are deep in thought on a project and facing a deadline, allow your phone to go to voice mail. In today's world if people have a true emergency, they will find a way to reach you, whether that means calling a colleague of yours or the receptionist or sending an instant message.

Never allow your tasks to be the excuse to ignore your body. Drinking plenty of water, exercising, and eating good food are the elements that fuel your physical body and give you the mental sharpness you require to succeed.

Don't forget to press your inbox-outbox into service. I have a client who works in an insanely busy office. He can't afford to waste any space on his desk so his inbox and outbox are two wall pockets mounted just inside the entry. It's amazing how you can cut down on traffic when people are stopped at your door.

Even if you're twenty years old and have a crackerjack memory, write things down! Use your brain to solve problems; don't overload it with details that your calendar or computer can remember for you.

If you get the urge to do something other than your assigned task, ask yourself what you are avoiding or afraid of.

Concentrate on doing fewer things well rather than multiple things in a haphazard, slapdash fashion.

Every person's day will look different, so I can't have a one-size-fits-all formula. And therein lies a great gift: You can craft your day with an eye to increased productivity but with the freedom to be creative. Set a schedule and try it out for a day or two. Tweak it until you find the optimum time you like to write or return phone calls or respond to e-mails. Allow your organizing skills to help you navigate through true emergencies with an eye to a return to normal. It won't take long for you to wonder how you ever allowed yourself to be buffeted by the needs and wants of others.

Next week we'll look at some of the schedule-interrupters you may have invited into your life as well as those that marched in and took up residence on their own. Over the course of a year, you'll build on your understanding of time management, ultimately ensuring your success.

WEEK FOUR

Identify Sneaky Schedule-Interrupters

This week, you can

- Recognize legitimate monkey wrenches in your plans versus the ones you invite

Time required: Sixty minutes

As I write this chapter, the flu is flying around Los Angeles. I've never had so many friends and colleagues so sick. I guarantee that priorities are being tossed about like ships in a storm. When illness, death, accidents, or other types of traumas and interruptions come to us, we have to scramble to do the best we can to keep up with our commitments. It's a delicate dance of eliminating as much as possible while delegating what we can.

CLEVER WAYS YOU MAKE YOUR WORK LIFE MORE DIFFICULT

Very often, we find ourselves burning the midnight oil because we have put ourselves in a time crunch. Let's look at a few of the ways people effectively make life difficult for themselves: procrastination, an inability to say no, a fear of success or failure, or a lack of devotion to one's own agenda.

What derails your best efforts? Is it one thing or several? Make a note in your journal; the act of acknowledging and then writing down how you make life difficult helps. You need to remember your personal tactic. Then you want to identify it the next time it happens. Finally you can stop it in its tracks! See if you find yourself in any of these statements. Would your best friend choose one and exclaim: "Oh my gosh! That's you!"

- "It never fails. Just when I sit down to work, the phone rings, an IM pops up, or a text message is sent and I can't get anything done."
- "I need to work with the TV or music on in the background. It doesn't in-

terfere. I take minibreaks to relax my mind."

- "It's so odd but I always get sick right before a presentation is due."
- "I have my priorities straight, but just try and get my spouse (or child or coworker or parent) to cooperate. I am sabotaged at every turn."

Wait a minute, you're saying. The problem is those other people. But the common denominator in all these statements is a *surrender of power* to someone else, to something else, or to a negative belief. Remember that you do not have to respond to every request for your time and attention the second it is presented. You don't have to instantly respond to an e-mail or return a telephone call right away. You don't have to allow your colleague to hang out in your office for half an hour telling you about her weekend. You have a choice. Unless the request is to perform an act that will save a life, you can complete your work before you respond.

My best friend, for example, works for a large corporation and in a different time zone. Very often I call Susie to talk just when she is in the middle of putting out fires on the workfront. A quick "I can't talk now" is all it takes to postpone a private chat. I can't think of a single time when this was a problem.

GET YOUR WORK LIFE BACK ON TRACK

It's always tricky dealing with people who view their requests as urgent when you realize otherwise. The first consideration is your relationship with this person. If your boss comes to you with a nonurgent request that has an urgent label, guess what? It's urgent! If it's a request from someone with whom you enjoy working and you can spare the time, help him out. Most of the time, however, the request will come from someone who has no boundaries, is clueless about the amount of time a task will take, or is so egocentric he feels you should drop everything to help him. No matter the scenario, take a moment to evaluate the request. Ask yourself these questions:

- How long will this take?
- Can I spare that time right now? Or will it toss a monkey wrench into my carefully planned day?
- Is this request easy to handle or is it more complicated than this person realizes?
- Does this person frequently come to me with nonessential requests? Is he trying to put some of his workload on my shoulders?

After a quick series of questions like this, you will be in a position to evaluate the request. Here are some possible responses:

- "I'd love to do this for you, John, but I have so much work of my own to handle, I'm afraid I can't right now."
- "Mary, is there some reason you can't take care of this? Perhaps I could

walk you through the process?" (This is especially helpful if the person is a new employee.)

- "Carl, I might be able to help you, but I am on deadline right now. Could we talk later this afternoon? I need to see how much progress I can make. Perhaps someone else can assist you?"
- "I understand you would like my help, Pat. Why does this have to be handled right this minute? Are you on a tight deadline?"

Rather than react from anger or annoyance (either outwardly and alienating the person or holding it in and hurting yourself), why not think of yourself as a mentor? It's your job to do one of three things: instruct the person how to do this task themselves; point him in the direction of someone who has the time to assist him; or inform the person that you are not his personal go-to person for every work crisis he has, whether real or self-created.

It may sound old-fashioned, but manners will almost always buy you time, help, and understanding. I can't say that's the expected result when you have a colleague who makes demands or feels entitled. Perhaps a way of expressing respect is to have firm boundaries and honor the ones others set. We all know bored or depressed people who will rob us of our work time if we let them. Saying no to them will not only empower you but also be a powerful example to them. Will they learn and change their ways? More than likely they will move on to the next willing victim. The important thing is that it won't be you!

REVIEW OTHERS' ACTIONS AND YOUR OWN

This week, keep an eye out for ways your fellow workers attempt to derail your work. Has the situation become worse since you began your organizing program? Don't be surprised if it has. Your efforts and your increased productivity will not be respected by everyone. You represent a threat to their status quo behavior. Keep your eye on the prize: an easier, more productive day and a more balanced life. This will take you through any rough patches.

While you are on the lookout for ways others are attempting to disrupt you, don't forget to look at your own actions! It's amazing how gracefully we can sabotage ourselves. At the end of this week, jot down all the ways *you* have tried to interfere with your organizing efforts. List at least three. Once acknowledged, watch out for them so you can stop them in their tracks.

At the end of the week, make another list of the three most common ways you let your schedule be hijacked by someone else. You can make notes throughout the day or week or jot them down on Friday afternoon. You will be amazed and amused to see in black and white just how often and how creatively you surrender your power to another. What is the antidote? Remember the validity and the power in this phrase: "Just say no!"

This has been another busy month for you as a Zen organizer. Creating priorities will become second nature over time. Don't be surprised if you find yourself putting things in order of importance wherever you are. Today it's your projects at work. Tomorrow you might prioritize the rides you want to experience at a theme park. You won't be able to stop yourself!

Every day we make large and small decisions about how we experience life. That's what a priority helps you do: make wise choices about your life. This is an important skill to develop, so be patient. Remember that the keys to success with any skill are increased knowledge and practice. Now that you have read this chapter, how have your priorities changed?

MAY SUMMARY

WEEK ONE

Understand why you have not been able to set priorities. Doing so will free you from the past and enable you to set a new, positive agenda.

WEEK TWO

Uncover the internal drama playing like a broken record in your head. It may be time to change the tune! Next, discover just how long things take.

WEEK THREE

The Magic Formula and the time-honored to-do list dance in concert this week to help you be more productive and realistic.

WEEK FOUR

Identify the monkey wrenches in your work life and file them away in your mental tool kit under "Sabotage: no longer needed."

6. JUNE

Dealing with People

The finest timber comes from the slowest growing trees. . . .
He who has the sincerity and courage to face whatever is in him, the
persistence to go on with his struggle in the face of obstacles within and
without . . . is certain to achieve something which he would not give
away in exchange for the whole world.

– SRI KIRSHNA PREM

LET'S FACE IT. OFFICE STRESS IS ALL about "them," isn't it? We'd be just fine at work if only *he* wasn't our boss, or coworker, or human resources rep, and so on. Or maybe it isn't someone in your company but rather someone who works for your most important client. You have to make this company happy, but who have they assigned as the liaison with your group? Why, it's the Wicked Witch of the West! Or perhaps it's a vendor. The local printer gives you prices you can't beat, but does he have to make everything else so difficult?

You may not turn into Mother Teresa after you read this chapter, but I'm sure you will have an easier time dealing with your worst nemesis. You may not be in-clined to invite him to dinner, but at least you won't be popping tranquilizers every time he walks by your office.

WORK HABIT OF THE MONTH: CHANGE YOUR ROUTINE

The last five months have been about creating routines. This month you're going to have some fun. I want you to think about something you have done for a long time one particular way. How could you shake things up and do it differently? For example, suppose that every morning you do the following in a set sequence: go to the bathroom, make the coffee, let the dog out, and wake your child. Shake up the routine. I want you to be open to change. Your workday begins at home, but don't forget to consider your office routine. Do you check your e-mail, open your snail mail, listen to your voice mail, and have coffee almost simultaneously? Do one thing at a time and give your nervous system a rest.

HOME HABIT OF THE MONTH: SAY THANKS

Let words be your action this month. If you live with others, make it your mission at least once every day to acknowledge them for something they do. Does your teenage son take out the garbage without being asked? Does your husband feed the cat when you're late getting home from work? Did your daughter set the table for dinner without a word from you? Tell them you noticed. Thank them.

Do you live alone? Every day acknowledge at least one stranger for an act of kindness. Did someone wave you into traffic? Did someone hold open a door for you, help you with a package, or pick up something you dropped? This attitude of gratitude can spill over into your work life. What about a word of acknowledgment to the postal carrier, a coworker, or even your boss? Let them know you are grateful.

The point of this month's action is to make encouraging others a natural part of who you are. We have a choice in life: We can either empower others or belittle them. This month, choose to empower.

WEEK ONE

Make Meetings More Productive

This week, you can

- Let the Magic Formula streamline your meetings

Time required: Thirty to sixty minutes

MEETINGS—YOU CAN'T LIVE WITH them, but you can't work without them. It's important to have meetings to keep colleagues in the loop, but they become a problem when they run too long and take over your schedule.

Ah, the wonderful Magic Formula (eliminate, categorize, and organize) is coming to the rescue this week. It will make your life easier whether you are a presenter at meetings or you run them. The steps you learned back in March when creating a file system can be applied to setting a meeting agenda.

ELIMINATE EXCESS FROM MEETINGS

Let's start with the scenario that puts you in the driver's seat: You are the person who runs the meetings. Here are some questions to begin your investigation. Do you find your meetings are generally productive? Do you get consistent feedback from employees to this effect? Or do you find that these meetings are scheduled by rote and produce few good results? What's the bottom line on your skill as a meeting leader?

Let's apply the first step in the Magic Formula, eliminate, to improve your experience and that of your fellow attendees. How do you feel you could apply elimination to your situation? Here are some ideas.

Eliminate some time: Perhaps these meetings run too long and everyone runs out of creative steam before the clock indicates it's time to exit. Or can you reduce the amount of time each participant has to give a presentation?

Eliminate some participants: Do you really need each participant to come to every meeting?

Eliminate some agenda items: Do you see eyes glaze over at the mention of some of the reports due? Perhaps these are non-critical matters that could be typed and e-mailed to everyone to read at their leisure?

Eliminate meetings: Is a weekly gathering key or would once a month suffice?

How would you play with the idea of elimination and come up with a better meeting plan? Please list at least three ideas and be specific.

CATEGORIZE YOUR MEETING AGENDA

Categories make us powerful. It's easy to see the benefit of categories in a pantry, an office supply closet, or a file system. Guess what? Categories work for meetings as well. Here are some ways to implement categories to streamline your next meeting.

First, make a list of all the points to be covered and then note the individual speakers for each section. It's going to make life much easier if all projects are reported in sequence. What do I mean by that? I would start with the most pressing matters and move down the food chain to the least important. If there's an emergency and time gets cut short, you will have covered the key points.

Within each project presented, there will also be logical groupings of information. Let's say a remodel is planned for one area of your warehouse. You might want to hear all the financial aspects first, then see the new design ideas, and end with the construction details (if the job is underway). Have you been organizing material in this way?

Here's another idea. Suppose you are the head of your division and several managers must report to you at these meetings. While the specifics for each project may vary, can you ask that all material be categorized in the same sequence for every project? For example, perhaps you begin with finance, then move to current status, and then close with projected goals to be achieved by the next meeting. You would be creating a department template for all employees to use.

ORGANIZE THE ELEMENTS OF A MEETING

Finally, look at the categories and organize them in the most efficient manner. The obvious choice, as noted, is to list your agenda items in logical sequence. It's easier for people to absorb information if one entire category is presented before you move on to another agenda item.

After you have created your agenda, make further alterations to it in your quest to streamline the presentation:

For example, how much time should each presenter have? Do you want equal time slots for a regular meeting? Or do you want to vary it according to the length or importance of the material to be presented?

What about the location of your meeting? Have you considered the creature comforts of your fellow workers? Is there a regular complaint about the temperature in the room? Do your meetings cover too much material or run too long or both? Are snacks and water available?

What about the time of day? Are you asking the parents of young children to appear at an 8 a.m. meeting that causes havoc in their personal schedules? You won't get the best performance from these people. Or if you do, it may be tinged with resentment. Have you ever polled your meeting attendees to see what time of day they function best?

Are you prone to hauling everyone in for surprise meetings at the end of the day? You may live down the road, but if you make them late and your team has to travel

in rush hour traffic to pick up their kids from school or day care late, you won't get quality work. You also won't inspire confidence in your leadership or loyalty to the company.

WHEN IT'S YOUR TURN TO SPEAK

Perhaps you are the worker who presents at meetings rather than organizes them? Your control over the situation is limited to your own performance. Why not streamline your presentation as a way of demonstrating what is possible? Here are some ways to use the Magic Formula for individual performances:

Eliminate all extraneous material from the presentation.

Categorize your material so everything is presented in a logical flow. Prioritize the order of your sections, most important to least. You don't want to be saying at the end of your presentation: "Oh! I forgot to mention when I began that . . ."

Organize your categories in ways that will best engage your listeners. Do they need a handout? Would charts, graphs, or illustrations make the material clearer? Should these be part of the handout or put in a PowerPoint presentation? Remember that technology is meant to serve you. If all it does is dazzle, your presentation will be like Chinese food: Your listeners will wonder why they are hungry for more content as they exit the room!

I once asked a client about her husband, who was famous as a leader who inspired incredible loyalty. I asked her how he did this and her reply has always stayed with me: "He honors who they are as human beings," she said, "and he perfectly matches talent to task." Can this be said about you?

WEEK TWO

Have We Met Before?

This week, you can

- Recognize someone from your past in your present issues with others

Time required: One hour

AT SEMINARS MY STUDENTS FREQUENTLY say, "Regina, you reveal so much about yourself in your books!" Well, if a story from my life helps spark a memory of a similar experience in your life, I say let the healing begin! However, the following story is a bit embarrassing. It's about a relationship. You know, one of those "what was I thinking?" moments most of us have experienced.

I'll call him Andy. He was charismatic more than handsome. He was also self-centered, arrogant, and a few tacos shy of a full platter. When the relationship ended, as it was destined to from day one, I went to my therapist, convinced we'd be doing a post-mortem for a few weeks.

After I told her what happened, she looked at me and said, "Well, we can sit here for at least six months and talk about what a jerk Andy is . . . and no one will dis-

agree with us. Or we can talk about why, out of all the men on planet Earth, you chose him for a relationship." I remember saying, "Oh no! It always comes back to the self, doesn't it?" And so it does even in the workplace.

Every person who presses your buttons does so because you have those buttons to press. Someone told me recently that he thought I was a saint because a mutual friend drives him crazy. I asked what about this person was so disturbing. When my friend finished his litany, I had to chuckle. Not one of those qualities bothers me in any way. I just don't have that particular set of buttons to push!

If someone at work is driving you up the wall, chances are good he is not only like someone from your past, he has showed up to help you heal yourself. If you can look at this irritating person in a different light, you may find he isn't so bad after all. As I said at the start, we empower these people with our reactions. If you've helped create the snake, you can also de-fang him.

REMIND YOU OF ANYONE?

Take out your notebook and answer a few questions. You're looking for clues and connections.

First make a list of anyone in your work life who drives you crazy. (I hope your list is short!) Next to each name, write a few words describing the upsetting behavior.

After this list is complete, see if you can find any common themes. For example, let's say you discover that the common de-nominator is critical behavior. You never feel safe around this person. Is there some-one in your past who treated you the same way? Don't forget to include your parents in this investigation. If one or both were highly critical of you, the residual effects, if left unchecked, can last a lifetime. Psychol-ogists have found that when we have unre-solved issues from our childhood with mom or dad, we often find ourselves work-ing with (or dating or marrying!) someone with whom we have the same issues. I like to joke that I've "dated" my dad for years in an effort to heal our relationship. He died when I was twenty-four and it wasn't possible to work things out with him directly. Are you working with "your parents"?

Most of us have had a series of jobs, if not serial professions. Make a list of all of them. Write briefly about each experience as if you were telling someone a story. Do you see the same difficult person or upset-ting scenario repeated in most, if not all, of them? Does a difficult person pop into only one story, or are you the new Stephen King with tales of horror wherever you go?

Very often we have big life issues to work out and manifest situations that af-ford us an opportunity to grow. In this context, the situations may be a series of jobs that seem unrelated until we realize, for example, that we consistently face the same difficult personality type. When we don't consciously recognize the opportu-nity, we may feel like a victim. Do you have low self-esteem? Do you have trouble speaking up for yourself? Have you left a series of jobs for the same reason? It's far better to address the reason than to spend your adult life on the move in the work-force.

Finally, if you have come up dry, why not ask your best friend or spouse if he or she see any links to the past with the per-son or persons treating you unfairly now. Very often others see a connection when we do not.

This may seem like a light week in terms of assignments. It won't take long to write out these responses. However, it will take courage to fearlessly examine your present situation to see whether you have something to learn or whether, as some-times happens in life, you've just run across a garden-variety jerk.

DISCOVER YOUR SITUATION

Instead of complaining about your job, let's discover the *specific* issues you have at this place of employment. Free-floating agitation will keep you enmeshed in the problem:

- What are your three top complaints about your current work situation?
- Do any of these have at their root a lack of communication?
- Would conditions improve immediately if the air was cleared with a frank discussion?
- Can you chat with a colleague in private?
- Can you schedule a discussion about communication styles? Are you more prone to send an e-mail while your colleague tends to storm into your office and be blustery and confrontational? Do you send instant messages a hundred times daily without noticing that your colleague calls you twenty minutes before leaving for the day? Your irritation may be based on different communication styles. A little compromise and a lot of understanding go a long way.

Do you have an issue with one person or the corporate culture? Have you tried to improve your relationship with direct communication? Have you enlisted the help of coworkers, your supervisor, or perhaps the human resources department? Often a transfer to another division in the same company is a desirable move. Have you investigated this possibility? Sometimes the only way to mend the situation is to find a new job where your communications style and the talents you have to offer are a perfect fit. The issues you have at work may be a great blessing in disguise, moving you to a better experience.

WEEK THREE

Reactions Are Always a Choice

This week, you can

- Ask others about their life story or work experiences so you can understand why they are different
- Employ new techniques for dealing with difficult people

Time required: Thirty minutes

THIS WEEK WE'RE GOING TO LEARN some tried-and-true techniques for dealing with difficult people. These come from the worlds of business and psychology. Before we consider them, however, I'd like to offer a technique that may at first blush cause you to roll your eyes. It sounds a bit corny, but I can tell you from experience that it's powerful. What is it I'd like you to do? Offer the offending people love.

Love? Love the colleagues who are making your life a living hell? No, I don't mean you should put them in your will, offer them your first born, propose marriage, or shower them with gifts. I don't want you to do anything differently. Love is an inside job. It means regarding them and their offending ways with compassion rather than anger. It means talking to them

in a way that elicits their story, that is, *why* do they act this way? Over the years, I've worked with people who made my teeth ache, but I made it my mission to understand them. We were, after all, going to cross paths on a regular basis and I didn't want to have to feel like war was imminent whenever they entered a room.

The amazing thing is that many of these good folks have actually become friends. This technique is not a magic bullet. There isn't any when it comes to dealing with human beings. Start with love and then move on to the psychological and business tools I'll be giving you in a moment. Resolution will be a different recipe for each person.

Finally a word of caution: Coming from love is not synonymous with coming from a place of superiority or turning yourself into the person's shrink. You don't need to do anything except be present without any hostile emotion and *listen*. You will be surprised what you will hear. In the end, all boorish, cynical, destructive, negative behavior comes from a person who has been broken in some way. They are crying out in pain, and they expect more pain. Love is the surprise healing balm you can offer. Miracles happen when we give the other guy a break.

TECHNIQUES FOR DEALING WITH DIFFICULT PEOPLE

My best friend is a genius at teasing. It's an art form to tease people without hurting their feelings. Her success comes from the fact she has a good heart. Her words are never meant to cause pain. But let's say you work with a guy named John who delights in the kind of negative teasing that makes all of us cringe. "Hey, Mary, what's with that outfit? You look like one of the Village People!" You know the guy or gal.

The best time to have a talk with someone whose behavior is troublesome to you is when you are calm and centered. The worst time is when you are emotional and out of control. Take that minute or hour or day to compose yourself. Work out how you will express your concerns. Don't be shy about asking them to set aside some time to chat with you if need be. Be sure the conversation is private.

"John, I'm sure you haven't meant to hurt my feelings in any way, but I've never been comfortable with teasing. Could I ask you to stop those jokes about my weight (or smoking, eating, tardiness, wardrobe, lack of organization, etc.)? I'm reading this new organizing book and I'd like to use my time more productively. When I hear those comments, I have trouble concentrating." Keep the focus on you and the reaction you are having to your coworker's words. Blame tends to shut people down and put them on the defensive. A series of "I" statements helps them understand the impact of their words.

Without whining or complaining, see if you can find out if other people in the company are bothered by the same behavior. It might be appropriate to speak with the office manager, a human resources rep, or your boss. If someone is causing a problem with several employees, the productivity of the company will suffer. The Magic Formula begins with elimination. Sometimes it's a person who must be eliminated. Be prepared to be that person if you go public. Perhaps you can simply transfer to a new division in the same company?

THE HOLY MAN AND THE SNAKE

Let me close this section with a fable from India. A holy man was traveling through the countryside. He stopped at a small village for some sustenance. The local townspeople told him of a king cobra who was terrorizing their village. "He's killing innocent children and eating our livestock." They asked the holy man if he would go into the countryside, find the snake, and speak to him. He agreed.

As the holy man walked in the local forest, suddenly the offending cobra rose up before him. "Wait!" shouted the holy man. "Snake, what are you doing? You should be ashamed of yourself for hurting the innocent. Please stop these evil ways at once." The snake heard the holy man, and his words resonated in his heart. He agreed to stop.

About six months later, the holy man found himself back in the same area. "I wonder how my friend the snake is doing?" he asked himself. He decided to go into the town to find out. Much to his surprise, there in the town's square, the once fierce king cobra was near death. Children were throwing rocks at him and taunting him. "Snake!" cried the holy man. "What happened to you?"

The snake looked up with weary, sad eyes. He summoned just enough energy to speak. "Well, you told me not to hurt anyone."

The holy man's eyes filled with tears. "Oh," he said, "but I never told you not to hiss."

Never allow yourself to become a victim of another's cruel, destructive, or unconscious behavior. You don't have to go to war with them. You might simply use a calm, firm tone of voice that suggests that continuing this behavior would not be of interest to you. Consider each situation and individual on a case-by-case basis. The bottom line is this: You do not want to allow anything or anyone to inhibit your ability to be productive and happy. Don't forget to hiss when necessary!

WEEK FOUR

Deal with Difficult People

This week, you can

- Develop specific strategies for the biggest offenders in your work life

Time required: Thirty minutes

THE KEY TO DEALING WITH DIFFICULT people is to recognize them for who they are. Even if you can't eliminate them from your life, you can categorize them. Have you ever known you were coming down with something but had no idea what illness your symptoms indicated? Didn't you feel better when you heard your doctor say: "You have such and such." Suddenly isolated symptoms had a name and you had a course of action to follow that would bring healing.

The same is true in the world of human business relationships; it helps if you can diagnose the personality type you're dealing with. If you can view this person in a particular context, you will take the onus off your emotional reactions. Instead of asking "What the heck is wrong with Sue?" you'll be asking "Wow! How does one deal with such a negative personality

anyway?" Isn't it funny how certain archetypes reveal themselves no matter what the profession or family setup? See if you recognize anyone in your office in the following sections. Oh, and don't forget to look in a mirror. You know, just in case.

THE NAYSAYER

I'm going to begin with the naysayer because I was raised by one. When I was a junior at Hunter College in Manhattan, a new series of classes was introduced. In lieu of a letter grade (A, B, C, D), you simply received a pass or fail. It was a way to allow students to experience educational material without the fear that a low mark would hurt their grade point average. I desperately wanted to take fencing. I thought it was a beautiful art and wanted to experience the class. My mother was aghast. She was convinced that I was doomed to fail because I was not considered athletic. Why would I want that on my record? We fought about that class for two weeks and then I gave up. Years later I studied fencing in Los Angeles. I wasn't a candidate for an Olympic team, but I certainly could have passed that college class. My mother's negative assumptions robbed me of a fun learning experience.

In the office, this personality type will tell you your efforts will fail. For the naysayer, the glass is never half full; it is habitually half empty. If they see you organizing your space, for example, they may even start an office pool to see how long the new order will last. (Yes, I have clients who have experienced this!) Of course they will be equally sure to note that your efforts to win a new account, finish the budget on time, or get a promotion are also doomed. Compassion is the antidote of choice. Consider how much fear you have to be living with to approach others this way.

The person isn't really thinking about your abilities; he is thinking about his own. If you succeed, will he have to? Nothing is more terrifying to this person than the thought of change. Defang this snake with determination to succeed. One day you may have a colleague who stands in your doorway and says, "Wow! I didn't think you could do it! Great job." Choose to become an example of what is possible rather than a victim of the naysayer's low expectations.

THE KNOW-IT-ALL

I once worked with a man who would have been king in the know-it-all court. Can you imagine how insecure you'd have to be to constantly assert your superiority? It can be exhausting to deal with this personality type day in and day out.

No matter what products you use in your office, he's going to own superior ones. All those sales you made last month—didn't you know he closed more? You like this book? He's using a better one. And so it goes. You can't win, so why try? You don't need to win. Like a great Judo or Aikido master, you can direct your opponent's energy be redirecting it elsewhere. Ask the know-it-all to share his wisdom. He'll be so delighted you asked. After all, he doesn't really care about you and your goals. He just wants to hear himself speak! While he's talking, you can be planning in your head. Where are you going to move the desk? What folders do you need? Which items will be going home with you? There's no end to the plans you can be hatching in your head while the hot air is being pumped into the room. Thank your king of information for sharing and then do your own thing.

THE CONTROL FREAK

Whether it's a boss or a colleague, a control freak is sure that he knows the best way for you to do your job. There are many reasons for this behavior, but once again, one of the most common is fear. What are they afraid of? They can't face that there may be another way to do something. It's their way or the highway because your submission helps to validate their choices. If the control freak in your life is a coworker, listen as patiently as you would to the know-it-all. You might find a kernel or two of information that you want to include in your approach. Perhaps this person has found a unique way to organize some aspect of your company's business. Tell the control freak that you'll be getting back to him because you want to mull it all over, and you're grateful he took the time to share. Then quietly do your own thing.

Now, if the control freak is your boss, you have an obligation to come to terms with what she wants. You'll have to weigh each item or aspect. Is her way better when it comes to handling e-mail? Okay. Adopt that method. Is your choice for files, as an example, more in line with the way you think about information? Ask if you can try your system first. If you're productive, it shouldn't matter.

THE UNDERMINER

If you're new to a company and haven't been given the skinny on fellow employees, the underminer can often do a great deal of damage. There you are innocently sharing your work or opinions or ideals with someone and suddenly at the next office meeting or in a company e-mail, your words magically flow out of someone else's mouth! It's a tricky situation. Be on the lookout for the following:

Does this person have a reputation for doing this kind of thing to everyone? Ask someone you trust to see if you can get the inside information on his standing in the company. If this is his usual way of operating, people will suspect that the great idea didn't originate with him.

If it's a small piece of information that has been taken from you, let it go. If it's a significant contribution to the company, you'll have to make a decision about letting the powers-that-be know what happened. I wouldn't communicate this in an accusatory manner. ("Do you have any idea what Robert did to me?") Rather I would ask for some time for a private meeting and quietly communicate what happened, asking for direction in how to handle the situation. People feel empowered when someone asks for guidance.

Keep communications with this person to a minimum and reveal nothing further. In addition to filching ideas, this type of person frequently finds a way to inappropriately share personal data you let slip.

The most difficult situation is when the underminer is your supervisor. No easy way exists to handle this situation. One reaction you need to avoid is bottling up your anger and resentment. If you never speak up, the energy will either be directed inward, making you sick, or fly out of you in an angry burst and do more damage. Direct, honest, nonconfrontational communication works wonders, unless this human being is so damaged he can't hear you.

As you consider these difficult people archetypes, what solutions could you create for your unique situation at work? Write down the names of the offending parties and identify their type. Take some time to write about possible ways of dealing with them. Do you have a friend who is a skilled people person? Whenever I'm stuck with a troublemaker in the workplace, I consult with my best friend. And don't get stuck using any one solution over another; you'll have to negotiate your way step by step. Remember: The bottom line is your overall productivity.

WHEN THE DIFFICULT PERSON IS YOU

I learned a big lesson many years ago when I was a professional actress. I was in a play and there was a lull in the dialogue. It was probably a heartbeat in time, but when you're on stage it feels like ten minutes of dead air. Just as I smugly thought to myself, "I wonder who the idiot is who has the next line?" I realized I was the idiot! I didn't have to jump in and cover for another actor. I had to cover for myself.

I had a client who was such a micromanager that she redid her highly capable assistant's work, no matter how minor the task, searching for errors. The company could not prosper; no energy was left to be invested in growth. My assistant and I

tried to point this out to her, but she couldn't see it. In a few months her assistant moved to another company, where her talents were appreciated.

We all experience this in different ways. You may have the realization that you are sometimes a difficult person to work with. After a few minutes of embarrassment, let the emotions go. It's time to deal with the issues.

It's beyond the scope of this book to obliterate a person's need to control, be negative, or be a know-it-all, or any other manifestation of emotional lack that appears in your life. However, it is possible to see how these tendencies crop up in your work life and affect those with whom you work. After all, if you are impeding someone else in your work community from contributing their best, it is neither appropriate nor fair to the business or your colleagues. And the greatest loss is to yourself.

Please answer the following questions in your notebook. It's important to take a fearless look at your own behavior. Playing the victim is a powerless role. Seeking to understand how your actions affect others and embracing a willingness to change will empower you beyond your wildest dreams:

1. What unfortunate experiences led you to embrace one or more of the destructive patterns we have talked about in this chapter? Could you have made another choice after this experience?
2. How difficult would it be for you to change? Write five specific things you need to do. For example, do you realize

now that you are a micromanager who stifles your employees? How will you foster creativity and give them more freedom?

3. Is it possible that instead of believing that *you* know how everything must be done, you could begin to question others about their approach to tasks? Could you make it your goal to grow and learn from this information?

4. If changing your behavior in the workplace is terrifying because it feels as if you are letting go of control, why not try these techniques in your home? Following are three examples of change at home.

• Have you been browbeating your spouse or children with your organizing expertise? Why not call a family meeting and entertain other solutions to the clutter issues facing your home? Do you have to be the only authority?

• Do you think you know better than anyone else how to organize your closet, create a morning routine, clean the bathroom, and so on ? Ask a few friends how they do these tasks! Be on the quest for new products, tools, or techniques. Be open to surprise.

• Do you deny your children the chance to do chores because they won't do things as well as you do? No child does a physical task as well as a more experienced adult—at first. Allow your children to develop a set of skills that will enable them to run their own homes one day.

Every home experience mentioned here has its counterpart in the workplace. Practice giving up total control in the safe environment of your home and then move into the office, if that is an easier transition for you. Sometimes you will be the mentor, other times the student. Reverse your roles often and your life will have balance and joy.

As we arrive at the midpoint of the year, I suspect you are feeling more in control. You probably have several new habits in place. How many minutes of exercise have you added? How much water are you drinking? Do you feel more in control of your time? Can you even remember when you *didn't* prioritize your projects? Pat yourself on the back: These actions mean you made the decision to change.

JUNE SUMMARY

WEEK ONE

Rethink your meetings.

WEEK TWO

Recognize someone from your past in your present issues with others. Doing so is the first step to effecting lasting change.

WEEK THREE

Realize that reactions are always a choice. You can more easily change yours if you strive to understand what makes the other person tick. Employ new techniques for dealing with difficult people.

WEEK FOUR

Develop specific strategies for the biggest offenders.

7. JULY

Take a Vacation!

Inner refuge is refuge in ourselves, in our ultimate potential.
– KATHLEEN MCDONALD, *HOW TO MEDITATE*

ALL WORK AND NO PLAY MAKES JACK a dull boy. That was the saying when I was growing up, although we never knew who Jack was. Well, all work does more than make you dull. It drains you of creative energy, joy, and the ability to focus. The stress of constant work can leave you open to every flu and cold bug that passes by, and it can lead you to the road marked "depression" faster than most things.

A recent Expedia study reported that 35 percent of Americans don't take all their paid vacation days! Constant work is a great excuse to avoid real life. Workaholics don't see their friends and family because—they're working. You can list any number of things you can miss because of work, including emotional responses. The person who is always at the office often doesn't have the time to stop and grieve when a relationship ends. The fast track to fame and riches is not the American dream; it's the American fantasy.

So relax. Go ahead and take those vacation days—or at the very least, devote more time to you. Zen organizing is about living a life where work and play are in balance. This month, as you will see, builds on skills you have already developed. Are you ready to get started? The first thing we need, of course, are some new habits.

WORK HABIT OF THE MONTH: TOSS THREE THINGS

I want you to play a game this month. Every day you need to toss three things. Reply to and delete an e-mail message; erase a voice mail message that no longer has pertinent information; toss a piece of junk mail before it can start a stack on your desk. On the weekend, continue tossing at home. Three items is a tiny number, but when you multiply it by twenty-one days you realize you will have significantly lightened your load. You will also be sharpening your elimination muscle.

HOME HABIT OF THE MONTH: MOVE YOUR BODY

Summer has arrived. The days are longer. It's time to add five minutes to either your current exercise regime or an additional new workout. The body gets used to whatever exercise it is asked to habitually perform. This is a great month to shake things up.

If you began with yoga, try some new postures. If you're walking or running, extend the distance and perhaps alter your route. How about five more minutes a day of stair climbing? Think how great your gluteus maximus muscles will look in a bathing suit on your vacation!

WEEK ONE

Beat Burnout

This week, you can

- Take practical steps to stay on top of your game all year long

Time required: One to two hours

CAN YOU GUESS THE MOST IMPORtant technique when it comes to staving off burnout? That's right: the power of making a decision. Victor Hugo said, "Nothing else in the world . . . not all the armies . . . is so powerful as an idea whose time has come." If you are ready to live a more balanced, stress-free life, nothing can stop you. This week you learn about some tips to give you a good headstart.

SELF-CARE BEGINS AT HOME

Wouldn't it be nice if we could go to a spa several times a week? We'd be continuously pampered into a state of relaxation, and doing our best work would be a breeze. Unfortunately, that luxury isn't in the cards for the average worker. However, I do have some ideas to achieve balance that we can all do. It doesn't take a huge amount of effort, and you just might find yourself enjoying the process.

Get Enough Sleep

Sleep has restorative powers the human body needs. But you can't deprive your body all week long and make up for the damage by sleeping in on the weekend. Nor can you power through the day on caffeine and sugar and think you have overridden your body's lack of sleep.

Why not make it easier to hit the sack? When was the last time you purchased new sheets? What about your pj's: Are they threadbare? Could your alarm clock wake the men and women at West Point? Try something a little softer.

Take your journal and go to your bedroom. Make notes on the improvements you could make to this room so it becomes the quiet retreat you deserve at the end of a hard day at work.

Eat a Balanced Diet

Here we are back where we began our journey, with a discussion of the importance of food. A long time ago a physician told me that the best way to eat was to consume a lot of small meals throughout the day rather than three large meals. In Chinese medicine, they advocate eating rice, pasta, or bread (especially after the age of forty) before 6 p.m. to avoid bloat. I'm not suggesting you embrace either of these ideas, but why not spend some time researching good nutrition? The "Resources" section lists some books for you to check out.

If nothing else, eat fruits and vegetables. Avoid excess sugar (especially high fructose corn syrup), processed foods, and trans fats. Swap your soda for water. And stock up on healthy snacks. When your energy is flagging, you want a quick pick-me-up; you don't need a candy bar and a soda! Start with your snacks and make new changes day by day.

Get Wet

Once a week, take a long bath as a treat. Fill the water with essential oils. Burn a candle, dim the bathroom lights, and grab a trashy novel. Let your mind do something other than solve problems. Have some herbal tea or water by your side because the heat from the bath can dehydrate you.

Do you suffer from leg cramps due to standing for long hours at your job? Try the healing balm of an Epsom salt bath to raise magnesium levels, as well as soften rather than dry your skin. And you thought a bath was a matter of indulgence! Gentlemen, you too can enjoy a long, hot bath. I won't tell a soul. There are also soothing products you can try in a shower. Aromatherapy isn't just for the females in your home.

While we're on the subject of water, how many glasses a day are you drinking now? You'll be amazed by the power of water to relieve stress. The recommended number is eight eight-ounce glasses a day.

Play

Grab your best friend, partner, child, or pet and go play! I'm thinking of two remedies here: laughter and exercise. Take your child to a silly movie or a children's museum. Learn how to make soap or candles. Raise a few caterpillars and watch the butterflies on release day. (I have a reference page for this activity in the "Resources" section). Leave the cell phone at home or, if you must have it with you, shut it off. You can take a bathroom break every ninety minutes and see if you have any urgent messages.

Take your child and your dog to the biggest park you can find. Nature has restorative and calming effects. When was the last time you went on a hike? What was your favorite sport in school? I bet there's an age appropriate team that needs you for pick-up games on Saturday mornings.

Finally, never underestimate the power

of your best friend to heal what ails you. I've had personal challenges as I worked on the manuscript for this book. My best friend Susie has kept me on the straight and narrow. No one knows me better. When was the last time you had a giggle fest with your best buddy?

RESTORE YOURSELF AT WORK

Life is lived at home and at work. One feeds the other. With that in mind, the previous tips are things you can do to prepare yourself for your days at work. But what can you do at work to relieve stress and prevent burnout? Here are some ideas.

Review Your Goals

Why should you review your goals? If you are suffering from burnout, you are probably an overachiever. A goal is an important way to give our lives direction and meaning. If we have too many goals or they are all difficult or both, we are burning ourselves out in the name of progress. Look at the goal-setting work you did earlier this year, and see whether you are trying to accomplish too much and setting yourself up for failure.

Delegate

You don't have to do it all yourself. You do need to find capable people who can lift the burdens off your work-weary shoulders. And what's the key ingredient? You need to be a good teacher or mentor and explain exactly what you need them to do.

Learn to Say No

Long before the details pile so high you can't see to the other side and have to delegate some facets of your work life, just say no. It takes practice, I grant you. Look at it this way: Every time you say no to something, you open a space in your life, to say yes to something that matters more.

Ask for Help

Have you become such a people pleaser at work that you have more work than anyone else? Did you do a little too much volunteering in an effort to help others? It's time to chat with your boss or office manager and have some of these things taken off your plate. Just as in any relationship, don't assume that everyone knows you're overworked. They are probably too self-involved to notice. And if they do notice, they may assume you can handle it unless you speak up. Remember: It's okay to ask for help.

Slow Down

The more we pile onto our already overcrowded schedules, the faster we feel compelled to move. This usually causes more exhaustion, which leads to poor decision-making. But we look so virtuous! Take a look at your calendar. Do you fit ten appointments into your day when six is the maximum you can handle with any kind of grace? You need to slow down.

Try this experiment. Set a timer and endeavor to do as many things as you can in five minutes. Give each action or task your full attention. Stop and check your body, mind, and emotions. How do you feel?

Make some notes. Read the rest of this week's lesson and then set your timer for another five minutes. This time try and do as many things as you can, multitasking when possible. At the end, how do you feel? Is there a remarkable difference? This last exercise should leave you exhausted, and I bet your work isn't the best. Write down your findings. You may not have been as productive but this kind of hyperactivity may have felt more comfortable because it's the norm for you. You can retrain yourself to work at a more nurturing pace. The bonus will be an automatic increase in the quality of your work.

Be Smart about Multitasking

And now a word about multitasking, an art form if ever there was one! If you are in the habit of doing many things at once, don't pat yourself on the back just yet. If multitasking has you in perpetual motion, you aren't doing it properly. On the other hand, if you use naturally occurring downtime to accomplish other tasks, you can go to the head of the class.

Here are four productive ways to multitask:

- When you know you're going to an appointment that generally involves a wait (think doctor's office, the dentist, your attorney), have a work project with you. This time is golden.
- If you have a long document emerging from the printer, use the time to do some maintenance tasks such as sharpen pencils or return quick phone calls.

- Do you need to download a long document? Or is a new piece of software being installed? While the mindless, mechanical part is being taken care of, why not read the instruction manual?
- By the end of the day, I always have nonemergency phone calls to return. The next morning while I am walking my dog, I return them using my cell phone. By the way, you need to be careful if you're calling a different time zone. At 7 a.m., no one in California wants to hear from me, while the good folks in New York are ready for a second cup of coffee because it's 10 a.m. there.

How do you multitask in your office situation? Make a list of at least three additional things you can do. Again, these are actions performed in concert that move your schedule forward. Do all the items you mention qualify?

You've made a lot of progress this week in your quest to restore and maintain sanity in the workplace. Stress can be our friend if we allow it in at our discretion and use it for good ends. When we are always under stress, however, it leads to burnout. Every day you make a choice to be organized, healthy, and sane or to live in chaos, fear, and exhaustion. The power of that decision is always yours.

WEEK TWO

Get the Office Ready for Your Departure

This week, you can

- Prepare your coworkers and clients for your departure

Time required: One to two hours

Wouldn't it be great if you could just get up and leave your office for a vacation and not do any prep work? In the real world, however, this isn't the case. Your coworkers need to be brought up to speed on your projects; they need to know what they will be responsible for in your absence; and they need to have an understanding of how your job is performed. After all, in an emergency, you want things to go smoothly. Remember that you continue to make an impression on the powers-that-be even when you are out of the office and far from home.

EXIT STRATEGY

Here is a list of the things you might need to consider as you prepare to take a vacation. Your tasks will vary depending on the scope of your responsibilities, at what point you started getting organized, and the amount of consistent help you have during the year. You may have to bend these tips to suit your situation. In the end you'll have a perfect exit strategy (albeit a temporary one)! Let's begin with a series of yes-or-no questions. A preponderance of yes responses means you have more prep work before your vacation than others:

- Is your desk a scary mess to your coworkers?
- In your absence, would coworkers be hard pressed to find what they need?
- Are the nooks and crannies of your office space filled with bags and boxes of stuff?
- Are your computer files saved on your personal hard drive rather than stored on a shared drive where everyone can access them?

- Are your computer files a jumbled mess instead of organized in a way that the makes the information both easy and logical to find? (See August, page 181.)
- Are your hard copy files unorganized and not available in a printed master file list? (See March, page 67.)
- Have you developed new systems for your job and kept them a secret so that no one else knows how you perform your job functions?
- Are you unwilling to delegate tasks to others in your absence so your projects continue on course?
- Do you secretly enjoy a feeling of power because no one really knows how you function?

If your office and desk are in a state of chaos, my guess is that one of three things is at play: You're starting this book with this month and have yet to do the work that has led other readers to this point; you did the work and backslid a bit; you decided to read the material but not take the time to do the work. Regardless of the scenario, the solution is the same. You need to make the time to put your work environment in order. The immediate result will be that you can delegate more easily and leave for your vacation with a free mind. The long-term benefits will include saved time, reduced stress, and better health. Are you ready to begin? Spend some time with Chapter 3, where I devote time to the organization of your desk. If your vacation is imminent, implement as many of the suggestions as possible. If your vacation is in the future, dedicate yourself to Chapter 3 and then return here at the appropriate time.

CLEAR THE DECKS

After you get your physical space whipped into shape so that your colleagues can maneuver in your office if they need to find something, you'll want to turn your attention to other aspects of your workday. A big concern will be your projects. And don't forget your colleagues in other offices and the vendors you deal with on a regular basis. You're going on vacation, but you still represent your company. You'll want everyone to feel important and everything to be handled.

Let's look at how to fashion your exit with ease. Here are some key items you'll want to consider:

Workflow: Looking at your daily workload, what tasks must continue in your absence? Do you have an assistant or coworker who can manage these while you are gone? Speak to him so that everyone is on the same page concerning your departure, length of time away, and the work required. If no one can cover for you, you need to address the issue with your supervisor. And if you are the boss, make a decision to delegate!

If you have developed systems and strategies, pat yourself on the back. If they are your secret, there's no time like the present to write up a quick set of instructions that will clue folks in not only while you are gone but when you are promoted or switch jobs. Remember: You'll be in a pickle if others start creating emergency coping strategies in your absence.

Projects: Now it's time to consider your special projects. What needs to be done while you are out of the office? Who can you trust with this work? Instead of fretting over the competency level of those around you, resolve to become a good teacher or mentor. Switching your focus from the negative to the positive will bring you relief and empower others to do their best.

E-mail and voicemail: Let clients know that you are leaving and who they should contact in your absence. People tend to feel abandoned in these situations if no communication network is in place. Don't forget to set up your out-of-office phone and e-mail messages.

Mail: Decide how you want mail and interoffice memos to be left for your perusal when you return. The visual of a stuffed and overflowing mail or inbox will be a demoralizing sight after a vacation. Set yourself up to be in control, not overwhelmed. Let's say you've cleared off your desk as you exit the door for your holiday. Why not leave a box for incoming mail on the floor? Ask your assistant or a close colleague to put the lid on it the last day before your return. You'll be entering the same calm space you created. You can deal with the new demands once you get settled!

When you return from vacation, the Magic Formula will help you blast through that box of mail. First you will eliminate the junk. As you do this, you'll be placing what you need to keep in related piles, or categories. As you deal with each area these piles represent, you can organize the material into your existing system for that project or ongoing responsibility.

Contact information: Finally, circulate to key people an itinerary with contact information. Ask that you be contacted only in an *emergency*.

It takes some time to put this plan in place. You may have to stay late one evening or take care of this over a weekend. If you can, schedule some personal time with anyone who is covering for you. You'll want to be sure he has seen your written instructions and heard your wishes as well. Remember that everyone learns differently. I can't read a computer manual to save myself but a good tech person can teach me anything. Understand not only the abilities of those you work with but their learning styles and strengths.

Time spent preparing your coworkers to handle your work is an investment in your vacation. The better the home team functions without you, the less the likelihood of being inundated by their calls. To avoid disappointment, be realistic in your expectations. After all, some coworkers are not going to do your work with the attention to detail you bring to the table. They may not deal with clients with the same level of finesse. Also be prepared to encounter a surprise of a different sort. You may have a coworker who is as good at your job as you are. Graciously thank them—after all, now you have an ally.

WEEK THREE

Use Your New Skills to Plan Your Vacation

This week, you can

- Apply the Magic Formula to your vacation plans

Time required: One to two hours

THE MAGIC FORMULA WILL ENABLE you to organize *anything*. We've used it extensively this year in the office. Now let's use it to plan your vacation.

GETAWAY TIME!

You're probably feeling stretched thin, because a vacation plan means adding another project to your busy schedule. Why not shift your focus? Instead of the work involved, think of the result. Will you be sitting under a coconut tree on a tropical island? Will you be showing the kids around a famous theme park? Are you going home to visit relatives? What is this vacation about for you? Choose the moment you can't wait to experience and, like a scene in a movie that plays on an endless loop, see yourself in that moment. Be specific about the details. What is the temper-

ature? What time of day is it? What are you wearing? Who is with you? Set the timer for five minutes and allow yourself to savor this vision of the future. This is one way to become inspired to get organized for the trip.

Take out your notebook—we need to get ready for some fun!

1. What is the purpose of this trip?
2. Is it a family obligation or a fun-oriented holiday? If it's the former, can you inject a little fun into the experience? For example, perhaps you are going to visit Aunt Gertie. She's your only living relative but you don't have much in common with her and you'd rather be staying in a hotel. How about doing a Google search of the area? Perhaps one afternoon you could investigate a museum or historic inn or explore a beautiful park? With digital video cam-

eras so inexpensive these days, why not ask Aunt Gertie if you can ask her some questions about the family tree? Who knows what treasures she'll share?

3. If your vacation is to an area you have not explored before, do you need to do any research regarding lodging, tours, or other local attractions? I've spent months doing research for some vacations. It was a treat to find myself in locations I had been reading about for almost a year. A few years ago I had the opposite experience. I took a tour to China and did no research! Every day was a surprise adventure. Do whatever is best for you under the current circumstances.

4. How are you getting to your destination? Have you made the necessary reservations on the various planes, trains, buses, or automobiles you'll need?

These are all the practical things you need to think about to make the trip a reality. Each yes response will be the starting point for a travel to-do list. For example, let's say you are driving to visit your parents. If you are using your vehicle, you'll want to have it serviced, so put that on your list. Take the car in early because unexpected repairs may cause it to be in the shop longer than you anticipate. Planning for the unexpected is one of the hallmarks of an organized mind.

Another attribute is being able to instantly organize details when emergencies arise. You'll be doing both of these by year's end. Experience will be your best teacher. Years ago, before I started traveling exclusively with a small suitcase I could place in the overhead bin, I remember waiting for my suitcase to come off the plane and land in the baggage claim area. It suddenly dawned on me that I needed to purchase a unique color suitcase to have it stand out in a sea of black bags being hurled onto the baggage turntable. Make getting organized a skill you acquire and a game you play.

BE REALISTIC AND ELIMINATE

Once you have your list, let's apply the Magic Formula to it so we can be sure it is lean and to the point rather than bloated and overwhelming! The first step is to eliminate, right? Could any tasks be crossed off the list? For example, what if you live in New York City and you're planning to drive to Dallas to see family. You have "car maintenance" on your list. When you chat with your spouse, however, you realize that it would be far more advantageous to rent a larger vehicle so you can transport some items home and then fly back to New York. Your spouse has enough miles on one airline to cash them in for two tickets, and you get an auto rental discount through your job. Now you have one less errand to run before the big day.

As you plan your route to Texas, you realize that some tourist attractions you had hoped to stop and see en route will have to be sacrificed to save time. If you have brochures for those sites, feel free to discard them. Remember that the latest rates will be available online the next time you plan this adventure.

We have eliminated some items from our list and itinerary. Now, what about delegating some tasks to other family members? Unless you're the point person in your family unit or among your friends for all travel needs (and you enjoy this position), get others involved! This is a great way to eliminate items from your list while safeguarding that they will be handled. If you have teens at home, it's a surefire way not only to involve them in the plans but to teach them some practical planning tips.

CATEGORIZE YOUR TRAVEL TO-DO LIST AND ORGANIZE

Now it's time to consider *categories*. See if you can group the tasks on your travel to-do list. You might have the following categories: flights to research and book, hotels or motels that need the same attention, sightseeing, packing lists, and home instructions. We're going to cover the latter next week. For now, make your logical groupings of tasks and then make appointments on your calendar for when you want to handle each detail. The Magic Formula's third step is organizing your categories. You're on the home stretch. It's almost time to leave home. We'll add some tips next week.

WEEK FOUR

Leave Your BlackBerry Behind

This week, you can

- Make sure the home team is as organized as the one at the office

Time required: One to two hours

RECENTLY I WENT OUT FOR A BIRTH-day dinner with a few friends. They are divided into two groups: those, like me, who swear by their electronic devices and those for whom such devices remain somewhere between a mystery and a nuisance. Two of the friends at my birthday dinner were in the latter camp. They got cell phones in the past year and turn them on for emergency calls only. Don't bother leaving a message because they have no idea how to retrieve it.

The other two guests at dinner are like me: entrepreneurs whose businesses are partially dependent on Web communications. One runs a Web-based business and services clients and media. The other is one of the top real estate brokers in New York City. As for me, I never know when a client or potential client will contact me. My electronic devices keep me plugged into the world.

While writing this book, I've been paying attention more to my own behavior. And during the course of that evening, I noticed that the three of us would quietly take out our electronic organizers or phones and check e-mail under the table! We're all good friends and no one was offended by this behavior. Actually, it was a source of amusement. But this anecdote should forever put a human face on all professional organizers. We aren't perfect!

The moral of the story is this: If you absolutely must take your communication devices with you on your vacation, be mindful of your traveling companions. This especially goes for young children. A friend of mine was on vacation recently with her eleven-year-old daughter, Melissa. They were at a mall when my friend took a call from the company she works for. Her daughter piped up and said, "Mom, this is supposed to be a *vacation*!" The younger the child, the more difficult it will be for them to understand that your willingness to work doesn't equate with your greater love of your job. Now that you are leaving your office and your projects so well organized, ask your colleagues to contact you only in the event of a true emergency. You might even designate a specific time to call. Keep in mind the monkey wrench that time zones can toss into the mix.

BEFORE YOU LEAVE THE HOUSE

You're going to need a to-do plan to get your home ready for your vacation. Let's create a separate section to last week's list. Very often we leave home preparation for last. I'm not sure why, but my guess is that it's purely emotional. We all long to get away because we need to leave everyday routines and experience something new. But home is truly where the heart is and our reluctance to leave is played out in the last-minute dramas we create. Let's make this a thing of the past. Wouldn't it be nice to leave home without being exhausted? And wouldn't it be grand to come home to a house that didn't need a lot of attention?

Let's get to work. This is an achievable goal, albeit one that takes a bit of practice.

The Departure Checklist

Here are some common issues that will need your attention before you go. Schedule the time to take care of them all. You don't want to be racing out the door at 5 am en route to the airport and suddenly realize that you forgot to put a hold on your paper delivery. Nothing is a more enticing sign to burglars that no one is home than a stack of unread newspapers on your lawn. Here's my list for you.

1. Call to put a stop on your daily newspaper delivery.
2. Have your mail held at the post office or ask a neighbor to take it in for you.
3. Lower the thermostat before you leave.
4. Pay all bills that will be due during the time you are away. I leave mine for my dog sitter to mail, with a Post-it noting the mail date. You may want to set up electronic bill paying or automatic payment.
5. If you have children or pets who will not be traveling with you, create a cheat sheet with emergency numbers for their appointed caretaker.
6. In the case of children, the list will include:
   - Local emergency numbers, such as relatives and friends who can act on your behalf in a crisis.
   - Medical information, including doctors, preferred hospitals, and copies of insurance cards.
   - A temporary guardianship letter granting your representative the power to make decisions for your child in an emergency.
   - School information.
   - Babysitters.
   - All of your contact information, including cell phone number, travel itinerary, and phone numbers at your destination.

7. For your pet, the list will include:
- Name and phone number of your vet.
- Name and phone number of the local Animal Emergency Hospital.
- Food, treat, and medical supplies. Include instructions for administering. If your pet requires daily care, such as insulin injections, your pet sitter needs to practice!
- A copy of your travel itinerary and all contact information left in a prominent place.
- Contact information for the person who would represent you in a crisis situation with your pet. This is probably the same person who would assume care if your pet sitter had to leave. Make financial arrangements for emergency care. I leave a credit card and a note granting permission for this person to charge emergency medical care.

Final Words of Wisdom

In addition to the checklist in the preceding section, here are some additional words of advice. Not every item in the preceding list or in this section will need your attention, so don't be overwhelmed. You're looking for what relates to you. Take a deep breath!

Be sure whoever is in your home knows the location of all the important household items and has practiced unlocking the front door. If you have an alarm, have them set and release it a few times. Your alarm company should be advised who is watching the house in your absence.

Why do I include this advice? Years ago I agreed to house-sit for friends and take care of their pets. When they handed me the keys, it didn't dawn on any of us that the lock was tricky and I should practice. For the entire two weeks I lived in that house, I was unable to enter through the front door. I had to go to the backyard and come in through the back door. I learned my lesson! Another time I was staying at a friend's house while my apartment was being painted. I was applying my makeup early one morning when I heard an odd sound. Suddenly hot water was pouring out of the cabinet under the sink. A pipe had burst! I called a handyman and he told me to go outside and shut off the hot water tank. But I had no idea where that was or what it looked like. Fortunately, he stayed on the phone with me until I found it. Be overly cautious with your pet, child, or home caretakers.

If you're a frequent traveler, you can create a contacts file on your computer and make any updates or revisions each time you leave town. When you leave a copy in your home, be sure everyone knows where it is located. You might want to print several copies and place them in more than one room. The most common location for this sheet is the refrigerator.

Are you traveling with children? Depending on their ages, you will need to pack special supplies for them. Make a list of these items. If the kids are old enough, consult with them on the books, games, and so on that they'd like to have with them. Ask them to gather the items from the list and then help them pack. If they are responsible for transporting their own suitcase, they'll be less likely to take extraneous items.

If you've asked the good folks at work not to disturb you and have purposely kept your destination a secret, be sure you clue in your babysitter, pet sitter, or house sitter. You don't want them innocently spilling the beans. Direct them to tell any callers that in an emergency, *they* will get in touch with you and ask you to return the call directly.

If you're like most people, you bring work home with you, although I don't advocate this. If you will feel more secure having some key documents with you for reference just in case, copy them to a flash drive and attach that to your key ring. It's hard to find a home or a hotel these days without access to a computer. If you're re-ally stuck, an Internet café should be nearby. I'd hate to see you schlep your laptop on vacation. Have I given you enough alternatives to make you feel secure about not seeing it for a week or ten days? I hope so!

Finally, every situation and every individual is unique, so no solution fits every holiday experience. The goal in this chapter is to offer you ways to modify your behavior, especially if you often come home from a vacation as exhausted as when you left! I love the work I do. I feel passionate about my clients and the books I write. No one knows better than I the temptation to work 24/7. It's important, however, to give your body, mind, and emotions a break. If you take a true vacation from the daily grind, you will return refreshed and ready to contribute to the work you have chosen to do.

JULY SUMMARY

WEEK ONE

Learn the simple steps that will prevent burnout. You will lose time and productivity if you never take the time to rejuvenate yourself. Sometimes a simple bubble bath does the trick!

WEEK TWO

Prepare your workplace for your vacation. If your colleagues are up to speed on your projects, you should be able to leave with a sense of security.

WEEK THREE

Use your newly acquired organizing skills to plan your trip. Whether it's your home or the office, being organized will save you time, money, and physical and emotional energy.

WEEK FOUR

Make your home as ready for your departure as your office. If you know that everyone and everything, including your home, is taken care of, you'll be able to be completely present no matter where your vacation finds you.

8. AUGUST

Organize Your Virtual World

Be nice to nerds. Chances are you'll end up working for one.

—BILL GATES

I AM IN AWE OF THE TECHNOLOGICAL advances of the past twenty-five years. Who could have imagined that we'd have *instant* communication with anyone on the globe or that snail mail would seem such an antiquated concept? But technology offers a gift and a trap. If we aren't vigilant, the roles of master and servant can be flipped. Whether it's your e-mail, your voice mail, or the files you have created on your computer, this month your virtual house will become as organized as your physical one.

WORK HABIT OF THE MONTH: SYNC UP

The importance of maintaining your calendar is without question. Many people choose electronic devices that will keep them plugged into the latest information in their business and personal lives. I have clients whose PDAs and Blackberries are

an extension of their hands! The key is to remember to keep your device up-to-date. Every night before you get ready for bed, connect your electronic organizer to your computer to be sure it's synced.

HOME HABIT OF THE MONTH: TIME YOURSELF

Everybody needs to unwind. After a long day at work, it's only natural to want to come home and decompress. However, downtime can become a great big time waster if we don't watch the clock. Please identify the big culprit you fall victim to in your home. We're going to eliminate it!

Here's one of the most common examples: After working hard all day, you sit down to check your personal e-mail. Then you decide to play a hand or two of solitaire or a video game. You neglect to watch the clock, and suddenly two hours have flown by and none of your chores have been completed. You're bleary-eyed with exhaustion.

Stop the madness! You need a timer or a self-imposed (limited) number of games you can play per evening. You may want twenty minutes to unwind; if it stretches to one or two hours, you've lost precious time you could spend communicating with family and friends.

What will you bring under control this month?

WEEK ONE

Uncover Your Communication Style

This week, you can

- Figure out what kind of a communicator you are
- List concrete ways you can work better with coworkers

Time required: Thirty to sixty minutes

LET'S BEGIN THIS MONTH WITH A look at the way you communicate in general. What do you think you would discover about yourself if you invited a loved one to describe you? You might find that you are wired in a way that makes you a difficult communicator. Or perhaps you would see how your style of communicating isn't in sync with your boss, coworkers, or a client.

EXAMINE YOUR WORK STYLE

Take out your notebook to chart a more refined course to your goals. If you aren't sure what the answers are to the following questions, ask your spouse or your best friend for some feedback—he or she may see you more clearly. Are you ready to begin? Here are your questions:

1. Do you prefer long conversations to brief ones? Does your preference change depending on the way you are communicating? In other words, are you best as a face-to-face communicator, a phone person, or someone who loves to send e-mails or text messages?

2. Has your style changed over the years or are you loyal to your ways? I have a friend who is a tenured professor at a major university. She checks her e-mail twice a week. If you want her, you have to pick up the phone. If you want me, you should send an e-mail. There is no right or wrong. It's all about knowing what you prefer and then letting others know how best to reach you.

3. Are you competitive at work or do you simply like the best man or woman to win? How does your competitive drive manifest itself in terms of communica-

tion? When you are assigned a project, do you instinctively gather a team and start delegating tasks? Or do you keep all the details to yourself and work alone to achieve success?

4. Would you describe yourself as an empowering person? That is, do you enjoy giving coworkers compliments on a job well done? Or are you a buttoned-up kind of person who doesn't like to make a lot of fuss about success—or failure for that matter?

5. Would you describe yourself as a person who enjoys communicating information to others? Or are you shy and reserved? Does your style change depending on who you are with? For example, do your coworkers think you never provide a detail while your Aunt Trish would swear you are a Chatty Cathy?

6. Do you like to work on projects alone or are you best with a group? Have you ever communicated your preference to your boss?

7. How about gossip? Do you recoil when you hear it or are you the first one to spread the word? This is the worst type of office communication. Sadly, it's the most common as well. Why not resolve to avoid it?

After you answer these questions, stop and review your responses. Do you realize something about yourself that you were unaware of before you began? What have you learned? Can you be specific?

How will this revelation change the way you communicate at work? Will you have to shift in terms of your entire approach or is it a matter of working a little differently with a particular colleague? Let me give you an example.

I have clients whose lives revolve around their cell phones. If I want to reach them, that's the number I call. Other clients love quick communications via e-mail. Within the world of e-mail communicators, however, there are variations. Most people dash off quick notes that are brief, concise, and to the point. Others use e-mail with the same format they once wrote letters that were sent via snail mail. Their communications are formal and woe unto those who do not respond in kind.

Many of us have one preferred style of communicating and can be rigid about how we approach others. Adapting a fluid approach can put you in a more powerful position: You invite others to communicate with you and share their knowledge in their preferred style. Seduction isn't something reserved for the bedroom!

WEEK TWO

Organize Your E-Mail

This week, you can

- Make e-mail a true business tool rather than a personal time waster
- House your e-mail messages in designated folders rather than allowing them to multiply like rabbits in your inbox

Time required: Thirty to sixty minutes

IT ISN'T UNCOMMON FOR THE AVERAGE business professional to receive several hundred e-mails a day. We've gone a bit insane, haven't we? We very often let our fingers fly over the keyboard without taking adequate time to think about what it is we want to communicate. What is the average recipient to do? Here is the perfect arena in which to practice the fine art of rapid decision making. If you don't, you will be forever inundated and constantly playing catch-up.

DEAL WITH INCOMING E-MAIL

We get e-mail messages at work. We get them at home. We can check them on-the-fly on our phones. It's important to develop the habit of dealing with them quickly, easily, and efficiently. No one can deal with a large number of e-mails without a solid system. Each e-mail needs to be sent to a designated place, where you will know to look when you need the information or are ready to address an issue. Your willingness to press the delete key is central to preserving your sanity. Let's get started!

If your computer alerts you each time a message lands in your inbox, either shut off the aural alert or ignore it, especially if you are in the middle of something else. When I'm writing, for example, I can't allow myself to get distracted. If I am not working on a project and am enjoying some downtime at the computer, those alerts are music to my ears. The bottom line is this: You set the boundaries. Don't allow everyone in cyberspace to be the boss of you.

With each e-mail message, you need to decide the following:

- Do I need to respond to this message?
- If yes, when is the appropriate time? Responses can be prioritized just like your projects.

Here's a page from my own morning routine. I open my e-mail first thing in the morning because I need to scan for business messages from the East Coast (I live on the West Coast). If I see any such communications, I open them without delay. If someone needs me ASAP and is on deadline, it behooves me to respond immediately. I call this putting out e-mail fires.

As I scroll down the e-mail columns looking for work e-mails, I delete junk mail as I go.

At this point, I can usually take my dog out for his morning business and return for breakfast. When I'm ready to work, I quickly scan for anything new that I can delete and any new business e-mails.

Did you ever stop and think about what the type face and size you use in your e-mail messages say about you? This is a little recognized (outside the world of advertising) way of influencing the reader of your communications. "It isn't what you say; it's how you say it." In today's world we could have a twist: "It isn't just what you say, it's how it looks that counts." I've included my favorite style book in the "Resource" section to check out if you want to tinker with the look of your communication.

Now I have a level playing field. It's time to address all the work e-mails, move on to any personal ones I want to take care of immediately, and file the remaining e-mail in the correct folders I have created for this purpose.

What is your Achilles' heel regarding communicating at work? For example, do you take time to answer less-than-critical e-mails in great detail? This is a classic waste of time, but it also makes us feel and look busy! From now on, you are going to prioritize your e-mail.

Here are some ways to deal with e-mail instantly:

- Delete the silly, the spam that got through, the nonessential.
- Does an e-mail give you information that should be kept but there is no need to respond to the sender? File it immediately in a folder with related information. You have a choice to save the e-mail or print the information and file the hard copy.
- Is a response required but you need time to pull together the material? Shoot a quick e-mail to the sender letting him know when to expect a response. Keep this e-mail in a general To-Do folder or a To-Do folder for a specific project. If necessary, make a note on your calendar or set your computer to remind you.

These choices should take only a few minutes. Watch your decision-making skill improve! You want to save your energy and time for e-mails that you must deal with ASAP. At the end of twenty-one days, you will wonder why you ever gave away time to nonessential tasks.

FILE YOUR E-MAIL

After you respond to an e-mail, remember that your e-mail is automatically saved on the computer. Do you need to keep a record of messages received or sent or both? If you need a copy of your response, why not cc yourself when you send your reply? You can keep your cybertrail by filing incoming mail and your responses in the appropriate folder as a record. Some e-mail automatically saves all communications as an ongoing conversation with each transmission.

If a received e-mail is a nonessential communication, press the delete key! And don't forget to delete any guilt you feel. If you believe this is key information, transfer it to a specific folder. This is important for projects that require a paper trail. It's possible to have e-mails sent to specific recipients automatically saved in a designated folder; check with your IT person about this.

You can create cyber files that function just like your hard copy files. For example, why not have a To-Do/High Priority folder and a To-Do/Low Priority folder? If you are working on multiple projects, you may want to further refine your ability to sort items that need your attention by having a To-Do folder for each project. This option replaces the two To-Do folders just described or can be used with them.

Most large corporations have rules for creating paper trails. Follow them. If you work in a smaller company, why not speak to the head person about creating a format regarding e-mails for all employees to follow? You'll be contributing to the growth of the company.

Your e-mail files work in concert with the hard copy files in your office. For example, you want to be consistent in the way you name files. You don't want one type of information to have one name in the physical world, another in your computer file cabinet, and a third online. Why not use your master file list as a guide and duplicate as many file names as possible? (See Chapter 3 for information on creating a master file list.) You've already done the hard work. Why reinvent the wheel?

Just as we moved hard copy files to archival storage, so should your old e-mails be archived at suitable intervals. This moves them from your hard drive to the server. You can have this set up to be done automatically. And of course you will need to schedule time to clean out these e-mails. This might be something for a really good assistant to do on your behalf.

Perhaps now more than ever you can see that the principles of organizing are truly the same. Whether it is cyberspace, your hard drive, or your file cabinet, the basic rules apply. Once you achieve mastery in one area, you've opened the doorway to all the others.

Let me close this section with a true story.

I taught a class recently and encountered a student who swore that she had over one thousand e-mails on her work computer and over three thousand at home. Can you imagine? We were all amazed that she had not one but two computer operating systems that continued to work under this heavy load. But the load is more than on her computer system; it's in her mind every time she goes to check a new e-mail and has to encounter all those messages! And what are they? Say it with me: unmade decisions! Do you have a situation like this? Get busy deleting, filing, and archiving! The past is eating up valuable real estate in your present experience.

WEEK THREE

More Communication Opportunities

This week, you can

- Decide how you want to keep track of your life
- Use communication tools such as the phone or instant messaging to increase your productivity rather than waste your time

Time required: Thirty to ninety minutes, depending on what technology you already have in place

Technology is a wonderful thing. Today just about everybody has some type of electronic organizer as part of their work life toolkit. A lot of my business is conducted over the Internet, so e-mail retrieval is key to my survival. My old cell phone enabled me to check e-mail; my new one opens up to a small keyboard and allows me to surf the Web. When I signed up for a new contract with this phone, the woman behind the counter offered me five hundred text messages for $5 a month and unlimited for $10. I took the $5 plan because I rarely send text messages. When she pushed me to upgrade, I laughed and said: "I'm not eighteen. I don't spend my time text messaging!"

No hard-and-fast rules exist as to what you need. It depends on the nature of your business and how interested you are in high-tech aids. I have a dear friend whose brain functions like a high-speed computer. He sits in the center of a circle of computers and other advanced technological gizmos that I don't even begin to comprehend. I call him Captain Kirk on the bridge of the *Starship Enterprise* whenever I visit. I have a client who has two computers running at all times so she can switch from one monitor to the other and never lose time. These approaches would exhaust me, but anything less would bore them. Where are you in this scenario?

This week we're going to continue our quest to harness the power of the most common communication tools. E-mail may be king but there are other members of the court. Who can live without a phone, instant messaging, or voice mail, just to name a few? Every one of these options can help you be more efficient. Without conscious direction, however, they can also allow you to fritter away time. Let's examine each in turn.

THE OLD-FASHIONED TELEPHONE

Let's face it. The phone is still irreplaceable. Why? Because it offers something critical to communication: the sound of the human voice. Isn't it funny how you can read an e-mail message or text message and be convinced that you have been insulted or slighted? And then you call the person and understand that you didn't read the note in the right spirit. Here's a word to the wise: Unless you know the person very well, keep humor and sarcasm under control in an e-mail. Be as polite as you were on any first date with someone.

Everyone who knew I was writing this book begged me to add the following tip: Don't whip out your cell phone during lunch or dinner with friends. You don't look hip. You look rude, insecure, and foolish. And, if you do need to use the phone, remember that no one else cares what your business is nor do they want to feel your pain if it's a personal matter. If you work in an open office where no walls separate cubicles, keep in mind that your colleagues might hear every detail of your personal calls. The other day at the post office, a young man in his twenties had a loud conversation with the receptionist in his doctor's office. By the time the call ended, every stranger knew his diagnosis and his medical ID number. It was indeed the quintessential too-much-information moment!

Set aside blocks of time when you can return nonessential phone calls. When your workload is lighter, you might be able to have established times for returning phone calls in general.

I have several home-based colleagues who turn off their computers and phones at 6 p.m. on Friday night and don't check voice mail or e-mail until Monday morning. If you can do that, great. I think it's critical if you have a family. I happen to be single, so my clients and colleagues have more access to me than if I had young children and a husband at home. Boundaries are important, but you should set them to suit yourself.

VOICE MAIL

Voice mail is another wonderful invention that can rule your life if you don't impose rules. The first rule is that you do not have to take the time to call someone back if you are not interested in their services or their information. Am I suggesting that you be rude? Never. But the people who thrust their communication in your face during work hours without a thought as to its appropriateness or importance aren't worried about you or your feelings. Don't waste your time taking care of them.

As you did with your e-mail, decide whether you have to respond. Is this a high- or low-priority response? Does your company need any completed calls to be archived or can you delete the message? Remember that you can respond using a different form of communication and save time. If you leave me a voice message, I might shoot you an e-mail with the information you requested.

I frequently have to communicate with people I know will want to talk my ear off. I try and respond when I know they are at lunch or I leave a message after hours. I have fulfilled my obligation and communicated. I have not wasted my time. Again this is important when you have one or more top-priority projects with impending deadlines.

If you find it difficult to leave well-organized messages, don't rehearse them beforehand but do jot down the key points you want to communicate. You can follow your list and be a much-appreciated voice mail user.

TEXT MESSAGES AND INSTANT MESSAGES

I see kids texting while I am in line at the post office and other public places. They can move their thumbs faster than my eyes can follow! If you're using these as fun communication tools, do whatever works best in your circle of friends. When you use text messages and instant messages in the workplace, be aware of the following.

Does the person know how to respond? Don't assume that everyone knows the technology.

Is there a company policy for communicating this way?

Are you wasting company time (even if you are the company owner!) to communicate personal or unimportant things during the business day? Do you believe because it's fast, it's okay? Add all the minutes you squander over the course of a week and be prepared to be surprised!

Are you communicating information that should be archived by the company? Text messages and instant messages don't have a paper trail. If necessary, state the information also in a formal e-mail or letter if you're dealing with legal issues.

Text messages and instant messages are great tools when a fire has to be put out or you have an emergency, but don't overuse them!

PERSON-TO-PERSON

Yes, it's true. Face-to-face communication is becoming a lost art. Never underestimate the power of looking another human being in the eyes: You can hear the voice, watch for facial reactions, and create relationships better than with any other mode of communication. Of course, don't appear every five minutes at someone's cubicle and wear out your welcome. Be judicious! Talk in-person when your physical presence can add weight and meaning to what you have to say.

STAY UP-TO-SPEED WITH TECHNOLOGY

It can feel almost impossible to keep abreast of the fast-moving changes in technology. Every profession uses technology differently. And every office makes use of certain programs to help everyone work more efficiently. Don't overwhelm yourself! Master the tools that serve your business needs. Here are some ideas to help you do just that!

If you work for a large business or corporation, are you up-to-speed on the technology that the company has available? If not, can you register for classes to help you catch up? If none are scheduled, can you ask your employer if something can be put on the calendar? Chances are you aren't the only person in this situation. We can all use a periodic review.

If the company is small or is your home-based business, do you have an IT person you can consult with about the latest software and hardware that might be of service? Is it time for a computer upgrade?

Many stores that sell computers have staff members who can help you learn more about what's available. Why not go over to your local Circuit City, Best Buy, or Costco and see who can assist you.

Apple stores have classes you can take for the Mac. Have you taken advantage of any of them?

Microsoft has online tutorials. Are you a person who can learn using this format?

Do you have a favorite company whose equipment you trust? All the large companies such as Hewlett Packard have Web sites. From there you can subscribe to newsletters that will keep you abreast of the latest technology they offer. Software makers have the same service.

When you have a specific need, such as a system for automatically inputting business cards into your computer, do you make use of Google or any other search engine as a starting place for your research?

If you own your business, don't let your fear of gadgets and gizmos hold you back. We're in the twenty-first century and you just can't opt out. However, you can hire someone with the skill set you need. Technology is moving quickly. Instead of being overwhelmed, why not view the constant learning as a way to exercise your brain?

Following is a series of questions to help you focus on your specific needs. The clearer your communications, the less intimidating your interaction with a more technologically savvy person will be. And never be afraid to ask for clarification of terms. You'll pick up the jargon in no time:

- What do you need to research this week?
- Who will you go to for advice and assistance?

- How much money is in your budget?
- Do you back up material on a regular basis?

I hope this week has empowered you. Your quest to master technology doesn't mean you have to become a technology nerd. It does mean that you can make the decision to move from a fear-based employee or business owner to someone who is willing to again be a student. Redirect your energy and you will be astonished how savvy you will become!

WEEK FOUR

Clean Out and Back Up Computer Files

This week, you can

- Clean out your hard drive
- Back up your computer files … before it's too late

Time required: One hour or more, depending on the complexity of your computer files

When I was growing up, our home was always clean and organized. I have said many times I never saw piles of stuff anywhere. My mom was on top of our environment so that anyone who came by and saw it wouldn't judge her harshly. It was literally what she lived for. However, she had a secret that only my dad and I knew about: The insides of her drawers and closets were a mess.

My clients often have organized offices but a computer hard drive so messy it could star in a horror movie. Their reactions remind me of my mom's: If no one can see it, why bother? The answer is easy: You should bother to make *your* life easier. You do it for you. Our focus this week is to do just that: clean up and clear out the secret world of our hard drive.

STREAMLINE YOUR DATA

If your computer files are a mess, there's no time like the present to get them in order. They need to work in concert with your hard copy files. It should be easy for you to retrieve what you need, whether it's in your file cabinet or on your hard drive. Don't think for a minute that the jumble of material on your hard drive doesn't make you crazy. Is it easy to find what you need? Or do you spend time thinking, "Now how did I file that?" "Which folder did I put this document in?" Do you waste twenty minutes performing a keyword search of your entire hard drive?

Here are some guidelines to help you tackle a vital job I realize no one wants to do!

- Delete as many files as you can. Old information is going to clog up the computer and make it run slower. If that isn't a metaphor for what happens in your physical environment, I don't know what is.
- Some companies have an electronic archive on a different server. Take advantage and store completed projects there.
- Create categories so you can keep related information in the same place. When we created the physical file system, I suggested you use box-bottom hanging file folders and put your individual folders inside if you had a large category of related information. You can do the same on your computer. Create a large folder and place individual files inside. Once again let your master file list guide you.
- Don't clutter your main screen with too many documents. They can't all be that important! Save that page for the files to which you truly need a shortcut.
- If you can, color-code projects on your hard drive with the same color you use for related files in your file cabinet.
- Carefully name your master file categories. If you do this quickly or off the top of your head, it will be difficult to remember how to retrieve the information later.

BACK UP EVERYTHING

Find a way to back up (keep duplicate copies of) your files—preferably in more than one format. It isn't a question of whether your computer will crash but when! In fact, my computer crashed one night as I was finishing this book. You can back up files in a cyber account. You can copy them onto a CD each week. You can have your computer automatically copy files you create to an external hard drive. Whatever your choice, be consistent. Understand how your backup system works. Practice retrieving files from this area so that you aren't caught flat-footed in a real emergency! (See back-up tips on p. 132.)

Some people trust the handwritten format. I think that a marriage of both is a nice compromise. The key to electronic use is to realize that information can be lost. A friend of mine who is writing a book installed some fancy software that was designed to automatically back up his work. This freed him from copying the material onto a separate CD each evening. Can you guess what happened? The software had a bug. It kept copying his material until the computer crashed! His IT guys are desperately trying to salvage the material. Have you ever had a nightmare experience like this? How did you handle it? How did you change your method or technology so that you could avoid it in the future?

When I work on a book, in addition to backing up material as I go along, I e-mail completed chapters to my best friend

Susie, who does my desktop publishing. Susie formats the chapter and it then goes to my editor. In the middle of the writing process, if the worst disaster possible should happen (I live in Los Angeles, so earthquake, anyone?), I would know that this critical information was in safe hands—both with another person and on my e-mail server. How do you safeguard your work?

Here are two simple yet powerful tips. One, get in the habit of saving your work as you go through a document. I tend to save every other paragraph. Have you ever been hit by a power surge and lost a document? Rather than pulling out your hair, just tap the save icon like a mad person. Or have your computer do this automatically at intervals you establish. By the way, these phantom files can create a bit of debris on your computer, so don't forget to delete those earlier versions when the document is complete.

My other trick is to include the date in every file name, for example, ReginaLeeds. 12-07-08.doc. The time you'll save when you're seeking a particular version is immeasurable. This is especially useful when sending documents back and forth to colleagues who may make contributions. My editor and I, for example, send each other notes on the chapters as I write them. Corrections, revisions, deletions, and additions fly back and forth across the Internet via e-mail. A date saves us a lot of time when we have to retrieve the latest version of a file.

When it comes to the information housed on your computer, remember to keep it as streamlined, logical, and organized as you do your physical files. Clutter is clutter even if it's floating around on your hard drive or in cyberspace.

AUGUST SUMMARY

WEEK ONE

Understand how you really communicate. Your issues with others may be due to a difference in communication style.

WEEK TWO

Make e-mail serve rather than enslave you. Make decisions, file appropriately, and don't forget to archive.

WEEK THREE

Use e-mails, instant messages, and text messages to your advantage.

WEEK FOUR

Keep the world of your computer as organized as that of your office. Learn to back up your material before the inevitable crash.

9. SEPTEMBER

Fine-Tune for Fall

Our imaginative minds add value to our lives by helping us think of our circumstances not in terms of what is but in terms of what might be.

—*DAILY OM*

SOMETHING ABOUT SEEING LABOR Day on the calendar and the memory of homework assignments and the first day of school seem to be tattooed on my heart. How is it for you? Even if we don't have school-age children at home, we certainly remember returning to school ourselves. In addition, we know the holiday season is on the horizon. Just as we're learning how to get organized and stay on top of everything, additional obligations are headed our way.

Summer is a time for fun and relaxation. Fall is the time of the harvest. If you have been working with me for several months now, you must have a beautiful harvest in terms of your organizing skills. If you're just starting, you can achieve quite a lot before the year ends. Let's dedicate the first part of this month to reviewing our efforts. This is something you'll do periodically for the rest of your life. Environments don't stay static and neither do our interests and needs.

The second half of the month deals with setting up a home office. Whether it's the location of a formal business or where you run your home and family affairs, having an office space in the home is essential. Finally, this month is about integrating new demands on our time into our already busy lives. We'll be working on this till the end of the year. Too often the holiday season is a time of exhaustion. Let's make this one a time you consciously create and enjoy.

WORK HABIT OF THE MONTH: FINISH OLD BUSINESS

We all have communications we'd rather not face. Are you delaying an e-mail response or a phone call? This month you'll grin and deal with it. Every day, at what-ever time you decide is the most appropri-ate, you're going to make one phone call, return one dreaded e-mail, or write that long overdue thank-you note. Do this small task at the time of day that represents your personal peak. Then be glad the task is crossed off your list! Do one unwelcome task a day, and they won't pile up again.

HOME HABIT OF THE MONTH: MAINTAIN YOUR HOME

While it's true that psychologists have found that it takes twenty-one consecutive days of repeating an action to form a habit, some important actions don't need to be performed every day. This month, exam-ine your home for a list of *periodic* actions that need to be performed.

To this end, make a list of at least four things you should do each month to keep your home running smoothly. Here are some ideas to help jump-start your think-ing:

- Check the filters, from the one in your water pitcher to the one in your air/heating system.
- Test the smoke detectors.
- Do you need to change the batteries in flashlights, baby monitors, and phones?
- Check the outside lights to see whether any are burned out.
- Make sure you have supplies to re-place bulbs, batteries, and filters.
- Check your car's fluids and air tire pressure.

What's on your list? Please schedule these important maintenance items by making a note on your calendar or having your computer remind you automatically on the day you designate.

WEEK ONE

Improve Your Commute

This week, you can

- Make concrete improvements to your commute experience
- Explore ways to help you pass the time

Time required: Thirty minutes

Is THERE ANYONE OUT THERE WHO enjoys commuting? As a native New Yorker who rode the subways daily for many years, I know only too well how a simple train ride from Brooklyn to Manhattan could color my entire day.

But for better or worse, your commute represents the bridge between home and office. It exerts tremendous influence over your workday. This week we're going to look for ways to improve it. Whether you travel by bus, train, automobile, or public transportation, let's see if we can't create a smoother, more organized, and therefore, more profitable ride for you. Have your calendar or notebook handy so you can make a list of items you'd like to purchase or investigate.

USE YOUR COMMUTE TIME

No matter what mode of transportation you use, my first question is, "What kind of person are you?" Here are questions for you to answer:

1. Are you a morning person or a night person? (A morning person is more likely to want a book on tape playing as he commutes than a night person, who probably wants to withdraw and recharge for the day.)
2. Can you read while you are a passenger in a moving vehicle or does that upset your stomach?
3. Do you like to work in public places? Could you snooze in a public place?

4. What is your sense of personal space? Does a crowd make you feel claustrophobic or comforted?
5. Is your commute a time for relaxation or do you like to review work for the day?

There is no one answer when it comes to commuting. Now that I live in Los Angeles, the car capital of the United States, I am much more appreciative of my life at home in New York City, where public transportation rules. There is much to be said for leaving the driving to someone else. Do you spend a great deal of time commuting to work? Can you improve this situation? For example, if you drive now, could you take public transportation and use the downtime to read or work on your laptop? Can you carpool? Thinking outside the box, how can you make a negative commute into a positive experience?

Whether you take a subway, a bus, a commuter train, or drive your own car, here are some things you can do to make your ride more enjoyable.

Your journey starts before you leave the house. Don't weigh yourself down with a heavy purse, messenger bag, briefcase, or tote. Clean it out each night and carry only what you absolutely need. Carrying excessive weight can make you exhausted before you get to work, no matter how much sleep you've had. Don't bring everything home with you at night. A rested brain will function better than an exhausted one. The same can be said of your physical body.

Wear comfortable shoes. Keep your dress shoes at work or carry them with you. You're going to be wearing your work shoes all day. Give your feet a rest and some variety.

If you don't drive to work and commute time is when you relax, think about buying an iPod, an MP3 player, or a Nintendo DS to help you pass the time. Read a good, old-fashioned book or a newspaper. If you prefer a book, carry a small one or a paperback to save weight. And, of course, you can always listen to a book on tape.

Never underestimate the power of doing nothing to rest your brain and nervous system. You'll be thinking all day, so why not people-watch now?

If your commuter train or subway has you packed in like a sardine, consider taking an earlier train. Those few minutes alone at work before everyone else arrives can give you the edge when it comes to planning your day or cleaning up your desk (on the off chance you didn't do it before you left last night). By the same token, perhaps a later train in the evening will allow you to do your homework at the office. Then when you get home you can relax and truly be with your family.

Many of us use time on the street walking to appointments or the train or bus for making phone calls. As mentioned, no one else is interested in the details of your private life or your business deals. As they say in preschool, "Use your inside voice!"

Be sure you have healthy snacks every day.

Even if you're lucky enough to work for a company that provides healthy fare, unless it's free you can save money by bringing your own. In the event of an emergency en route to work, you'll have some provisions. I always keep a sixteen-ounce bottle of water on hand as well.

SAFELY ON THE ROAD AGAIN ... AND AGAIN

I don't set too many reminders on my computer calendar. One reminder I do suggest is to have your car serviced. The price of gas is rising to new highs as I write this, so have your vehicle serviced regularly to conserve fuel—and keep you safe on the road.

Speaking of safety on the road, invest in a road security or assistance program. The Auto Club has one and so do many automobile manufacturers and unions. On Star is a subscription service geared to keeping you safe in the event of an accident. If your car is stolen, On Star will find it and direct the authorities to it. The service provides help in many forms, including unlocking your doors from the satellite should you lock your child, pet, or keys inside. It also provides hands-free telephone calling while you are driving. I have it on my vehicle and have found it an invaluable tool.

Your registration and proof of insurance should be handy in your glove compartment, in case you are ever stopped by the police. This is not the time to be fumbling around while you mumble, "Officer, I know they are here somewhere. Just give me another minute, will you?"

Take a minute each week to clean out your vehicle. Remember when I said that stuff makes a "noise"? You're affected by all this debris and chaos.

Keep emergency supplies in the trunk of your car. New cars come with an undersized spare tire called a donut. It will get you to a gas station. Do you know how to change a tire? Is there a jack in the trunk? This is one great reason to join an emergency roadside assistance program. Let them change the tire! If you have an older car, check your spare tire every six months.

Here are some items to store in your car:

- Jumper cables
- Water (change out every six months; use the old water for your plants)
- Nonperishable food items
- Extra food and water for pets
- Flares, a first aid kit, a radio, and a flashlight. Check the flashlight batteries every six months as well. There are radios you crank for service, eliminating the need for more batteries.
- If you are handy and work on your vehicle, have a basic toolkit.
- Extra fluids for your vehicle, such as oil and window washer fluid.
- I live in earthquake country so I carry extra shoes and a blanket. You can get a lightweight emergency blanket that is about the size of a pack of cigarettes at your local camping store.

- If you might be working on your vehicle in an emergency, have some paper towels or cloths to wipe your hands, a hand sanitizer, and perhaps a ground cloth.
- If you travel with children and deliver them to a bus stop or to school, stock up on the supplies every parent needs, including Handi Wipes, emergency snacks and drinks, and entertainment such as books and DVDs (if you have a portable player in the car).

As you go through this list, you will remember things that are important to you. Note them. We've been working on eliminating procrastination, so set aside the time to shop for and assemble any tools or toys you need to make your commute better. While you're checking equipment, see whether any kitchen tools might make the morning easier. I have many clients who invest in automatic coffeemakers with to-go cups. When they enter their kitchen in the wee hours to begin their day, they are greeted by the delicious aroma of coffee—and taking it to go eliminates a stop at Starbucks on the way to work, saving time and money.

Getting organized is one of the ways we nurture ourselves to success. If your commute is perpetually difficult, you may still be addicted on some level to drama and self-sabotage. This week I invite you to make this important time a period of ease and an opportunity to rest your mind. The day will bring its challenges and triumphs. Use your commute to get ready for anything!

WEEK TWO

Organize Your Home Schedule

This week, you can

- Consider the merits of job sharing, flextime, or part-time employment
- Revisit your children's activities and social demands to be sure their year is not overwhelming
- Craft a wise family plan, especially in terms of commute schedules

Time required: Varies

THIS WEEK IS DEDICATED TO WORK-ing parents. While all of us try to lead a balanced life that includes alone time, fun with family and friends, and time for household chores, working parents have another full-time job. As with all growth, let's begin with a look at ourselves. When we heal ourselves we're in a more powerful position to help others.

If you began this program way back in January, you may have been overly enthusiastic in setting goals. As the New Year begins, a media frenzy eggs us on to change. And although it's change for the better, it can be overwhelming. Is there something or perhaps several things you'd like to remove from your schedule? Is your

exercise program too ambitious? Did you sign up for classes after work only to realize it's not the right time to go for your master's degree? If your schedule is organized within an inch of your life, drop something. You can always pick it up later when the time is more appropriate.

TRY FLEXTIME OR JOB SHARING

There may be creative ways to ease your work burdens. Would your company allow you to telecommute? Why not examine the possibility before you speak to your supervisors? Instead of just asking whether it's possible, you can come up with a concrete way this would work. If you can work at home even one or two days a week, you'll be saving wear and tear on your nervous system, not to mention your car if you drive to work. You'll need a room dedicated to work and a professional setup. We're going to spend the last two weeks of this month creating the perfect home office for you. (Don't worry, you don't need to have it this minute to consider telecommuting!)

What about flextime? If your normal work week is Monday through Friday, could you accomplish your work if you came into the office three or four days a week but arrived earlier in the morning and worked into the evening? In general you need to have been at the job and established yourself before you can ask for a flexible arrangement like this.

Have a well-thought-out plan before you go to your employer. Has the company tried this before? How would your job change in terms of output and working with others? If this is a new idea for your company, ask for a trial period.

Job sharing requires two people who not only have the same work ethic but are compatible in terms of communication and skill level. It requires careful planning. You don't want to share a job with someone who so outshines you that he ultimately replaces you or who lacks good follow-through so all the work is dumped in your lap.

If your job is causing you more stress than it's worth, can you switch to a part-time schedule and still survive financially?

If you can do that for a few months, you can use your downtime to search for a full-time job that's better suited to your talents and perhaps closer to home.

EXAMINE YOUR KIDS' SCHEDULE

I have to admit it: I am bewildered when I look at children's schedules these days. Their lives are planned to the minute. They are urged to be scholars and athletes. And that's just preschool. Examine your child's life before you launch into the new school year. Is everything necessary? We seem to have developed into a society where downtime is a negative concept and children find themselves in an overly committed, exhausting regime that robs them of their only chance to be kids. Find a balanced approach.

After you and your children know what their school schedule looks like this year, it's time to figure out something even more important: How will this schedule work in terms of commuting? Who in your family will deliver the children in the morning? Or do they go to a school bus stop? What happens after school if you are still at work? Will another parent take your child with theirs to an after-school activity? Does the school have extended care? Who will pick up your child and bring him home? Who is the homework monitor in the home?

You may be thinking that these are obvious questions and indeed they are. But what usually happens is that people fly by the seat of their pants. Instead, figure out the logistics and have a backup plan. Be sure that the schedule is readily available for your spouse, your older children, your designated caretakers, and anyone else involved with your child's care. "Where is that phone number?" should never be uttered in an emergency.

Craft a solution that's works for you, your family, and this particular school year. After all, your child will only be young once, you will only be the parent of this child at this age one time as well. Organized, balanced living will enable you to enjoy this time in life rather than fight your way through it.

Are you a devoted computer geek who can't wait to take out a spreadsheet and get started? Or are you devoted to your daily planner's calendar? Regardless of your communication style, adopt a solution that suits your needs. And if your spouse or your children have different styles, guess what? Once the schedule is worked out, you can transfer the information to any format that works for the individuals in your home. I've seen several wonderful versions of a family plan. Why not try the following and see if it works?

Create a contact sheet on your computer. You want everyone in the family to know key phone numbers at a glance: schools, police, fire, doctors, hospitals, work contacts, relatives, and friends. Do you have this information programmed into your cell phone? Although that makes life easy, what do you do if the phone is lost or stolen? Keeping an electronic ver-

> Are you a visual person? If your family would like a fun solution and you have the wall space, hanging a large calendar can make it easier to keep track of everyone in the family. You can buy a plain one at an office supply store such as Staples or get a fancy one at a store such as Pottery Barn. The latter will be most likely in a chalkboard format that you'll need to update regularly.

sion will offer everyone a way to stay in touch and make updates and changes easy to handle.

Then work out the basic schedule of each family member. Just as mom and dad need to know that Johnny is at baseball practice on Tuesday after school, Johnny needs to know where mom and dad are.

If one of you hits the road for business on a regular basis, you can alter the basic document for each trip to show dad or mom's present location. Indicate the time zone as well so your child can begin to develop a sense of time and travel. Don't hesitate to show a young child a map and indicate where the traveling parent is that night.

Print your contact sheet and keep it accessible for all. Place it in a reference binder using sheet protectors or use magnets to attach it to the refrigerator. E-mail it to your spouse and to anyone else in your family network that needs to have this information.

Family dinnertime is an ideal time to check in about schedule changes. It also affords an opportunity to find out how everyone is doing in their various activities. If a nightly meal is a fantasy for your family, try and plan dinner at least once a week. Nothing beats face-to-face communicating over a good meal!

WEEK THREE

Plan Your Home Office

This week, you can

- Plan to transform a room in your home into a place to do business, whether you have a personal business, telecommute, or run your own home
- Make sure all needed office equipment, furniture, and supplies are on hand

Time required: Approximately ninety minutes, plus an additional ninety minutes if you need to shop for supplies

MY SMALL BUSINESS HAS EVOLVED over the past twenty years in ways I could not have imagined. As my job expanded, so did the physical space dedicated as my home office. For many years, my office was my guest room. I love to entertain out-of-town guests, so when the time came to make the transition to a home office, I felt a touch of sadness. The room is small, so there was no way to combine both functions.

Once I made the commitment to the space, it seemed to effortlessly grow and change in concert with my business. In the end, having a home office has been a blessing. I have experienced the truth of one of the Zen organizing principles that I teach

my clients and students: We succeed in direct proportion to the respect we give our projects. (And my guests seem comfortable on the blow-up air mattress in my living room.)

In Eastern philosophy it is important to dedicate a place solely for meditation. On those days when you don't feel like meditating, the energy in the space itself will draw you in to meditate. We can extrapolate a great truth from this wisdom: Areas in our homes should be used for specific purposes. When mail, work, school papers, and all manner of paper debris generously litter our kitchen counters, the dining room table, and the nightstand, we are inviting procrastination and less-than-stellar work results. We're also setting an example for our children that will make good grades more difficult to achieve. Let's remove all these obstacles and create a great home space dedicated to the work of our lives.

We begin with a few questions to help clarify your needs and how you will use the space available to you. Use your organizing notebook. Are you ready? The better the plan, the easier it will be to set up the perfect home office for you.

DECIDE HOW TO USE
YOUR SPACE

Why do you feel you need a home office? Will you be completing work you can't get to at the office? Or is this space for a home-based business? Are you a stay-at-home parent who needs a set place to pay bills and run your home? Be specific about all the activities that you want to do in this new setup. After you know your activities, take a realistic look at the space. Can it support everything you're asking of it?

Will the space be a dedicated home office or will it be a room with a shared agenda? The most common combo is home office and guest room or home gym. If your combo is guest room and office, how often do guests sleep over? Will the prolonged presence of someone in this room negatively affect your ability to run your business? How much room does the current bed take up in the space? Can you down-size to a futon couch, a daybed, a Murphy bed, or a pull-out sofa?

Will more than one family member be using this room? The most common example here is a wife running the home from this room during the day and the husband finishing up work-related items in the evening. But what if each of you runs a separate home-based business? How will you handle the noise factor when you are both on the phone at the same time? Or what if one of you is on the phone, while the other struggles to complete reports due on a deadline? Is this setup realistic?

THINK ABOUT
THE PHYSICAL SETUP

You will probably spend a considerable amount of time in your home office, so making it inviting as well as functional is important. In this section we go through a list of needs and concerns so you can develop a plan that's tailored to honor the work to be accomplished in this space.

Is there a need for two desks? Perhaps more to the point, is there room for two? If the answer is yes, will they be different or compatible styles? If you have inherited some furniture you'd like to use, why not give it some snap with a coat of paint?

Can you convert a closet into a storage area for office supplies and archived material? Built-in shelves are wonderful, but simple bookcases will do the trick as well. If the closet already has one shelf, see if you have room for one more shelf between the existing shelf and the ceiling. You can use a plain piece of lumber with a brace on each side to hold the shelf in place. If the shelf will house heavy materials, it must be reinforced!

If the room has no closet, do you have space for something like a dresser? You might have inherited one of those as well or you could get one from Craigslist (www.craigslist.org) or Freecycle (www. freecycle.org). Once again, a coat of paint will bring a fresh perspective to a piece of furniture that looks a bit tired. Make it yours and don't be afraid to be bold! Stores like Ikea or Home Depot can also offer inexpensive solutions.

Do you need to paint the room? What about the floor? Does the carpet need to be cleaned? Or could the wood floor use a rug? Do you have plastic runners for under your seat so you can slide in and out of your desk with ease?

What about your walls? Put up some things that will give you joy to look at and inspire the work you want to do in this room. For example, I loved the Russell Crowe movie *Gladiator*. I framed the movie poster, and it inspires me daily to be courageous in my work. What image would do that for you?

Is there a window? Does it need new blinds, drapes, or curtains?

If possible, follow this simple but powerful Feng Shui rule: Never sit with your back to the door but rather face it. (However,

don't sit in direct line with the door.) Try this out for yourself. You really will be in a power position. Be forewarned, however, that you may become addicted to the power position in every room. My friends make fun of me because I can't sit with my back to *any* door! When we go to a restaurant, they always ask, "Regina, where do you want to sit?"

Stock up on supplies so you have not only what you need but a modest backup stash. Don't go overboard. You don't want paper to turn yellow or pens to dry up. Here's a list of some common supplies you will need.

Scotch tape
Stapler and staples; staple remover
Paper for the printer and fax machine
Large and small paper clips
Sharp scissors
Pens, pencils, highlighters, and
    Sharpies
A letter opener
A ruler
Small drawer containers for your drawers or one preset drawer organizer you can simply pop into place and fill with supplies
Binders, tabs or dividers, and sheet protectors are useful for many
Note cards
A good-sized wastebasket
Lighting: If there is space, put a lamp on your desk rather than relying solely on overhead lights. If you have spotlights in the room, can one shine directly onto your desk?

A file cabinet: The most common is a two- or four-drawer metal cabinet with a lock, but you can find cabinets in other materials such as wood or buy individual containers in wicker or some other natural fiber.

Make a list of the equipment you will need and use. A common list today would include the following:

Computer or laptop
Speakers
Printer
Shredder
Scanner
Fax machine

And last but not least, set up your office so that you don't waste time. I can't tell you how many of my clients have their printer across the room from their desk rather than nearby! If you have the room, a cart on wheels can hold all the basics: your fax, printer, and scanner. Try and keep your desk clear so that when you aren't using the computer, you have space to write or spread out a project. You don't want to feel cramped. Think about this as you place each item in the room on your floor plan. Play with some sketches. Your room should be efficient and visually inviting. The month of March (page 67) covers desk and file setup in detail. That material will serve you well as you prepare to establish a home work area. If you are beginning with this month, please take a minute to read that chapter.

By the end of this week, you should have a clear vision for your home office. Now, create a shopping list and have those items in place before you attack next week. Time to make the transition happen!

WEEK FOUR

Create Your Home Office

This week, you can

- Put together a functioning home office

Time required: Two hours or more depending on your situation

Now that you have a plan, let's implement it! For our purposes, we're scheduling all this work in a fourteen-day window. If you need more time to paint or wait for furniture delivery, for example, schedule the steps of this project so that it stays on track. Very often we begin a project with great gusto and then get bogged down in the details. You don't want a room in limbo for months to come. All it takes is making appointments on your calendar. Note delivery dates. Schedule the time to paint. Figure out what items you still need to shop for, if any, and make a date to shop.

This week, you need to clean out the room. Have some sturdy garbage bags on hand. If you need to move furniture to other rooms, have some extra hands on deck. And if you're offloading furniture, make an appointment with your local char-ity for pick up or place an ad on an online service such as Craigslist or Freecycle.

WATCH A FUNCTIONING OFFICE MATERIALIZE

Here are some guidelines to help with the transition from spare room to real office.

If your office will be a dual-purpose space (office and guest room or office and home gym), have office furniture on one side of the room and a guest bed or gym equipment on the other. This physical separation will reinforce the separation of activities. Besides, you don't want to be sitting at your computer trying to write the great American novel while your spouse is sweating over your keyboard. Rugs are a good way to note separate zones in any room.

Please move the furniture now. If your bed is large, it might be best to store it and use a daybed or futon couch that opens up. If you can't store it, think about selling it. Tell your friends what you are up to and you might find a buyer close to home! If you own your home, consider a Murphy bed. The room will stay clear and still be ready to give any guest a good night's sleep. (A Murphy bed pulls down from the wall. I sleep in one whenever I go home to New York and stay with friends. They are amazingly comfortable.)

If you are using the room for a double purpose and have a closet, it too will no doubt have to do double-duty as well. In lieu of built-ins, a bookcase is probably going to be your best bet in terms of office supply storage. You might also be able to use one or two rolling units made of heavy-duty plastic with three or four drawers. The top drawers are shallow and can house small office supplies and the deeper drawers can hold paper and binders. This isn't my first choice, but it will help in a pinch.

If your desk lacks drawers, you can have one unit like this and roll it out from the closet when you sit down to work. You can also use two two-drawer file cabinets to hold up a large, finished piece of wood to create a desk with a lot of workspace. A plain door will also do the trick and you can feed your computer wires through the opening for the door handle. Your local home store will put the wood stain of your choosing on the wood. You'd be amazed how well this solution works!

DRESS FOR SUCCESS

If you are running a business from home, it will be tempting to work in your pajamas, not make the bed, and let the kids run wild in your office. Treat your office space and the work you hope to accomplish here with respect. Would you go to an office outside your home without taking a shower and dressed in your sweats? Of course not! Unless it's an emergency, don't do it at home either.

Do you use the closet to house out-of-season clothes? Or if the room is also a guest room, do you want at least half the closet reserved for your guests? Whatever your situation, the closet should be organized. In the case of off-season clothing storage, why not keep your clothes in hanging canvas storage bags? You can get large ones that hold many garments. This will keep them clean during off-season months. Go through everything before you transport items here. If you didn't wear something this year, it may be time to donate it to charity. If it's worn, torn, or tattered, thank it for the good service you enjoyed and then chuck it!

Many of my clients want a home office and a place that functions as a craft center. Hobbies such as scrapbooking take up lots of room. You'll want to sit at a long table rather than use your desk. Use a

> If your children are young and you have no child care, they will have to be with you. But be sure they can amuse themselves and that their paraphernalia leaves when they do. Or have a basket of toys they can use only in this room. Fido deserves a dog bed and his own basket in this room if space allows. Fluffy the cat will want some items dedicated for her use as well.

beautiful wood table, a folding table, or a plain door sitting on two multiple-drawer storage units or two simple sawhorses. With choices like to this, you experience the creativity inherent in the organizing process.

I love to use the storage towers featured in the Exposures catalog to house photos and supplies. You can find suitable solutions at The Container Store as well. Every hobby has its own world of magazines and tools. Check out Creative Memories online or your local scrapbooking store for more storage ideas.

MAKE YOURSELF MOBILE

By midweek, the physical space should be transformed. In closing, let's consider how you can make yourself mobile while at home. It's easy to have a wireless Internet system installed. That way, you'll be able to take your laptop into your backyard on summer days or park yourself at the dining room table on winter days while dinner is cooking. You can also take advantage of this mobility if you are sharing the space with a spouse who also works at home. While one of you is making deals on the phone, the other can be taking care of company business on the laptop. Take full advantage of what technology now offers us.

As a Zen organizer, I must ask you to make one promise: Don't leave your paperwork or laptop in your temporary work zones. At day's end, everything should be returned to your office. This is important if you live alone but especially if you have children. It's so easy to allow your work to dominate your life. But nothing should trump family time. It's critical to teach your children by your example that there is a place for every item and a time for every activity. These are superior skills to take into the busy time of year that lies before us.

Now, congratulate yourself on a month of hard work. What is your reward going to be? You certainly deserve one.

SEPTEMBER SUMMARY

WEEK ONE

Use your commute time to make yourself more productive.

WEEK TWO

Decide if job sharing, flextime, or a shift to part-time employment will benefit your situation. Are your children overcommitted? Check their schedules. Be sure all family members stay connected.

WEEK THREE

Would you like to work at home? Carefully plan for your office.

WEEK FOUR

Turn your home office plans into a reality.

10. OCTOBER

Ease Business Travel

Who looks outside, dreams; who looks inside, awakes.
—CARL JUNG

Once you are organized in your office setting, it can be a challenge to maintain the same level of order while traveling on business. This is a common problem and simply requires two things to be successful: a solid plan and some experience. In this chapter you'll find all the tips and tricks you'll need to create a plan that works not only in concert with your office setup but also with the way you think while you travel. After all, not every businessperson is a born road warrior.

WORK HABIT OF THE MONTH: UPDATE YOUR CONTACTS

I've rarely met anyone whose contact list was up-to-date. Are their Post-its on your computer or desk with current numbers that need to be logged into your computer or written in your address book? Do numbers need to be added to your cell phone? Have folks left your office, your life, or planet Earth and need to be deleted? The time has arrived to make short shrift of this task. Every day, enter as many contacts as you can in five minutes. In three weeks, when this has become an ingrained habit, you may be caught up. Then it will be easy to keep up these contacts.

HOME HABIT OF THE MONTH: BE GRATEFUL

Each evening before you retire, take a minute to review your day. I'd like you to jot down three things for which you are grateful. If you can, create your list from the activities of the current day. This list will help foster an "attitude of gratitude" in your life. And remember that your list can include the most mundane things. Here are some examples: I am grateful that I was waved into traffic on the freeway this morning, that my relationship with Pam the receptionist was pleasant all day long, and that I was able to complete all my sales calls with ease this morning.

WEEK ONE

Get in Sync

This week, you can

- Put together the various tools at your disposal to serve you

Time required: Two hours (or more depending on your situation)

THIS WEEK IS ALL ABOUT BRINGING the various tools you use in your work life into sync. Your laptop, office computer, files, calendar, and briefcase may currently function as individual moons orbiting around Planet You. Let's make them pieces of the same solar system.

DECIDE WHETHER TO TRAVEL WITH FILES

If you're working the months in sequence, you already have a functional file system. If you haven't organized your file system yet, do so this week (see page 67). Your files are meant to be creative storehouses of the material you need to have handy in your life, but file cabinets often become unintentional archival storage containers or memorabilia holders.

When I work with high-level executive clients, I rarely find a single file in their possession. They don't need to store and access information; they have an assistant who does that for them. In a way, when you have an active, working file system, it functions as your assistant. Without question, creating a file system is one of the most time-consuming, labor-intensive organizing projects. But there is equally no doubt that over the course of a few months, the amount of time and energy it will save will make the endeavor worthwhile.

When it's time to travel, you may be tempted to take important files with you on the road. But have you ever been faced with the decision about what material you will need and thought, "I can't decide what I need. I'll just take *all* these files with me." Taking a minute instead to make those decisions will spare your back as you lug your briefcase or shoulder bag with you.

Once you have the files you know you will need, see whether you can pare them down to the exact papers you need to reference. Better yet, make copies of pertinent material and take only those pages with you. Some professions are paper intensive and this may not be possible. However, unless you are an attorney or working in real estate, you will probably be able to whittle your stack down to the precious few items you really need.

If your files are organized and you leave something necessary behind, it shouldn't be difficult for someone in your office to locate the material and either scan the pages and e-mail them to you or fax them to your location. All major chain hotels have business centers now, making life easier for all business travelers.

YOUR BRIEFCASE: HELPER OR HERNIA INDUCER?

As strange as it sounds, I rarely see an organized briefcase. And I find the most intriguing items inside the compartments, such as old candy, broken office supplies such as jammed staplers, and materials from projects and conferences from months earlier. What's in your briefcase? Take a minute to clean it out. Don't put anything back unless you know it will either serve you no matter where you go (such as a working mini-stapler) or relates to the work you need to accomplish for the current trip.

Here are some guidelines to help you repack your briefcase.

Food items: We all need quick pick-me-ups when we travel—trail mix and health food bars top my list. Never put any food items in your briefcase that can spoil, ooze, leak, or pop. I once carried a bottled cappuccino drink on a flight from L.A. to N.Y. The pressure of a quick descent into New York caused the lid to pop up just enough to seep. I didn't realize this until I got to the city. In the cab, the coffee leaked slowly onto my slacks. Let's just say it looked like I had had an accident. Worse, I smelled like a coffee emporium. Learn from my mistake. And when you return, be sure to clean out any food items from your bag.

Office supplies: If you find you use common office supplies such as a stapler, tape, rubber bands, or paper clips, by all means carry a few. Just don't pack that full box you picked up at Costco. Make sure your small supplies can't fly all over the inside of your briefcase. At a craft store like Michael's, you can find an assortment of plastic bags that seal. They are like the Ziploc bags you get at the grocery store, except you can get them in every size imaginable. Also available are minikits with small versions of a stapler, tape dispenser, and the like in a handy container. Buy one only if you will use it, not because you think it's cute!

Papers: By now, the papers in your office should be organized and in their designated place. Keep these papers likewise separated in your briefcase so that they are organized at your destination, as well as easy to file when you are back in your office. You can use individual travel file folders or something as simple as a paper clip. I like to use plastic travel pockets, which are plastic file folders that can be closed to safeguard the contents. When you're on the road, you'll find it calming to have all related information in one place. Take only what you need (eliminate), keep it all together (categorize), and then your on-the-road organizing will be a breeze.

The bag itself: Take an honest look at your briefcase. Is it tattered, worn, and old or outdated? Is it something you got for free at a conference? Is that the image you want to project? You want to have tools that make you feel good when you use them. Examine your briefcase and see if it needs to be replaced. Empty your briefcase regularly, at least once a week and preferably each night when you get home. Divest yourself of papers and files you no longer need. Trash, recycle, or shred the minute you can. The next day, file papers that must be returned to the office. Be sure material that will be archived is removed and sent to storage.

YOUR LAPTOP

There you are on a plane or in a hotel room ready to do your work when suddenly you remember that you haven't kept your laptop in sync with your computer. The latest version of the Jones file is back on your office computer, not your travel laptop. What's the point of being mobile if you don't have the correct information at your fingertips? If you're traveling back and forth from home to office working at both ends, this is probably not an issue. It usually rears its ugly head when your laptop is used just for travel and that isn't a big part of your work life. By the way, how old is your battery? Don't forget to take a cord and a cable if needed.

When you travel, remember that you can use a flash drive to transport your electronic files, provided you have a computer to use at the other end.

Sync up, e-mail, or transfer via flash drive whatever you need while you are traveling. Keep your laptop organized in the same manner you do your office computer. I can't tell you how many times I've encountered a client who is trying out different organizing systems or programs to see which one works best. Try something new on your home system but keep your laptop in sync with your office computer.

If you work for a large company or corporation, procedures, protocols, and computer programs will be in place. If you are self-employed, work with an IT person or a friendly, knowledgeable sales person or tech support person who can guide you in selecting the software that will make your business life much easier.

We've been developing habits all year. As I have mentioned in previous chapters, psychologists say it takes twenty-one consecutive days to turn an action into a new habit. When you try out a new computer program, organizing system, or tool, give it twenty-one consecutive days before you decide to abandon it. One or two days won't tell the tale. You'll be giving in to your natural resistance to change.

DON'T FORGET THE LITTLE GUYS

No, the little guys aren't your short relatives and friends; I'm referring to your PDA, cell phone, and any other small electronic device you use. For example, if your business trips are all done via automobile and you have purchased a GPS system, don't forget to download the latest updates before you hit the road. This is the kind of detail you can note in your calendar, put on a travel to-do list, or have a computer calendar program such as Outlook send you a reminder.

Sync up your electronic devices so they all talk the same language and also have up-to-date information. I once dropped my cell phone in a puddle, which meant I lost my address book. Later, I learned that my carrier could have updated my address book automatically and stored it in cyberspace. It sounds so pedestrian, but reading the manuals that come with our electronic tools is a good idea. Or if you have friends who enjoy the latest technology, ask them to show you what to do. If you have a Mac, Apple has classes you can attend. In the long run, it will be worth it.

Before we leave this week, let me say that once your tools are organized along the same lines as your office setup, the biggest investment of time is over. Going forward, you need to devote only a few minutes on a regular basis to maintenance. Do you find maintenance a pain in the neck? Well, maintenance is what life is about. Nothing remains static, does it? You need to maintain your weight, your friendships and relationships, your garden, your home … the list is endless. No point complaining about something that's just a fact of life! Turn your attention instead to how much better you're going to function now, knowing that all your tools are working together.

WEEK TWO

When You Have to Get Ready at the Last Minute

This week, you can

- Get yourself and your office ready for your departure

Time required: Two hours or less

THERE YOU ARE, ALL READY TO TACKLE the business of the day, when your boss informs you that you're going to a conference in another city. You think briefly about the additional air miles or the chance to stay in a lovely hotel. If you're really lucky, the information offered at the conference will interest you! Then your stomach drops with a sickening thud. What about all the work on your desk? What about those special projects that are moving along with what feels like constant prodding from you? In addition, you shudder to imagine your family's reaction when they hear you are leaving town. An opportunity suddenly becomes an albatross around your neck. This week we take a step back and make a plan.

Your preparation is twofold: Identify what needs to be done at the office to keep your projects and daily work moving forward in your absence; and decide what

special plans need to be made on the home front. If you are a working parent, you have the most demanding situation of all. Let's take each one in turn.

PREPARE YOUR OFFICE FOR YOUR TRIP

Preparing your office for your departure on a business trip is similar to what you did last month to prepare your office for your vacation. Your desk, files, and office space should be organized by this point, making it easier to direct others to whatever they need to access in your absence. The key difference is that now you will plan to be in contact, rather than hoping those holding down the fort will be able to cope without you.

If information in your office is for your eyes only, find a way to keep it in a locked drawer. Whether it's a file cabinet drawer or a desk drawer will depend on the size and the quantity of the information. Separate any personal papers, such as details for your 401K plan, and keep those at home.

Remember that a key tenet of Zen organizing is that the whole of anything is overwhelming. You always need to break things down into manageable chunks to succeed. In this case, make a list of the tasks you perform every day. Decide which ones can wait for your return (label with the letter *A*) and which can be given to your assistant or a coworker to perform in your absence (label with the letter *B*). Make your requests for the items that need to be handled in your absence well in ad-

vance of your trip and not as you're waving good-byes to everyone. If the person has never covered for you, he or she may require some training, and you'll have to factor in the time to do that either in person or through written notes.

The next order of business is to tackle the projects you are working on. Make a list of every project on your plate. Next to each, write the due date for the submission of your report or the final completed project. How many will not be affected by your absence? Set those aside for the moment.

Focus on the projects that need some work completed while you are gone. Will someone be able to cover for you? Do you need to work an extra hour or two to handle some items before your departure? Can you work on the plane (or whatever mode of transportation you are using)? Will you be able to work at the hotel?

The next step is to list the information you need to take with you to accomplish the project assignments that are due (both self-imposed as well as company-assigned deadlines) while you are away. I would work this out on paper if it gets too overwhelming to do in your head. Once assembled, these items should fit nicely into your newly organized briefcase.

Let's say you have five current projects. Three do not require any attention while you are away but two have multiple assignments you must take care of either before you leave or while you are on the road. As you pull papers and make notes, remember to separate the projects in your briefcase. You might want to use large envelopes or plastic holders that close with a tie.

It's important to remember that life is never perfect. In the daily grind, it's about keeping those balls in the air with as much grace and dignity as we can muster. Your projects may fall behind in your absence. Perhaps you'll burn the midnight oil one or two nights upon your return or have to spend a Saturday afternoon getting caught up. But the aspect of Zen organizing that will save you over and over is that you have a system in place. The system may need to be reworked to restore order or help you catch up, but it's in place. And the Magic Formula's three steps—eliminate, categorize, and organize—will help you be in control no matter the situation or circumstance. As business travel threatens to upset your newly organized apple cart, remember your Zen organizing philosophy and the Magic Formula. You'll be in control again in no time.

Getting organized will certainly help you meet your deadlines. Remember, however, that you have a personality type to deal with in terms of work style. My mother, for example, was naturally moved to tackle the most difficult assignment first so she had it crossed off her list. This was how she prodded me with my homework assignments right through college. On the other hand, I have many very successful clients who thrive on the adrenaline rush of completing tasks at the last minute. If this sounds like you, getting organized will at least put everything you need at your fingertips as you burn the midnight oil to reach completion.

During the year you may decide that you want to try out some of these new systems. You might find that knowing that your work is ready to turn in with time to spare is a nice feeling. Who knows? You may join my mother's camp of "achieve early" before the year ends.

PREPARE YOUR HOME FOR YOUR DEPARTURE

Hands down, if you have children at home and are about to hit the road, your journey is more complicated. You not only have to organize your household for your departure but also deal with the emotional reactions of others.

Your home is not unlike your office: It must continue to function in your absence. Whoever is in charge, whether it's a spouse, family member, or babysitter, needs to know the location of key items.

Stock up to avoid as many last-minute emergencies as you can. If your trip is soon, however, we'll have to do some quick measures to get yourself on the road. Roll up your sleeves and set aside some time. Grab some sturdy garbage bags and a timer. We're off to the organizing races!

Set your timer for ten minutes in each room and grab whatever you can toss. Remember to set aside items that belong in other areas. Return them when your ten minutes is up and don't allow yourself to get sidetracked. You're on the move. If it helps, put on some rock-and-roll music.

Make a list of what has to be done before you leave. Will you need to stock up on food, extra diapers, or juice? Don't go to the store without a list. This is not the time to give in to impulse shopping.

Make a list of everything your representative (spouse, babysitter, or relative) will need to know in your absence. This includes emergency numbers, after-school activities, and sleepover arrangements. If you need permission slips for school or medical care, be sure you have these signed and in plain sight. Keep a copy with you just in case you need to fax someone the information. Make sure all your contact information is readily available.

You might want to print the preceding information, place it in sheet protectors, and put it in a binder. If it's several pages long, you don't want to take the chance it will be misplaced. Have copies in more than one room, if that makes you feel more secure. Have all emergency numbers programmed into your cell phone so that you can access the information yourself while on the road.

Provide instructions for your animal companions as well. When you were creating your shopping list, did you add food and treats for them? Be sure your rep knows how to contact your vet and the location of the nearest animal emergency facility.

Now it's time to check your bills. Do any need to be paid before you leave? What about while you are gone? You don't want to incur late fees and jeopardize your credit rating.

Have you sent an RSVP for any social functions? Be sure and let your host know you will not be able to attend.

Is there anything else you need to take care of that I have forgotten or that is unique to your situation? When you leave home, you want to be able to leave knowing that everything is in place. This will better enable you to be truly present wherever you go rather than being a body in one location whose heart, mind, and soul are still at home.

What I am about to suggest isn't easy but I hope you will give it some thought. Your children are going to miss you. One day they will probably be road warriors themselves. Show them by example that this is part of what being an adult is all about. Tell them the work you do is how you provide for them. Purchasing expensive gifts to assuage your guilt teaches your loved ones how to manipulate you and the situa-

tion. Instead, pick up a $20 T-shirt at the airport that lets them know where you've been. Let the latest $100 computer gizmo wait until a major holiday comes along. When you get back, the best reward will be to plan some special one-on-one time with your loved ones. Research some local activities before you leave. Put a date on the calendar. Let your children look forward to that as their reward for surrendering you to your work life on the road. And oh yes, when that special time arrives, be in the moment, not on your BlackBerry!

UNPACK

When my clients return home from conferences, something magical happens to them. It's as if a Work Fairy came by and cast a spell over them. What do they do? First, they never unpack the canvas bag that they are given as a souvenir. Gum and candy turn rock solid. Paper that might be of use in their daily lives languishes in the canvas bag, which usually gets tossed in the back of a closet. When asked why it's there, the answer is almost always, "I'm saving that in case I get audited and have to prove I was there." Somehow I think Uncle Sam wants to see your hotel bill or your airline ticket receipt, not your conference notes.

The other most popular excuse is, "It's a nice bag. Someday I might use it again." The fact that it shares the company of several bags from other conferences doesn't deter my clients from realizing that these bags have become business memorabilia.

We unconsciously feel we need to hold onto items like this because we paid for it in the conference fee. Trust me. You don't. Because now you are paying a higher price: You are giving up valuable real estate in your office to what will surely become junk in time.

You're also creating or inviting a mess, which means soon you will once again be working in chaos. Why not give the bags to a school or charity? If it's a sturdy canvas bag and the right size, you might use it to transport groceries. Why not take out the papers you received and see if anything needs to be added to your file system? Or perhaps you have some names, numbers, or facts you want to keep track of now that you're home? Plug that information into the correct computer file or cell phone log and toss the paper. Remember, conference presenters want you to feel that you got your money's worth, so they often provide a lot of printed material. Enjoy the feeling, then toss the trash!

WEEK THREE

Pack for Business

This week, you can

- Learn to travel lean like a true road warrior

Time required: One to two hours

PLEASURE TRAVELERS TEND TO TAKE huge suitcases filled with everything but the proverbial kitchen sink. I don't think I've ever seen an experienced business traveler lugging a gigantic suitcase. The more you travel, the more you realize how little you need on the road—and the more creative you become at supplying what you do need. Never have the words "less is more" had more significance. If you are new to travel, this week is for you. If you're an old hand, why not give a quick read and see how many of your secrets I share here.

TRANSFORM YOUR BUSINESS WARDROBE THE EASY WAY

Earlier this year we talked about packing for vacation. Remembering that hotel clerks and family members do not need to be dazzled by your wardrobe, it's okay to mix-and-match; sightseeing isn't meant to be a fashion experience. When you're traveling for business, you can probably make do with two suits: the one you wear on the plane and the one in your suitcase. If you want to go crazy, pack an extra.

What transforms your suits (and for our purposes I'm considering men and women wear suits) are the accessories. Men change their shirts and ties and nobody blinks an eye. Ladies, it's the same for us. Change your blouse or use a sweater instead. Make use of jewelry and scarves. Take a second pair of shoes. Years ago, I was a speaker at a conference, and I stayed the weekend to enjoy some of the other presenters. I wore one pantsuit. Every day I changed my top, scarf, and jewelry. No one, not even my hostess, realized it was the same outfit with new details.

I've learned to be more liberal about shoes and now carry at least two pairs with me. It was on a trip to China that I discovered that one pair of comfortable shoes for twelve straight days is more than even I can bear. The average business trip is short and rarely includes a gala evening event. If the latter is on your itinerary, you'll need to be prepared.

If you are staying in a hotel you haven't been to before, check to see what amenities they provide. Now that we are restricted as to the liquids we can bring on board an aircraft, why not use the shampoo provided by the hotel? You can probably receive samples of other products just by asking.

Let me close this section by saying that a client of mine who travels the world swears he is frequently upgraded just because he shows up at the airport in a suit and tie. In our society, clothes make the man or woman. Apparently it can also bump you up to a premium ticket.

THE TO-PACK CHECKLIST

As you assemble your toiletries, don't forget the restrictions imposed by the FAA. In addition, it's wise to check with your airline carrier's Web site the day before your flight for any last-minute changes.

Basic Grooming

Contact lens solution and a few extra pairs of contacts
Glasses (as a backup if you wear contacts and an extra pair in case something happens to your favorite)
Reading glasses, if you need them
Sunglasses
Deodorant
Disposable razor
Fragrance
Lotion (body, suntan, and face)
Nail file or emery boards
Nail polish (for repairs)
Nail polish remover wipes
Shaving gear
Soap (liquid or a bar and soap leaves for your purse)
Toothbrush, floss, mouthwash
Toothpaste
Small packets of tissues for your purse or pocket

Makeup and Hair Needs

Shampoo
Conditioner
Hair gel or mousse
Eye shadow
Eyebrow pencil
Face color, blush
Foundation
Hairbrush, comb, pick
Hairspray, gel
Lipstick, lip gloss
Lip balm
Mascara
Powder
Tweezers

First Aid

Band-Aids
First aid cream in a tube
Antiseptic wipe packets
Oral thermometer (nonmercury and
    nonglass)
Moleskin for blisters
Scissors (leave out if traveling by plane
    unless you plan to check a bag)

Prescription Medications

Extra written prescriptions in case of
    emergency (for life-saving medica-
    tions)

Over-the-Counter Medications

Antacids
Headache medication
Sleep aids and ear plugs
Vitamin supplements
Motion sickness pills or patch
Allergy kit, if needed
Birth control pills
Insect repellant and after-bite cream

Clothing

Blouses and shirts
Sweaters
Slacks and jeans
Dress pants
Suits
Skirts
Dresses: day or evening
Shoes: dress, sport, casual
Socks: dress, sport, casual
Nylons or tights
Shorts
Bathing suit, sandals, aqua shoes
Exercise clothing

Jacket
Coat

Undergarments/Sleepwear

Bathrobe and slippers
Bras
Pajamas or nightgowns
Underwear

Documents

Emergency I.D. list and personal
    contact info (preferably laminated)
Memberships that provide discounts,
    such as your auto club
Directions and maps
Driver's license
Addresses of friends and family
Insurance documents: medical, travel,
    etc.
Itineraries, hotel and contact informa-
    tion
Immunization record, if applicable
Passport, if applicable, and copy of
    passport
Tickets (airline, bus, or train, as well as
    theater or show tickets)
Photo ID if you don't have a passport
    or driver's license

Money

ATM card
Cash
Credit card and debit card
Foreign currencies, if applicable
Traveler's checks, if applicable

Miscellaneous Items

Camera, batteries, and battery charger
Cell phone and charger (use cell phone
    as your alarm clock)

Converter or adapter set, if applicable

Feminine hygiene products

Jewelry

Laptop computer, extra battery, and charger (unless you're wireless)

Small travel umbrella and raincoat or disposable rain poncho

Small, flat carryall for souvenirs

Reading material (magazines and paperback books)

Puzzles, games, deck of cards

Travel notebook and pen

Sports equipment, such as gym attire

Suitcase locks (FAA approved for air travel)

Travel umbrella or rain poncho

Emergency sewing kit

Work documents, if applicable

Binoculars

Flashlight

Calculator for foreign currency (check your cell phone)

Extra Ziploc bags (various sizes)

Wet wipes (for your purse or pocket)

WEEK FOUR

Complete Those Expense Reports

This week, you can

- Set up a system to deal with reporting your expenses

Time required: One hour

EXPENSE REPORTS TAKE AWHILE TO properly fill out, document, and submit. Many people feel they can't take time away from special projects or their daily grind to perform this task. This week I'd like to offer a few tips that will make expense reporting easier. After all, you want to be reimbursed, don't you? Here are some guidelines to help.

CORRAL THOSE RECEIPTS!

Take a large envelope (8 1/2-by-11) and label it for the upcoming trip (such as "New York City, April 3–7, 2009"). On your trip, empty your purse or briefcase every day and tuck all receipts into the envelope. Or place your receipts in a small zippered compartment in your suitcase and transfer them to your waiting envelope when you get home. By having all

your receipts together, filling out the reimbursement claim form will be much easier.

Every day, note the purpose of the purchase directly on the receipt and circle the date and total. This will help jog your memory when it comes time to fill out the form—especially if the receipts are in another language or currency.

Make a copy of your expense report as well as all receipts. If anything gets lost in transit or during processing, you won't be up the creek without a backup paddle.

File your expense report as soon after your return as possible—ideally the day after you get back. The faster you submit it, the faster you will get your money.

You will also have business expense receipts not only on business trips but also on a day-to-day basis. Whether these are reimbursed or written off your taxes, you will want them in one secure location. Keep a file folder for this purpose in your desk file drawer. Because receipts are small and can easily slip out of an ordinary file folder, use an expanding file folder with closed or accordion sides. The technical name for this type of file is a heavy-duty expanding file pocket.

Finally, if you love cashing the expense checks but just can't make yourself fill out the form, see if you can't get someone in your life to do it for you. I have a client whose sister-in-law keeps him up-to-date when it comes to travel expense reimbursement. He travels the world for his company, so we're talking about thousands of dollars in expense reimbursements. In exchange for her bookkeeping efforts, she gets treated to dinner whenever the family goes out for a meal. It's win-win for everyone involved. Is there a brainy teen in your house? Be willing to turn this task over to someone who is qualified and responsible.

OCTOBER SUMMARY

WEEK ONE

Sync all your work tools (computer, laptop, PDA, and files) to make your life easier. Just as with humans, they need to communicate.

WEEK TWO

When you're about to go off to a conference, make preparations at the office so that you won't be swamped when you return.

WEEK THREE

Taking too much when you travel adds physical and emotional weight to your experience. Learn to pare down to the basics.

WEEK FOUR

Be sure you are reimbursed for all out-of-pocket expenses when you travel. It's worth the time and effort.

11. NOVEMBER

Move Forward

All our dreams can come true, if we have the courage to pursue them.

—WALT DISNEY

I hope that by this point in the year, you are feeling an increase in personal, creative momentum. The real reason to set aside time to get organized is that it frees you to soar into the future, accomplishing the goals of your heart along the way.

November is full of good times with family and friends—you have to love Thanksgiving. Embrace the attitude of gratitude on which this holiday is built. And, with thanks for all you have learned to date from your job or career, let's move forward to a new level of awareness, creativity, and productivity.

HOME AND WORK HABITS OF THE MONTH: REVIEW YOUR ROUTINES

You have been working on new habits for ten consecutive months. This month I'd like you to take a few minutes to review how far you've come. Which ones do you enjoy? Which ones were not your cup of tea?

This month you have a choice at home and at work. You can do one of two things: go back and revisit a habit you were not able to develop at the time. Try again. Or, if you have done everything, how can you put a few habits together to create a new *system*?

What will you do this month? Make a decision and write it in your notebook. Otherwise, it might fly away with other good intentions. I want you to make a commitment.

WEEK ONE

Harness the Value of Professional Networking

This week, you can

- Consider the benefits of networking
- Learn creative ways to connect with other professionals

Time required: Thirty to ninety minutes

NOTHING REPLACES HUMAN INTER-action in the workplace. Friendly contacts build relationships. Who do you want to work with? The vendor you like and trust or the irascible guy with a great widget to sell? It's not what you know but who that counts. And, unless someone like Bill Gates is your uncle, you'll need to look outside the family unit for your best connections.

You never know who can open a door for you. The receptionist at your company or the guy you met at the convention last month might just be related to Bill or Steven (Spielberg, of course). And if you've been gracious and fun to work with, you could be in line for an introduction. Opportunities for career advancement are just outside your cubicle. You simply have to make the effort to create or find them.

You may be the conduit for advancement for someone else. When people entered ancient walled cities, they encountered someone called a gatekeeper, who directed them where they needed to go and to the people they needed to see. Why not fashion yourself as a modern gatekeeper and become the go-to guy or go-to gal in your work community? Be the person who knows where the best people are in your profession.

Networking can seem like a job in itself, but it doesn't have to be. This week we endeavor to become the worker everyone wants to interact with, from industry colleagues to the mail room clerk in your own company. And we'll do it all with grace and dignity. Are you ready?

MEET COLLEAGUES FOR LUNCH, DINNER, OR DRINKS

Depending on your business, the size of the city where you live, your available time, your age, and a host of other factors, you can pick and choose some networking options from the following list. Then, see whether you can come up with three additional ways to network after you read my suggestions. Make the decision to implement one or two of these ideas this month. Initially, you may have to make some phone calls or do some research on the Internet. Before the week comes to an end, however, you will be on the road to a better work experience. This week is about giving, and it never fails that as we give, we receive more than we imagined.

It is easy for me to fall into workaholic mode. I am an only child so I thrive on my alone time. I also happen to love my job. The time flies and I am always astonished to look at the clock and realize I have been writing or working with a client one-on-one for most of the day. I have to acknowledge, however, that a balance of work and social time is good for my soul and makes me far more productive in the long run.

What about you? Are you known as the gal who locks herself in her office during lunchtime? Do you find whenever you cross paths with someone you wind up saying something like, "Gosh, we should really go out for lunch sometime." If you enjoy the company of certain colleagues, make that call or shoot over a quick e-mail invitation. A greater understanding of this person may help you get through the inevitable difficult times at work. If this person works for another company, one day you may network for each other if one of you finds a job change is in order. And, if nothing major comes of this connection, at least you will have walked away from your work for an hour.

Try a new restaurant. Go to lunch at a different time and avoid the crowds. Walk to the restaurant rather than drive. Shake up your daily routine every once in awhile and you can't go wrong.

VOLUNTEER FOR COMPANY-SPONSORED COMMUNITY SERVICE PROJECTS

Most large corporations sponsor some sort of charity involvement. If yours does, sign up! If your company has never had any type of community outreach, why not start something yourself? There are runs or walks in most communities to benefit a host of health-related charities. You wouldn't have to reinvent the wheel; just get the word out to your fellow workers about a fun way to help others and spend time outside the office.

Perhaps someone in the office has a child or other relative facing a health crisis and you could raise money to help the family cover their extended medical bills? Charities such as Habitat for Humanity may be building a home in your community and need a few good men and women to wield some hammers. If you live near a body of water, it probably needs cleaning up from storm and tourist debris. What a great way to spend a few hours on a Saturday morning. Think outside the box and see what your community could use.

Investigate some charities that you think would be appropriate and talk to your supervisor. If you have a knack for PR, remind your supervisor that this is also a great way to build community recognition for the company. It's truly a win-win situation. Your local newspaper and TV station probably have specific columns and airtime set aside to publicize such events.

Set up a committee to assist you. Does someone on staff long to be the new Steven Spielberg? Put him in charge of documenting the day. What a perfect movie to show at the year-end party! Be open-minded and creative in the ways you seek to help. Your efforts will without a doubt yield rich rewards.

JOIN ORGANIZATIONS FOR YOUR INDUSTRY

One thing that never fails to astonish me when I work with my clients is that no matter how esoteric their business, a cottage industry is devoted to it. Magazines and newsletters I have never heard of support this work, and countless organizations exist so that like-minded individuals can network. And *network* is the key word. When you join associations, you not only spread the word about your company but also create relationships with other busi-

ness people who might one day need your services at their companies either as a consultant or full-time employee. And of course you might be able to fill a slot at your company should a vacancy arise.

There are also organizations devoted to networking either at breakfast once a week or in the evening after work. When I started my business in 1988, I was a member of a breakfast group for a year. It was a great way to build a client list. Each week, your entrée to the group was part financial and part the referrals you were able to find for your fellow businessmen and businesswomen. Ladies Who Launch is a great example of such an organization for women entrepreneurs. And don't forget to check out the Chamber of Commerce in your area.

KEEP YOUR BUSINESS CARDS WITH YOU

Keeping business cards nearby, even on weekends and holidays, sounds like a no-brainer, doesn't it? Well, you would be surprised how often I meet people socially or in a public place such as the airport and they don't have a card with them. Always keep a few in your wallet to pass out no matter where you are going. I am not suggesting that you become an obnoxious person who never stops trying to network everyone in his vicinity. I am suggesting that you be prepared to be of service to someone who might need you or your company.

LEARN NEW SKILLS

Would you like to make more money at your current place of employment? I bet one of the key things you can offer is to increase your skill set. Take a class after work or on weekends. Learn the latest computer program for your industry. Enroll in a community college and get your undergraduate degree or gain credits toward an advanced degree. These are like chips you would toss on the table in Vegas: the more chips, the more likely you are to win.

If you have considered networking a necessary evil or something you don't have time for, I hope this week has opened your eyes to new possibilities. I started my organizing business because I truly loved being a catalyst for change in the lives of my clients. I had no idea that I would form deep bonds and be introduced to folks who now populate my world as mentors and friends. Give networking a second look. It's worth it!

WEEK TWO

Make the Most of Conferences and Sales Conventions

This week, you can

- Aim to generate contacts from whatever business activity you pursue

Time required: One hour

WHEN YOU ATTEND CONFERENCES and sales conventions (which usually occur far from home), there are some benefits right off the top: airline miles and car rental and hotel points. If you travel a lot for your business, you might come up at the end of the year with enough dividends to offset some of the cost of your next family holiday. A word for the travel wise: use the same vendors all the time so your points can accrue and yield dividends.

BE OPEN TO OPPORTUNITY

Conferences and sales meetings present you with a large cross-section of people working in various aspects of your profession. These are wonderful opportunities to learn more about how their companies function. Do they use systems that your company might employ to streamline widget manufacturing or in-house proposals? Do they use new software that would benefit your group? Do you see marketing techniques you might employ? In the last week of this month, we will address your desire for a raise as well as how to prepare for your annual performance review. These large gatherings offer you an opportunity to gather material that will benefit your company. This is a concrete, clever, and creative way to prove your worth.

If you are actively seeking new employment, a sales conference or convention is a bonanza. Gathered in one arena are hundreds of potential employers. Of course, you need to be judicious in your approach. You don't want your current employer to hear that you are on the move.

We all know business people who never shut down. They work the room wherever

they go. It's exhausting, isn't it? I am not advocating this approach, but I do suggest that you remain open to possibilities wherever you are.

HONE NEW SKILLS

Let's consider some ways you can artfully make the best use of your conference time.

Are you shy? I know I can be at times. Is making introductions for others or yourself a test of your nerves? Practice in every unimportant, nonthreatening arena you enter. Introduce yourself while standing in line at the post office. Make small talk over the fruit in the market. Chat with other parents at school. Do it until it's second nature. I talk to strangers wherever I go. The more you do it, the more you discover we're all just people. The nice ones will embrace you. The others don't matter all that much, do they?

If we met and I asked you what you did for a living, would you have one or two succinct sentences for me? Or would you ramble incoherently while my eyes glazed over with boredom? You have only one chance to make a first impression. Make it count.

Speaking of first impressions, we are a visual society. Is your wardrobe up-to-date? A Hollywood stylist gave me an invaluable tip a few years ago that I'm delighted to share with you. Plan your basic wardrobe around a few classic, timeless pieces and then each year, study the trends. Are ani-

In your file cabinet you may want to have a section labeled Travel. This is usually where my clients keep articles about areas of the world they would like to visit. Some also keep notes about places they have enjoyed. Keep your travel benefits statements here. Toss the old the minute the latest arrives in the mail. If you receive your benefits statements online, create a Travel section in your electronic files and folders for the different entities offering you rewards.

mal prints in this season? Buy an inexpensive pair of shoes or a scarf and use that accessory with your basic black dress. You'll look trendy without spending a fortune.

A jewel is waiting to be tucked into your business success arsenal. What is it? Cultivate the art of listening. It's rare and will separate you from the pack. When we are truly present and listening, we get all kinds of cues as to the direction we should take to truly connect with this person. And, let's face it, don't we all love it when someone allows us to chatter on about ourselves? Use this tool wisely and it will open doors for you.

Take a minute when you return from your conferences to write a personal note to anyone who contributed to your time in a meaningful way. Yes, I know that e-mail is faster and cheaper. But it will never make the impression a handwritten note can make. In addition to your words, it says that you felt this person was worthy of

your time. You'll stand out from the crowd this person just connected with.

As you unpack your conference bag, enter your new contacts in your address book or file them wherever you will be able to locate them easily. You don't want the energy you expended on making connections to be for naught.

Something about leaving home allows us to view our current situation in a new light. Take advantage of your time away and remember to see your home and work life with fresh eyes. You will find more appreciation for what is good and less apprehension about what needs to be changed. Consciously channel the energy for change that infuses you the minute you leave home. Make your next conference an adventure rather than a burden. And don't be surprised if your attitude and enthusiasm rub off on others.

WEEK THREE

Update Your Resume and Other Important Documents

This week, you can

- Start keeping the key documents in your business life up-to-date and in order

Time required: One hour or more, depending on your circumstances

AT CERTAIN MOMENTS IN LIFE, WE feel tremendous frustration because we have not made adequate preparations for the future. This week we take advantage of our newly streamlined schedule and dedicate an hour to the yearly maintenance required to keep our business ducks in a row. We'll begin with that time-honored document that gets neglected the minute we find a job. You know the one I mean. Your resume of course!

UPDATE YOUR RESUME YEARLY

Even if you're at a company or a job you love, keep an updated resume handy. Opportunities come when we least expect them, so why not be prepared? The format and style of resumes change with the times, so your best bet is to do a little online research. Although many books are devoted to the subject, type "How to write a resume" into any large search engine such as Google and you can access the most current guidelines.

Writing your résumé may not seem like fun, but that's usually because people wait until they're unemployed to deal with it. If you update this document each year, it will be a snap to keep it current. Even if your job doesn't change, your accomplishments at work surely have. In fact, think of this update as a way to consciously plug into and acknowledge your accomplishments over the past year.

What is the underlying skill set you used to achieve the results you are proud of? How did your contributions affect the company's bottom line? The skills you used and developed will have universal application to all employers. Acknowledge yourself and your growth. You never know how this will open future doors for you. Not sure what your accomplishments are? Are you by nature a self-deprecating person? Have a talk with a colleague or good friend who can help you see the particulars when you are overwhelmed or too shy to do so for yourself.

In addition, wouldn't a prospective employer be impressed with the charity work you organized this year at your current place of employment? The classes you attended to increase your skill set or the ones toward a degree also carry some weight. And if you end up retiring at this job, updating your resume will be a way of reminding yourself of your work accomplishments. It's easy to get mired in the sorrow of what we feel we should have done. Instead, pat yourself on the back for the things you did do.

If applicable to your career, another document you might want to have on hand is an updated CV, or curriculum vitae. This document is used most often in academic circles and has more personal information on it. Again, a bit of research using your favorite search engine will show you the latest format. What if a foreign company wants to hire you as a consultant? They will be accustomed to a CV rather than a resume. Be prepared for the best and those opportunities will be drawn to you.

Many of my clients have a reference section in their file cabinet. This is a business reference, but it is often divided into three areas: Reference/Business, Reference/

Company, and Reference/Personal. Reference/Business holds reference material about your field of work. Reference/Company contains information concerning your specific organization. For example, remember the volunteer information I suggested you gather? It would reside here. And Reference/Personal is the ideal place to keep items such as your resume or CV. You may also have award citations, continuing education credits, letters of recommendation, and fan letters from vendors and clients. They should all have a folder in this section. These are additional ways to prove your worth come review time or if you want to seek a job with a new company.

EVALUATE YOUR 401K, ROTH IRA, AND/OR OTHER ACCOUNTS

Whether your company offers a 401K plan, you've personally established a Roth IRA plan, or you have both, it's important to keep this information current and easy to reference. These investments usually manage themselves and run automatically. You fill out the initial paperwork and then watch your retirement savings grow. However, as with all financial matters, schedule periodic reviews. Your money is a commodity that you should manage and direct. You want to evaluate what you are investing in and the percentage you are deducting from your paycheck.

In this Financial area of your files, you may also want to have another subdivision for stock transactions, money market funds, real estate investments, and any other money-generating areas of your portfolio. These individual sections may be very large and complicated for some of you. Because investing generates a lot of paper, check with your financial planner, tax attorney, tax preparer, or stockbroker to be sure you are saving the necessary documents for your tax records. Shred the rest. The fear of making a mistake often causes people to save every communication they receive. This causes serious bloat in your file cabinet!

Many of my clients keep this information in binders. In fact many regular reports are printed on three-hole-punched paper. If you have the shelf space, take advantage of this format and keep everything, no matter what form you use, in chronological order with the most recent at the front.

This type of information is private and the setup I am suggesting would be for your file system at home, not the one you keep at your office.

REVIEW MEDICAL RECORDS AND INSURANCE INFORMATION

One of the most important sections in your file cabinet is the one for your medical records and insurance information. If you're starting your organizing journey with this chapter, please see Chapter 3 for detailed instructions on how to set up a file system.

The following elements should be separated into individual folders:

- The company's current benefits booklet.
- The insurance carrier's current coverage booklet.
- Blank medical claim forms to take on doctor visits.
- Pending claims for your periodic review to be sure you are reimbursed.
- Claim forms and information related Section 125 (Cafeteria) Plans (flexible medical spending withheld from your salary pretax).
- A file for every member of the family, with pertinent information about their health history, including immunization records, pathology reports, and test results. Be judicious, however, and don't feel that every communication from a doctor's office is important. Keep whatever information another physician may want to reference. (He or she can request your file.) If you are a worrywart and feel it's all important, scan the older test results and store the information on a disc.

Keep an up-to date-medical ID card in your wallet at all times. And, in the event of an emergency, leave a copy for your children's caretaker while you travel. This will keep all the material in one convenient location.

Schedule a monthly reminder in Outlook or whatever calendar system you are using to check and see if you have submitted all your medical claim forms for the month. This, like expense reports, is money waiting for you.

Finally, I suggest you review your medical plan yearly to be sure it's in keeping with the needs of your family. You may want to invest in supplemental insurance if you see the need on the horizon. By the same token, everyone may be in such perfect health that you can significantly raise your deductible and thus lower the portion of the premium you must contribute.

At the end of this week, you're going to be flying high knowing that you have crossed these important but—let's face it—boring tasks off your yearly to-do list. Simple actions like these save time and money, and, oh yes, raise our self-esteem. I'm wondering what reward you have chosen. You deserve one.

WEEK FOUR

Prepare for a Review and Ask for a Raise

This week, you can

- Get ready for the yearly performance review
- If appropriate, make a case for a raise

Time required: One hour plus

REMEMBER WHEN YOU WERE CALLED into the principal's office at school? Did you break into a sweat? Were your hands clammy? Was your stomach in an uproar? Well, the mere mention of an impending performance review and the desire to ask for a raise will probably propel you back in time to a similar physical response. Let's prepare for them this week. If these tasks are an intellectual, nonemotional activity, they won't be painful at all.

RATE YOUR OWN PERFORMANCE

If you are new to the company, ask some of your colleagues exactly what you should expect during your performance review. In fact, the Human Resources department may have a specific checklist to make the process easier. Talk to them before you begin. It's also wise to know as much as possible about the person who will be doing your review. Company policies vary and so do the personalities of those in charge. Forewarned is forearmed, as the old saying goes.

With that said, you should have a good idea what your review will reveal:

- How well are you getting along with your colleagues?
- How productive are you?
- How consistent are you?
- Are your projects on time?
- Have you rated kudos from supervisors?
- How have you and your projects contributed to your division?
- Are you on time for work?
- Do you volunteer to help others when work is slow?

- Are you willing to stay late if circumstances dictate?
- Do you frequently get caught up on work from your home? An easy way for an employer to track that is to check the time on e-mails you send.

Aside from your performance, do you stand out as a well-liked employee? Do you think of doing little things such as celebrating a colleague's birthday or the birth of a child? Have you initiated some activity that promotes the company position in the community or world at large, such as a charity event? If the company has a long-standing presence in the community, have you volunteered time and services as a way of showing support? In other words, are you a year-round team player or someone on the fast track just breezing through this company until a better offer comes through?

The more positives you toss on the table, the better your review. And the more outstanding your review, the more likely that your request for a raise will be approved. Let's say you came up short when you read the preceding list. No problem: Take out your notebook and make some notes. What are the accomplishments you *have* made? Where and how could you improve your status as an employee? Maybe you need two alarm clocks in the morning to end your tardiness. Perhaps you need to rework your schedule to fit in some volunteer work that the company sponsors. Or maybe the work you are doing this year on getting organized will show up in better organized proposals and

presentations. What concrete steps will you take?

Some of you were no doubt enthusiastically shaking your heads yes as you read my introduction to this week. "Yes, Regina. I do all those things!" Well, guess what? Your supervisor is a human being. So why not write down all the ways you believe you have done a good job and contributed to the company? During the review, if you think you have not been perceived in the same light that you regard yourself, you can whip out your notes and use them as talking points on your behalf.

A word of caution: Business has no emotion. A review or meeting for a raise request is no place for tears, anger, tantrums, or any other display of emotion. No matter what your supervisor says during this meeting, say thank-you for his or her guidance. And if you can't be unemotional during the review, ask for some time to consider not only what has been said but how you might change your performance. At a later date, you can calmly make your case. This last paragraph is the most important piece of advice I can give you in this chapter. Say it with me: Business has no emotion—and neither should you when you are conducting it!

ASK FOR A RAISE

You get a great review. It's just what you expected. You want a raise. You have more homework to do! Asking for a cost-of-living increase in these difficult economic times, with the price of gas skyrocketing and food prices going through the roof, is a no-brainer. However, why not ask for more? Before you make up a figure based on your dreams or economic need, find out the salary of other people in your field who do your job. Don't forget to find out more than just that figure, however. You'll want to know what degrees the higher paid individuals have, how much extra training they've had, how many years of experience, and how their company compares to yours. If you work for a small company as the CFO, you aren't going to make what the same person at Microsoft does. Begin your research at a site such as Salary.com. Professional associations are also a great resource for this information. Remember to be cognizant of the location of the companies you are researching. If you live in the Midwest, for example, your job will not pay as much as it might in, say, New York City or San Francisco. The cost of living in the city you call home is a factor.

Investigate your own company as well. Is it thriving or barely surviving? If it's the former, what have you contributed to this growth? What about the division in which you work? You want to put yourself in your employer's shoes. How would you react to your request if you were the head honcho? A company is ideally a team. It isn't just about you. This global understanding will be an asset.

Make an appointment with your boss. Thank him for your good performance review. Be direct in the purpose of the meeting and base it on the current salary guidelines you have researched. In fact, enter the meeting with a specific dollar amount you want to receive. You can negotiate down but not up!

Remind your boss of your accomplishments as well as your unique skills. This is no place or time for emotions; do not mention other job offers or threaten to quit. These strategies can backfire. If the response is negative, calmly ask exactly what would be required for you to receive an increase. Then ask how much time should elapse before you revisit this matter.

If your company can't offer you more money, take heart. Come into your meeting with a backup plan. What about more vacation or sick days or some of those innovational work concepts we discussed previously such as flextime? People never think about our situation with the same passion or detail that we do. Your boss hasn't been fretting over your situation at his family dinner each night. Be creative on his behalf. Then all he has to do is decide!

This month requires a great deal of introspection and research. Being prepared and ready to grow isn't easy, but you can't deny the rich rewards they bring. Speaking of rewards, you will probably have a long weekend for Thanksgiving, so pat yourself on the back and plan a nice one. Maybe it's just a day with the family in a park without your cell phone. Be creative and do something that appeals to you. Thanksgiving is about more than the meal.

NOVEMBER SUMMARY

WEEK ONE

Turn professional networking into a pleasurable experience that can benefit you and your company.

WEEK TWO

Make use of all the benefits and perks at sales conferences and conventions. You have to go, so why not look beyond the work to the silver lining?

WEEK THREE

Stay current with all your personal business documents, such as the all-important resume.

WEEK FOUR

Take the sting and fear out of performance reviews and requests for a raise.

12. DECEMBER

Balance Your Work and Life

Your imagination is your preview to life's coming attractions.

—ALBERT EINSTEIN

Drum roll, please. Here's the question of the month. How will you celebrate the holidays: relaxing with joy or suffering from burnout? We both know which one is the most common outcome, but you know my choice for you.

Keeping your home life balanced with your work obligations isn't always easy. There is no question that being organized will take you to the finish line, but being organized isn't a destination you reach. It's a journey you take. And the journey you imagine is often interrupted by other peoples' needs and plans, not to mention societal demands. When else in the calendar year does society demand so much of us? Chart your course and, like any good ship's captain, navigate the sudden swells and choppy water with finesse.

Energy is like the ocean tides: It ebbs and flows. Sometimes work will be insane and other times it will be all but dead. Sometimes your family will seem as if they don't need you and other times you will feel as if you're on the FBI's Most Wanted list. You'll be using the Magic Formula every day in clever and creative ways. When the ball gets dropped, you'll pause for reflection rather than panic, and then you'll resume once again in control. Chaos was the choice you used to make. A Zen organized life is the choice you made the day you began this book.

This month I have ideas that can transform the way you celebrate the season. Let's balance our need to celebrate with the way we go about incorporating the holiday into our daily lives. If we don't take charge, our emotions will and you know what that means: bloated credit card bills, too much food or alcohol, and complete exhaustion. There is a better way. We're going to deal with those December demands that get added to already full plates. Do the words "end of the fiscal year" strike fear in your heart? Don't panic. You're ready for all challenges because you've learned how to prioritize.

And finally, we're closing out this year with a look back on all you've accomplished—and a look forward to the New Year on the horizon.

WORK HABIT OF THE MONTH:
SAY "NO"

This month I'd like you to strengthen an old habit rather than acquire a new one. With the special demands of this season, this habit will be a crucial tool in your survival arsenal. What is it? Our old friend, "Just say no." Take a stand for what is important for your career, your sanity, and your available time. How will you use it? Here are some ideas:

"No, I'm afraid I can't cover for you while you are on vacation. My workload is too heavy at this time of year."

"Thank you for asking, but I won't be able to attend your party."

"Can we schedule this meeting for after the first? I'm not able to prepare fully before then. Will that work for you?"

"Oh my, thank you for asking me to head the decorating committee, but I must decline. I have too many obligations with work and family to do my best."

Get the idea?

HOME HABIT OF THE MONTH:
CHOOSE HEALTHY SNACKS

This month we are lured by extra food around the office. Not just any food, but high-calorie, stick-to-your-hips cookies, chocolates, and caramel corn. Each day this month, spend a few minutes thinking about which healthy snacks you will eat that day. Once you have completed your mental plan, take action! Cut your carrots, wash and bag those veggies, grab a slice of cheese, or toss that apple into your purse. You'll find if you are full of good food and your blood sugar is balanced, you won't be tempted to dive into the sweets. Sugar gives a temporary lift. Healthy food will take your through the month with ease—and no extra pounds to lose in the New Year.

WEEK ONE

Streamline Your Holiday Experience at Work

This week, you can

- Decide what type of holiday experience you want and set a plan in motion to bring it to fruition
- Be creative in your gift giving without breaking the bank

Time required: Thirty to sixty minutes

THINK BACK TO YOUR OFFICE LAST year around the holidays. Is December a fun time at your place of employment? Or is there a lot of pressure to get into the holiday spirit? Do you try to avoid it all in an attempt to devote yourself solely to your work? Or are you the spirited one surrounded by Scrooges? This week we make a plan that's tailored to your personal desires as well as the reality of your situation. When your emotions threaten to take over and derail your holiday, you can whip out your trusty plan and be back on track in minutes. Your plan will include sane holiday gift giving, decorating, and entertaining. Let's get started.

ROAD MAP TO THE HOLIDAYS!

Write down two or three things you would like to incorporate this year at work in terms of celebrating the season, as well as two or three things that you want to avoid. Are your items achievable?

The key thing to remember is that you have a choice. If Mary in the next cubicle loves to deck out her space using every holiday ornament she can find, that's her choice. You needn't duplicate her efforts. Often people will unconsciously pressure us to do what they are doing to validate their own choices. You can be gracious but firm when Mary asks where your decorations are this year. And should you be in a contest to outdo Mary, be just as firm when Stan down the hall asks why you bother. Don't be afraid to set boundaries. The clearer you are about what you want to achieve, accomplish, and experience this season, the less influenced you will be by others' needs, wants, and opinions. Your plan helps you establish healthy boundaries.

Every action you take this holiday season requires physical, mental, and emotional energy. Do you have the reserves for everything you want to do? Take each item (gift buying, decorating, entertaining, and so on) and break it into the steps that will make it a reality. You've been doing this with work projects. It a rule of thumb for everything you want to accomplish. Let's look at one of the most common holiday challenges we all face, gift giving.

GROUP GIFTS

When it comes to your colleagues, is a rule in place about personal exchanges? Here are some common but effective ways to handle group gift expenditures:

Secret Santa: A great way to conduct gift exchanges in a large group is Secret Santa. Everyone puts his own name into a container and then draws one name. This is the only office colleague for whom you need to purchase a gift. It's prudent to add a monetary limit, such as $10 or $15. Consider a contest to see who got the best value or made the silliest purchase for the designated amount.

White elephant: A white elephant exchange, or regifting party, can be fun. Each person brings in the silliest, most useless gift he has received in the past with the intention of passing it on. After the story of the gift is told, it can be claimed by someone. The third time the gift moves to a new owner, it has found its final home. If you're having a casual in-house office holiday party, this makes for lively conversation. One word of caution: Never, ever bring a gift that has been given to you by someone in the circle. No matter how silly you find the gift, there is never any reason to humiliate someone.

Donation to charity: Make a group donation to a charity. Charity donations can work in multiple ways besides the obvious cash donation. Here are a few ideas for you:

Help an individual family in your city through a local house of worship or community outreach program. Some charities share details about the family (age, clothing sizes, and so on) so that your group can supply presents for specific family members.

Aid a family in a far-off country through an organization such as Heifer International. They give families animals such as chickens, an ox, or a cow to help them feed themselves.

Your company may openly support a charity in the community. When a friend of mine worked at a large movie studio, for example, they arranged for employees to help out at a downtown mission in Los Angeles the week before Thanksgiving. The year I went with her, several famous faces were dispensing food to the homeless.

Donate to a charitable organization such as Habitat for Humanity or the Search and Rescue Dog Foundation in Ojai, California, in a friend's or colleague's honor. Let them know that you have done so rather than purchasing individual gifts. Most organizations will supply a certificate you can share with those on your gift list. It may even inspire them to do the same.

INDIVIDUAL GIFTS

If you decide to purchase individual gifts, you'll want to plan before you shop. The first and most important step is to know your budget. Put that figure in the upper-right corner of a blank sheet of paper in your notebook. And be sure it's realistic. This time of year, too many people make emotional decisions when it comes to things that affect their finances. You've learned to think ahead while you organized all manner of projects this year. Imagine yourself fearlessly opening your credit card statements in January because you know you stayed within your limits. Work backward from that moment.

Next, list all the colleagues for whom you'd like to purchase a gift. Remember to include colleagues from other companies with whom you regularly interact as well as those in your office. You can list every-

> Let me say a word about holiday cards. While it isn't as personal, save time by printing labels with the names and addresses of the colleagues and vendors to whom you want to send a card. It is now possible to put a personal imprint or photo on a stamp. I know several companies who promote themselves this way; it's a unique touch and will take the attention off a computer-generated label. The "Resource" section lists some companies that provide custom stamps.

one to start and whittle it down later if it's an economic necessity.

Next to each name note one or two ideas and the amount of money you presume would cover either gift. When you are finished, add the individual figures. In most cases, this total is greater than your budget. What to do? Start eliminating folks or choose less expensive gifts for some until you are in line with the figure you know is within your financial comfort zone. Keep in mind that you can always send a card!

To save time, shop online or through a catalogue. Should you actually enjoy shopping during the holidays, group your gift ideas according to the stores where they are most likely to be found. See if you can find a mall that has as many of the stores you need as possible.

Unless you enjoy wrapping presents, have your online, catalogue, or brick-and-mortar retailers do it for you. If you consider how much you are paid per hour, you will realize how valuable your time is and see the fee you might pay in a new light. You might also find a teenager adept at gift wrapping who would like to make some extra money during the holidays. Some malls have wrapping stations whose proceeds benefit various charities. Where there's a will, there's a way!

WEEK TWO

Office Parties

This week, you can

- Get ready for the office holiday party
- Use your time wisely rather than allowing fear, bad management, or the needs of others to rob you of this precious commodity

Time required: One hour

LAST WEEK YOU WORKED ON A BUDGET for your gift giving so that you wouldn't overwhelm your finances. This week let's consider your time budget. You've been working on time management all year using different skills and tools to achieve mastery. During the holidays, your best intentions can go right out the window and time will once again be frittered away. Why? For the same reason budgets are blown: Our emotions and expectations step into the driver's seat of our lives. You'll find that the more you develop the ability to say no, the fewer problems you'll have.

This week deals with the most likely time suckers you will encounter this month—holiday parties.

HOLIDAY BUSINESS PARTIES

It often seems that every business entity we deal with decides to throw a party during the month of December. It's certainly an understandable way to thank colleagues, employees, and vendors for their good service. And goodness knows some of these gatherings are even fun! But they occur on top of your events with family and friends. When holiday gatherings become more of an obligation than an enjoyable experience, they can rob us of precious time.

Time can be lost at work because a particular party is a considerable distance away. Commuting in heavy traffic is wasted time if you're the driver. An easy antidote is to arrive midparty so you can leave your office after rush-hour traffic has cleared. On the other hand, if you're in a large metropolitan city and rely on public transportation, you might want to be one of the first to arrive so you can work for an hour when you get home.

You might arrive at the party famished and overindulge in food and drink. Why not eat something before you go so that overindulging won't be an option?

Increased demands on our time often seem overwhelming, and instead of dealing with these demands, we seek escape. And where better to escape than a party? You tell yourself that you had too many obligations piled on your plate this year and you need a break. When the year ends, you are surprised to find that you managed to appear at every business holiday party to which you were invited. While everyone at work thinks you're the life of the party, they are also disappointed with your work performance.

Early in this program we talked about the importance of conscious decision making. Delivering your projects on time will make you far more valuable than any appearance at a party. It will also build your self-esteem.

TO PARTY OR NOT TO PARTY

You are probably fairly adept now at prioritizing because you've been working on that for several months in one form or another. It's time to see that everything in life, not just work projects, must be weighed and valued on the priority scale. Remember the basic tenet of organizing: The whole of anything is overwhelming. The bottom line is that you need to balance the importance of your appearance at each event to which you are invited against the work deadlines you have before the holiday vacation.

Here are some questions to ask yourself so that you can stay on track.

- How important is this party or social gathering to your career?
- Will the client or your boss be offended if you don't at least make an appearance?
- Are you the point person at work who should represent your company? Or are you simply looking for some holiday fun? It's important to understand why you are considering saying yes to this invitation.
- Will you have to shift some work obligations to other days to buy the time for this gathering? Can you realistically still make your deadlines? If you can, rework your schedule for the week. Obligations get met not by magic but by careful planning.
- Do you have a history of overindulging at parties? On the day of the party, can you make plans to have a healthy, filling snack before you go? I am a vegetarian with food allergies. I cultivated the habit of eating before I go to social functions years ago.

You'd be surprised what a relief it is to not be tempted by fattening foods! If alcohol is your nemesis at these functions, decide how may alcoholic drinks you can safely allow yourself and stick to that number.

PLAN THE OFFICE PARTY

I have a client, Jen, who is always the designated office party planner. We're not sure if this is due to her party planning skills, her take-charge attitude, or the fact that she loves to celebrate birthdays and other festive events throughout the year. Are you like Jen? If you are, more power to you. If you aren't and you feel that your office would be a happier place with a small celebration, here are some tips to help you get started. These guidelines are for all in-house parties throughout the year. They are especially useful, however, around the holidays when gatherings expand in number:

Is a specific room set aside for these celebrations? Are you allowed to decorate it? Book this room ahead of time when you need it. You wouldn't want to spontaneously put up balloons and streamers only to find that the company president is coming down for a big meeting in the next fifteen minutes.

Buying paper plates, cups, plastic cutlery, napkins, and decorations ahead of time and in bulk can save you money. However, this is practical only if you have a place to store these items. And *your* office, desk, and bookcase are out of the question. If the company isn't large enough to have an area for these supplies, buy as you go.

Will you need flowers? Most supermarkets supply lovely and affordable bouquets. If you have an account with a florist for large company events, see if they will offer a discount for small celebrations. (As an aside, one of the biggest sources of clutter in every company kitchen I have ever organized is inexpensive vases left over from floral deliveries. Save one or two but toss the other fifty to make room for necessities, such as those party supplies you thought you had no place to hide during the year.)

Large chain stores such as Costco have great premade party platters. Poll the attendees and see if they want to chip in and go this route or if they would rather have a potluck. For most small celebrations, you can be specific and have, for example, just desserts. Aim to suit the situation and satisfy the crowd.

If your office holiday party is held in-house, as I indicated, you can expand on these suggestions, adding holiday decorations, music or some other entertainment, and drinks. If your party is held off-site and you are the point person for those plans, create a file folder to house the materials you need to reference as you plan. You will probably have outside vendors to contact, such as a caterer and a DJ. Keep a file in the project area of your file drawer labeled Holiday Party. Next year, when it is time to plan the festivities again, you can

DECORATE

If your office likes to go all-out, I presume there's a decorating committee. The size of the staff dictates how holiday planning is handled. If there is no designated person or persons, why not go to your supervisor and create a committee or take on the assignment yourself? This way, the decorating task can be given to different people each year. The key concerns are choosing a decorating scheme that pleases everyone and finding a place to house it all.

One clever solution I saw in a CPA's office would work well anywhere. They stored decorations in my favorite opaque container on wheels with a locking lid from The Container Store. They fit two of these containers in the space between a high cabinet and the ceiling. Because the containers were opaque, no one could tell exactly what they housed. The material was safe and out of the way until needed. Do you have any unused space like this in your office? Why not walk around and use the fresh eyes technique to see what reveals itself to you.

pull out your file, discard what is not relevant for the current year, and add whatever is pertinent. Over the course of the year, you can collect flyers or postcards from vendors you might want to try at the next party. One-stop shopping makes life easy no matter where you use it!

With a little effort, you can take the sting out of your business holiday obligations this week. Next week we're going to tackle the business time suckers that traditionally pop up at the end of the year. We're waging an all-out campaign to be sure what we need to do is accomplished in a timely fashion this month. This will give us the opportunity to enjoy what we've chosen to put on our plate.

WEEK THREE

Banish End-of-the-Year Business Madness!

This week, you can

- Manage the new and perhaps unexpected demands on your work schedule

Time required: Thirty to sixty minutes, depending on the complexity and number of your projects

IF YOUR COMPANY HAS A FISCAL YEAR-end that coincides with the calendar year-end, you may have an onslaught of work to finish before the end of the year. In addition, some of the companies you're working with may also be handling end-of-the-fiscal-year business, which means they need more input from you. What's a person to do? Prioritize, prioritize, and just for good measure, prioritize! When we are young we learn to count starting with one. As a Zen organizer, you begin at the end date, where the goal will be fulfilled, and count backwards.

One of the biggest surprises my clients encounter is the realization that, while regular maintenance is key to daily survival, once you are organized, the system we have created is not written in stone. Depending on the rapidity with which you accrue new material and change projects, you need to revise your files and day-to-day systems on a periodic basis. The holiday season provides a prime impetus for change.

HANDLE INCREASED DEMANDS

If you suddenly experience an increase in work demands, your old knee-jerk reaction may have been to sleep less, work more, and push through. But that was your past. I'd like to offer an alternative. Here are some steps for you to consider:

1. Place the new projects you have been asked to work on either in order of importance or by due date.

2. For each project, create a list of steps that must be taken to reach your goal of completion.

3. With list in hand, schedule each step on your calendar. This should begin to give you a feeling of control and reduce the feeling of being overwhelmed.

4. As you examine your calendar, you will almost certainly see that the schedule has to be altered. Some previously scheduled appointments and deadlines have to be moved to make your December 31 deadlines. Rescheduling appointments and deadlines will take some time, but remember that most of your colleagues are under the same time pressure and may very well welcome your request to delay the delivery of material.

5. Do any of your new projects need files? Create them now so that as additional information crosses your desk, it all has a home.

6. Can any facet of your most pressing projects be delegated to an assistant or another coworker? This is especially viable if you work in a large corporation and each division is busy at different times of the year. Your request might rescue someone who is twiddling his thumbs.

Again; preparation like this takes time. You may want to barrel ahead without doing this step. Stop in the name of your sanity. Crunch times like this bring up all the fears we harbor about our ability to succeed. And the holiday season exacerbates this by tossing a bundle of home-related deadlines and obligations onto our already bulging plates. Isn't it astonishing that a season meant to help us embrace goodwill for ourselves and others winds up being the season when depression is rampant? Take a deep breath and a step back. Then give yourself the time to plan and watch how easy this step makes the fulfillment of your deadlines. Who knows? You may find yourself at more holiday parties than you initially thought possible.

HOLIDAY ILLNESS AND TRAVEL

You might be surprised to see holiday illness and travel in the same category. One represents a problem and the other (I hope) a joy. But both are a double-edged sword in terms of your schedule. December is the month you're likely to be out of the office—whether you're taking vacation days or sick days. If you are traveling, you needn't panic. In Chapter 7 I gave you the tips and tricks that will help you take a vacation from your job knowing that your deadlines will be met in your absence.

In the same chapter, you can learn how to be sure that everyone has easy access to the parts of your work (files, binders, information stored on your computer, and so on) that affect them. Once you are organized, a cold or the flu may throw you for a loop, but your colleagues will be able to carry on in your absence. It's a great comfort to be able to direct others to the exact spot where the information they need is located. When you are vested in the fantasy of "my desk is piled high with papers but *I* can find everything," you won't be able to empower someone else in your space.

What if you have a colleague who is not organized? What if he decides to take a holiday trip or is sidetracked by the flu and you need to cover, but you have no idea how he has set up his office? If this is someone with whom you interact on a regular basis, you would be wise to ask him now how he maintains any information that has an effect on your work. Someone like this might have no clue how to organize his work, and his secretiveness is a cover for this flaw. You might want to share with him the work you are doing in this regard. This is the "Hey, we're all in the same boat" approach.

Many people, who are insecure at heart, set up a secret and mysterious system so that no one will be able to access information except themselves. When I encounter this attitude with clients, I strongly suggest they write a detailed job description. At the very least, when they leave the company, the new person will have some clue as to what systems are in place.

Here are some tips to help you handle holiday travel interruptions at work:

If you know of your colleague's intention to travel during the holiday season, be sure you understand exactly how your work and your deadlines will be affected by his absence. Ask him for the specific information you need to continue with the project. If the information is not forthcoming, ask how you can help make it available.

People often feel insecure about sharing information, perhaps because they're afraid of being shown up by your performance. Assure him that you are all on the same team and that your offer is meant to help both of you. Not only will the project move forward if you have this information, his workload will be lighter when he returns from vacation. Who wants to return from a vacation with a mountain of catch-up work to do?

If there is still no response, it may be prudent to involve a supervisor. Do this as a last resort.

Sometimes when we work closely with another person it's possible to set up a buddy system: I'll cover for you if you will cover for me when my vacation time comes around. We all have different strengths and weaknesses. A buddy system allows two people to work in concert and have increased productivity when they align their strengths.

If you have an assistant, be sure he is kept in the loop about your project deadlines. He is there to assist you, so make good use of him. Your job will run more smoothly if you have someone who has access to your calendar and runs your business errands. When he is also in the loop and understands the big picture, he can better assist you in time of true need. You won't lose power if you share knowledge; you'll be more powerful. And who knows? This person may have a perspective that will benefit the project.

Finally, if you see some previously unforeseen event will derail your project deadlines, don't hide under a rock. Speak immediately to a supervisor or to your client. Often clients can easily alter a deadline, especially during the holidays. With similar holiday pressures at their end, a changed due date may be appreciated. If this is not possible, you will at the very least have several people trying to implement a quick resolution. Fear often stymies our ability to think clearly. Communication is the perfect antidote.

WEEK FOUR

Enjoy This Week and Prepare for Next Year

This week, you can

- Make a plan to achieve more in the New Year now that your work environment is streamlined
- Enjoy the holidays!

Time required: Thirty to ninety minutes

IF YOU BEGAN THIS BOOK LAST JANUary, "you've come a long way, baby." Are you aware of your accomplishments?

Take a minute and look back over this year and consider how much you have achieved. How many new habits did you acquire this year? How many positive actions do you now perform without thinking simply because you appreciate and treasure the outcome? Whether it's saving time, money, or energy, you have taken steps to be more productive. It was a choice. No. It was a *decision*.

As much as the same old routines and habits may not serve us, their familiarity produces a feeling of comfort. If you haven't become as organized as you'd like, don't beat yourself up. It's the human condition. The great thing to remember is that

if you apply yourself, what is new today will be tomorrow's norm.

This last week I know you are frantically tying up loose ends and getting ready to celebrate the holidays. So I don't have any physical tasks for you, just a few questions.

ASSESS THE SITUATION TO DATE

It's time to look into the future. In many cultures, the week between Christmas and New Year's day is the time to clean out the old and make way for the new. This can be an outside job that involves sweeping and tossing, but it should also be an inside job that clears the inner cobwebs and makes way for the life we dream of living. This opportunity is yours every year, not just this December.

Here are some written exercises that will help you create the New Year as you would like to experience it:

1. Which work and home habits changed your daily experience the most? Ideally, I'd like you to list at least five habits for the home category and five habits for the work category. Could you expand on any one of these habits and make it more applicable to your experience? Have you thought of ways to weave some of these habits together into *systems* that will help make your day run more smoothly?

2. Did you quickly abandon any habits? Do you have any idea why you decided not to pursue these particular habits? If an interruption, a distraction, or an emergency took your focus, can you go back now and incorporate these habits into your life? Or did you feel that your situation was unique and you would not benefit from them? It's okay not to incorporate all the habits but it's important you know why. If you said that you skipped some because they were too difficult or you were feeling lazy, I'd tell you that being human is allowed. Each habit was chosen for a particular reason and they do work in concert. Why not give them all a chance to influence your day-to-day experience for the better?

3. What are your work goals for the New Year? Please be specific.

4. What is different now from a year ago? Again, be specific.
   - Do you feel more at home in your work space?
   - Is your new file system making life easier for you?
   - Has the incorporation of systems streamlined your work flow and increased productivity?
   - Do you find that you prioritize automatically?
   - Is there less stress in your life? Are you surprised to find that a little meditation and exercise go a long way to uplifting your daily work experience?
   - Did you make a change that influenced a coworker?

This may be the most important exercise this week because it will make you focus in a direct way on the effect that Zen organizing has had on your work life.

Now that you are organized, you must keep your eye on daily maintenance. But I hope you won't have to redo your entire file system or spend a day cleaning out your office for quite some time. You created your foundation. You learned new skills. You acquired new habits. It's time to fly! What do you want to accomplish now that a year of hard work is behind you? Are you ready to go after that promotion, or do you want a new job? Have you always wanted a degree? You can work toward achieving a goal only after you have identified it.

And, if your organizing efforts this year haven't yielded the success you wanted, continue in the next year. Honor your achievements to date. For example, if your office is clear and the envy of everyone who passes by, pat yourself on the back. If your file cabinet, however, is still a mess, there's no time like the present to focus on that project.

At the heart of Zen organizing is a desire for balance. I would urge you not to fall into a common organizing trap: You *don't* want to spend the rest of your work life getting organized. You want to acquire the skill of organizing and then spend the rest of the time making it work for you.

THAT OLD ZEN PROVERB

"The way a man does one thing is the way he does everything." I introduced this proverb at the start of our journey. At the beginning of the year, I made a guess that your home and your office were likely mirror images. Now that your office is organized, you may feel uncomfortable in a disorganized home environment. Don't be surprised if one of the impulses you feel in the New Year is a desire to clean out your closet, make room for the car in your garage, or make your bathroom cupboards as beautiful as your new file system! It's the old Zen proverb at work.

As I travel around Los Angeles, I am always delighted to see familiar faces. There's my favorite bank teller, the de-

SEEING IS BELIEVING

You may have noticed that although I mentioned the creation of a dream board in the Introduction, I never assigned the task of making one during the year. It was always an option for you to embrace. Now, however, is the perfect time to make one so that you can see in pictures the future you'd like to create for yourself. You have acquired skills you didn't have when you began your organizing journey. But you may still find your future difficult to envision. As you search through magazines for images that speak to you, clarity about your goals may be instantaneous as you see a photo and think, "*That's* what I want!"

lightful coffee shop employee at my neighborhood Starbucks, and the sweet man who buffs my car with relish at the car wash. I couldn't survive without the person who prepares my taxes, the attorney who watches over my business affairs, or the caterer who helps me entertain. Whether you are a carhop or the CEO of a large corporation, your contribution to the whole is needed, appreciated, and vital to the world. We all matter.

I hope this book has made your day-to-day work experience easier. Once the noise of the chaos is silenced, you'll be able to hear the inner direction that guides us all. With an organized work space and a calm mind, you'll be able to implement those impulses with ease. At its core, Zen organizing is about helping you make the contribution you were born to offer the world. After all, there will never be another you.

Twenty years from now
you will be more disappointed
by the things that you didn't do
than by the ones you did do.
So throw off the bow lines.
Sail away from the safe harbor.
Catch the trade winds in your sails.
Explore. Dream. Discover.

—MARK TWAIN

DECEMBER SUMMARY

WEEK ONE

Help your office create a holiday experience that benefits everyone. Keep giving under control.

WEEK TWO

Spend your time wisely rather than fritter it away.

WEEK THREE

Let the power of prioritizing and your trusty calendar beat the end-of-the-year work onslaught.

WEEK FOUR

Have specific goals in mind as the New Year dawns.

Never say in weakness, "this task is too difficult,"
for perseverance will give the ability to accomplish it.

Beware of leaving any work undone, for the world
will abandon those who abandon their work unfinished.

The pride of profuse giving dwells only
with the dignity of diligent effort.

—TIRUKKURAL, 62:611-613

ACKNOWLEDGMENTS

Writing a book is at first a solitary effort. After the manuscript is delivered to the publisher, however, an army of people are engaged to help you realize the potential of your words. In the case of my publisher, Perseus, these are not ordinary people. They are angels. And I am forever in their debt. It is my pleasure to acknowledge them in a public forum so that their contributions to this book can be known by all.

The first bouquet goes to my editor, the incomparable Katie McHugh. Where Katie is cool, level-headed, and intellectual, I am emotional, impetuous, and spontaneous. As a team we create the perfect balance. Katie is a tough taskmaster without ever losing her gentle manner. She knows when to prod and when to give me a wide berth. Thank you, Katie, from the bottom of my heart.

Once again Christine E. Marra guided the manuscript through the often rocky waters of postproduction. If you enjoy the interior layout of this book as much as I do, you have Christine and her team to thank. Christine is skilled, gracious, intelligent, and kind. She takes you across the finish line in style. I might have done it without her, but it would never have been as good, as much fun, or as meaningful. Thank you, Christine.

I can write a book. I have little concern for or knowledge of correct punctuation. Remember how I described myself? I could say the same of my use of commas: emotional, impetuous, and spontaneous. If this book is perfectly punctuated, it is due to the enormous patience and expertise of one Susan Pink, copy editor extraordinaire. Susan never once tampered with my writer's voice. For this gift most especially, I am in her debt.

We take it for granted. And yet without it, finding a remembered reference would be impossible. What is "it?" The index at the back of any book. Donna Riggs does the impossible: She creates an amazing, easy to use, and comprehensive index. And she does it with amazing speed. I'm in awe of her tenacity and the careful way she reads a manuscript.

A book of this nature takes the reader on a journey of self-discovery. Having worked one-on-one with clients for over twenty years, I know this can be an emotional rollercoaster. What better to discover along the way than the whimsical faces of a duck or two! Thank you to Jane Raese for placing them with care and precision.

I loved the cover design of *One Year to an Organized Life,* but I was totally knocked out when I saw the cover for this book. One day I hope to meet Jon Resh in person and give him an enormous bear hug in gratitude. The ducks on this cover remind me of the Village People. I sing a chorus of *YMCA* every time I look at them!

The greatest book in the world will languish on a shelf without a skilled PR team to guide its birth. Wendie Carr and Lindsey Triebel work tirelessly to promote my books. They are not only skilled at what they do but also a delight to work with. I can in no way adequately express my thanks to them in words.

Of course I wouldn't know anyone at Perseus if my agent, Marilyn Allen, hadn't opened the door for me. Marilyn believed in me from the literal minute we met. I owe her my career. And I thank her for her friendship.

I wish to thank my clients, many of whom grace the pages of this book. Some are identified (with their permission) and some are anonymous. Their willingness to open their lives to me is a constant source of inspiration.

When I sign a contract to write a book, my closest friends joke that it is time to head for the hills. If they ever do head into the hills, I'll be lost. It seems I get a bit cranky the deeper I get into the process. I thank them *all* for their love and support. Special kudos are given to Susie Ribnik, Ann Walsh, Lynn Hernandez, and Tanya Russell.

And last but not least, I extend pats, hugs, and all my love to the ancient golden retriever who shares my life. Spirit had been tossed on the street like so much trash when we met. From the day I adopted him, we were a team. He fills my life with laughter. Who could have imagined that the man in my life would shed, have almost no teeth, and suffer from canine dementia? I thank God for him.

And I also thank God for you.

RESOURCES

CONSCIOUS GIVING AND VOLUNTEER OPPORTUNITIES

American Red Cross
www.redcross.org

Heifer International
www.heifer.org

Mercy Corps
www.mercycorps.org

National Search and Rescue Dog Foundation
www.searchdogfoundation.org

Oxfam
www.oxfam.org

Six Degrees
www.sixdegrees.org

The Hunger Site
www.thehungersite.com
(This site will also link you to other charity sites for breast cancer, literacy, animals, and more.)

Volunteer Match
www.volunteermatch.com

CREDIT REPORTS AND IDENTITY THEFT

Free Annual Credit Report
www.annualcreditreport.com or
call 1-877-322-8228

Created by the three nationwide consumer credit reporting agencies (Equifax, Experian, and Transunion), this centralized service allows consumers to request free annual credit reports.

Equifax
www.equifax.com or call 1-877-576-5734

Experian
www.experian.com/fraud or
call 1-888-397-3742

Transunion
www.transunion.com or call 1-800-680-7289

Identity theft
www.consumer.gov/idtheft
For detailed information about identity theft.

DONATIONS

Clothing and Household Items
Career Gear
www.careergear.org
Provides professional attire for job interviews to disadvantaged men.

Dress for Success
www.dressforsuccess.org
Provides professional attire for job interviews to disadvantaged women.

Goodwill Industries International
www.goodwill.org
Sells clothing and household goods.

One Warm Coat
www.onewarmcoat.org
Collects and distributes coats for free to those
in need.

Salvation Army
www.salvationarmy.com
Sells clothing and household goods.

Computer Technology
The following sites refurbish and distribute
computer technology (laptops, desktops,
and printers) to economically disadvantaged
youths in the United States and around the
world.

Computers 4 Kids
www.c4k.org

National Cristina Foundation
www.cristina.org

World Computer Exchange
www.worldcomputerexchange.org

MIND, BODY, AND SPIRIT

Beliefnet
www.beliefnet.com
Inspiration, spirituality, and faith.

Daily OM
www.dailyOM.com
Nurturing mind, body, and spirit.

Health Journeys
http://www.healthjourneys.com
Belleruth Naparstek Guided Imagery Center.

Light on Yoga
Book by yoga master B.K.S. Iyengar.

Mysteries.Net
www.mysteries.net
Meditation and yoga site.

Self-Realization Fellowship
www.selfrealizationfellowship.org
Meditation and yoga site.

Transcendental Meditation
www.tm.org
Meditation and yoga site.

*You: Breathing Easy: Meditation & Breathing
Techniques to Relax, Refresh & Revitalize*
Dr. Mehmet Oz & Dr. Michael Roizen (audio
book)

ADHD/ADD Information
www.add.about.com
www.oneADDplace.com

*Driven to Distraction: Recognizing and Cop-
ing with Attention Deficit Disorder from
Childhood Through Adulthood,* Edward M.
Hallowell and John J. Ratey

Health and Exercise
Prevention
www.prevention.com
The Web site has current information on
health, fitness, and exercise. A great source for
developing a walking program. You can also
sign up for a free newsletter.

Real Age
www.realage.com
Excellent source of practical health tips including diet and exercise.

Dr. Mehmet Oz and Dr. Michael Roizen
Books by Drs. Oz and Roizen:
You: On a Diet
You: The Owner's Manual
You: Staying Young et al

MISCELLANEOUS ITEMS

Butterflies: Raising and release
www.butterflynursery.com

Creative Memories
www.creativememories.com

www.educationalscience.com
www.naturepavilion.com

Give the Gift of Sight
www.givethegiftofsight.com
Provides free prescription eyewear to individuals in North America and developing countries around the world. Drop off eyeglasses or sunglasses at LensCrafters, Pearle Vision, Sears Optical, Target Optical, BJ's Optical, Sunglass Hut, or Lions Club.

Hungry for Music
www.hungryformusic.org
Distributes used musical instruments to underprivileged children.

Luggage
www.suitcasesforkids.org
Provides luggage for foster children who move from home to home.

The New Designer's Design Book, Robin Williams

Reader to Reader
www.readertoreader.org
Accepts books for children and teens and distributes to school libraries nationwide.

United States Stamps personalized
www.photo.stamps.com
www.zazzle.com/custom/stamps

OFFICE AND FILING SUPPLIES

Day Runner
www.DayRunner.com

Exposures
www.exposuresonline.com
Offers binders, magazine holders, et al.

Fitter
www.fitter1.com
Fitter Active Sitting Disc transforms your chair. Check out other ergonomically correct products.

FLAX Art Design
www.flaxart.com

Levenger
www.Levenger.com
Binders, calendars, magazine holders, and more.

Office Depot
www.officedepot.com

OfficeMax
www.officemax.com

Relax the Back
www.Relaxtheback.com
Ergonomically correct office furniture.

See Jane Work
www.seejanework.com

Staples
www.staples.com

The Geek Squad
www.geeksquad.com
Computer and IT help.

ONLINE AUCTION AND SALE SITES

Cash for CDs
www.cashforcds.com

Craig's List
www.craigslist.com

eBay
www.ebay.com

PROFESSIONAL ASSOCIATIONS

Clutterers Anonymous
www.clutterersanonymous.net

Codependents Anonymous
www.codependents.org

www.Ladieswholaunch.com

Messies Anonymous
www.messies.com

National Association of Professional
Organizers (NAPO)
www.napo.net

www.salary.com

RECYCLE

1-800-GOT-JUNK?
www.1800gotjunk.com or
call 1-800-468-5865
Removes just about anything (furniture, appliances, electronics, yard waste, and renovation debris) and makes every effort to recycle or donate items.

Rechargeable Battery Recycling Corporation (RBRC)
www.call2recycle.org or call 1-877-273-2925
Recycles used portable rechargeable batteries and old cell phones.

REDUCE AND STOP UNWANTED MAIL

Direct Marking Association (DMA)
www.the-dma.org
Reduces your total volume of mail when you register for the Direct Marketing Association's Mail Preference Service (MPS).

Opt-Out of Preapproved Credit Card and Insurance Offers
www.optoutprescreen.com or
call 1-888-567-8688
Official Web site of the Credit Reporting Industry to accept and process consumer requests to opt-in or opt-out of prescreened credit card and insurance offers.

SHOP

Bed, Bath, & Beyond
www.bedbathandbeyond.com

Costco
www.costco.com

Exposures: Celebrating Life's Memories
www.exposuresonline.com

Michael's Arts & Crafts
www.michaels.com

Target
www.target.com

The Container Store
www.thecontainerstore.com

Wal-Mart
www.walmart.com

TRAVEL

Flight, Hotel, and Car Reservations

www.cheaptickets.com
www.expedia.com
www.hotwire.com
www.orbitz.com
www.sidestep.com
www.travelocity.com

General Travel Information

Automobile Association of America
www.aaa.com

Centers for Disease Control
www.cdc.com/travel
Provides travel health information.

Department of Homeland Security
www.travel.state.gov/passport
Apply for a passport or get information on
traveling abroad.

National Weather Service
www.nws.noaa.gov
Weather reports on destinations in the United
States.

Transportation Security Administration
www.tsa.gov/travelers
Updated information on items a traveler is
permitted to bring on an airplane.

Weather Channel
www.weather.com
Weather reports on destinations in the United
States.

Weather Underground
www.wunderground.com
Weather forecasts for destinations in the
United States and abroad.

INDEX